Peter Hardy has spent much of his long career as a foreign correspondent and travel writer reporting from distant corners of the world for the *Daily Telegraph*, *Daily Mail*, *Daily Express*, and *London Evening Standard*. In the 1960s he lived briefly as a hippy in San Francisco, becoming the friend and lover of Janis Joplin.

His colourful life has not been without some landmark mishaps – as a small child he lost an eye to a bow-and-arrow, and while reporting in Idi Amin's Uganda he narrowly escaped execution after receiving a death sentence for espionage. More recently, he was seriously injured in a tragic accident while ski mountaineering in the French Alps. But despite it all, he claims that travelling with James Blunt has undoubtedly been his most dangerous assignment to date.

Peter is the editor of the website welove2ski.com and its sandy sister welovethebeach.com. When not travelling to concerts, mountains or beaches he lives in Hampshire with his wife and children.

Different Country, Same State:

On the Road with James Blunt

Peter Hardy

headline
review

First published in 2010
by HEADLINE REVIEW
An imprint of Headline Publishing Group

First published in paperback in 2011
by HEADLINE REVIEW

1

Cataloguing in Publication Data is available from the British Library

ISBN 978 0 7553 1995 4

Typeset in Adobe Garamond by Palimpsest Book Production Limited,
Falkirk, Stirlingshire

Printed and bound in Great Britain by
Clays Ltd, St Ives plc

Headline's policy is to use papers that are natural, renewable and recyclable
products and made from wood grown in sustainable forests. The logging and
manufacturing processes are expected to conform to the environmental regulations
of the country of origin.

HEADLINE PUBLISHING GROUP
An Hachette UK Company
338 Euston Road
London NW1 3BH

www.headline.co.uk
www.hachette.co.uk

Contents

To Felice, for her love and encouragement in making
my journey possible

Foreword

'We call him Weird Uncle Peter. He's just that – weird – but he's also sort of wise and if there's an echo of truth in just half the things he says have happened to him, then he's had an amazing life. I also have a Gay Uncle Dave, but he's a real relation who became a raver in his late forties – after a messy divorce from Mad Auntie Clare. Weird Uncle Peter, on the other hand, just turned up one day claiming he was a family friend and soon became part of the furniture. But what's he actually *doing* here on the tour? That's the question I keep asking and the band keep asking, everyone keeps asking. When he first appeared on the scene, we told people he was our drug dealer. Then, as his own addiction really began to kick in, it seemed inappropriate, and so he became Weird Uncle Peter on account of his appearance – he's a lot older than us and his body had just about given up.

Dragging one leg behind him as he moves, he can be a frightening sight, the benefit being that children run screaming. He damaged the leg in an avalanche; lost his hearing in an IRA pub bomb, and lost an eye in Vietnam or a dog attack as a child or something like that.

It's taken me a while to learn to talk to his left ear and look at his left eye. It's not that the glass eye is unconvincing; it's just that both look pretty bad. Every few minutes, he'll pull out a brightly coloured handkerchief from his right-hand trouser pocket with which to clean the false eye. It doesn't look like it needs cleaning, but maybe glass eyes cause more abrasion and so more mucus than the real thing? Maybe he's suffering from Lady Macbeth syndrome? I don't know. We never got to see, as we were always beaten to it by the handkerchief.

Anyway, for much of the tour he was just hanging around with us, drunk, stoned and scaring groupies. Often he would disappear for a few weeks, and then, unannounced, turn up again. He never explained where he'd been and we'd never ask. We'd just cheer as he walked through the door in whichever country we were.

James Blunt,
August 2010

Introduction

Don't believe all that stuff. OK, maybe some of it is true. Fact is, as Blunty has apparently noticed, I *have* been hanging around with him and his band on chunks of the world tour to promote his *All The Lost Souls* album. It's been one of the greatest pop marathons of all time: 213 performances, if you include TV appearances, and double that if you include radio, in 58 countries in 15 months.

I'll Take Everything, goes the song. We did, and more. It's been said that touring with James Blunt makes Led Zeppelin seem about as excitingly excessive as a Buckingham Palace garden party. I've only done two of these so I'm in no position to judge. James Walsh of Starsailor, the support act for James during part of the *Bedlam* world tour, said: 'This is the most rock 'n' roll tour of all time.' James reminds me that Starsailor has toured with Oasis: 'So they're used to people who are all fart and no poo.'

After a punishing schedule like that, Blunty, the chances of any one of us retaining even the vaguest traces of sanity are as remote as me seeing your hairy face through that false eye that you're so fond of talking about. So, I forgive you.

OK, so I've got a lot more years under my belt than James and his close-knit band: Paul 'Beardy' Beard on keyboard, Karl Brazil on drums, Benny Castle on lead guitar, and Johnny Garrison (previously Malcolm 'Splitter' Moore) on bass. To start with I guess we were understandably wary

3

of each other. They, of course, more so than me. I have the edge in having known James since long before he became famous.

I'd better put my cards on the table. I'm a veteran Fleet Street journalist and a writer who's been around the world a bit, sticking my nose into all sorts of situations that interested me during the past four decades. I also happen to be a close friend of the family. I first met his dad, Charlie, and his mum, Jane, when she came to work for my wife and me as a picture researcher.

Blunty, at the time, was away at university, wondering how he could make it as a singer-songwriter, while at the same time maintaining the Blount family tradition of joining the army for at least a few years. You get the idea that the army was a temporary measure when you see the title of his sociology dissertation: 'The Commodification of Image – Production of a Pop Idol'.

About the first thing he did when he started in the music business was to drop the silent 'o' from Blount. It made pronunciation easier but also earned a new entry in the dictionary of rhyming slang, with James Blunt replacing Berkeley Hunt. 'I remember I was at primary school,' he told me, 'when people first recognized that my name rhymed with c**t. I can promise that no one has ever said that to me since primary school until I got into the music business. Through boarding school and university and army no one had ever reminded me of that.' But that's showbusiness.

At family gatherings we'd sort of nod and smile at each other. James and I did – and do – have in common a passion for skiing so we always had one subject to talk about. But in those days, it was his sisters Emily and Daisy whom I saw much more of and knew best.

In what seems a lifetime ago I once even sang with the young Blunty. But I have to confess that it was 'The 12 Days of Christmas' and not 'You're Beautiful'. The audience, apart from my wife and children and his mum and dad, was a stuffed French turkey and a rightfully unimpressed First Choice chalet girl in the ski resort of Val d'Isère.

While James did go to war with a guitar strapped to his tank, he seemed on the surface to be an extraordinarily unlikely candidate to become a celebrated international pop star. So when he suddenly and emphatically hit the big time – No.1 not only in Britain, but also in the USA and around the world – I was intrigued to discover what made James tick. As a trusted family friend I tried pulling a bit of rank and won. I found myself in a unique position to ride the inside track.

James seemed quietly amused at the idea of someone of my age tagging along in his life. His humour works in mysterious ways. So since May 2006, on and off, I've been travelling around the world, living intimately on a day-to-day basis with him and the band, sharing their highs and lows. I've snapped a few thousand photos along the way, written part of the tour brochures, generally tried not to get in the way, and usually failed to do so. After the release of *All The Lost Souls* in September 2007 and the start in earnest of the world tour in January 2008, I regularly dipped in and out along the itinerary all the way through to the final concert in Athens in March 2009.

It's not been an easy journey. I am, after all, of a different generation and old enough to be father to Blunty and all of his band. Perhaps it helps that I've seen it all before. Mostly I've been there, I've done that, and I'm difficult to shock. Slowly, over days and nights that turned into months, we got to know and then to trust, to like, and even to love each other. They remind me that my behaviour at times didn't fall far short of theirs and I'd like to think that the generation gap almost closed.

OK, so I'm not as athletic – not as fit, some would say – as any of them. But that doesn't mean I haven't been able to grab a little insight from, shall we say, a more mature perspective as to what goes on when the Blunty show comes to town. I mean, I've got eyes in my head – well, one, anyway.

For me it's been a curiously rewarding yet addictive experience. The more I travel with James and Co., the more I feel myself becoming absorbed by the journey and the less certain I become of the destination – to the point where I wonder if for Blunty, and indeed for me, there really *is* a destination at all. The whole purpose and fulfilment seems to lie in the getting there, wherever 'there' is. It's forced me, for the second time down the years, now that I have drifted into the autumn of my life, to entirely reassess my values.

James is a deeply complex person. As a character I find him intriguingly attractive and infuriatingly frustrating. He's all fuzzy question marks and no clean answers. The more time I spend with him, the closer he becomes as my friend, the more I realize that the less I know him. It's as if the more paint I add to my canvas, the more the true portrait is obscured.

He's a singer and songwriter, an artist with undeniably proven talent, whose music and lyrics strike a chord with which millions identify. But time and again I ask myself: 'What separates Blunty from the herd of singer-songwriters out there who never make it? Why does he evoke such passion in his supporters and such vicious, venomous disdain in his army of detractors?'

Where did he suddenly come from? Where is he going? It's as if an enormous forefinger, like the one in the original National Lottery adverts, whooshed down out of the sky one day – around the time James left the army – and juddered to a halt about a centimetre from his face. It was his Road to Damascus (a city that is as yet absent from his tour calendar). A celestial voice boomed through the ethereal amplifier: 'James Blunt, you have been chosen to create some quite extraordinarily sad songs that will sweep around the world to make millions of people very happy.' Trouble is, He forgot to tell the music critics what was going on. Perhaps He had already decided to which hot destination they were all headed.

Why do many of them in Britain hate him so vehemently and tell their readers to do the same? Yet 3.1 million people at home bought *Back To Bedlam*. It's now officially gone down in history as the biggest-selling album in the UK of 2000–2009. At the time of writing James has sold around 18 million albums worldwide. It just doesn't add up. So who's got it right here – a handful of British critics or the general public? That's what I wanted to find out.

Indeed, is Blunty really worthy of all that conflicting emotion? I've asked these questions of lots of people who've been professionally involved with him, from Elton John to veteran technicians who've worked with the biggest names in the business over the past 30 years. Without exception, I get a resounding, but still confused, 'yes'. The music industry, the professionals, utterly endorse him. They have not a single doubt about him.

He's good, he's even great, because he's so bewitchingly different – but they can't explain why. The most honest assessment comes from a world-famous sound technician whose opinion I respect: 'When I first started working with James, I thought OK, so here's another guy from a public school who's all promise and no delivery. There's lots of them around who have the nous or the nepotic influence to get to that first rung on the ladder. On meeting him, it took me around ten seconds to change my mind.

'For a start, he's not posh, not in the least. He's instantly likeable, easy to work with, and always professional. His closest friends, the people he likes to spend the most time with, are his band and you don't get a more diverse bunch of social criminals than that.

'Anyway, music is the ultimate leveller – we judge on our own scale. He's good enough to be where he is: at the top of that scale. To me the secret to his success is his refreshing musical naivety. He comes from a family that didn't own a stereo. Fact is, he hasn't listened to much music, he prefers making his own. He didn't grow up with a backdrop of conflicting musical influences, so his work is quite extraordinarily original. I'd go further, I'd say it's unique.'

Me? What do I think? He's one of an increasingly rare

kind – an artist who performs at his best live, with a band, without a band, it really doesn't matter. He doesn't need to rely upon any electronic gadgetry. He never hits a wrong note. I don't know a lot about music, but down the years I've learned quite a bit about people. So who is James Blunt?

I have to confess that, after living by his side over many months in 29 different countries, I'm only marginally nearer to coming up with the definitive answer. On the surface he's polite, charming, good company, and armed with a bone-dry razor-sharp wit that can thrust deep. It's lost in translation, even from UK to US English. Beneath the surface? Well, we'll come to that.

But James Blunt has one particular quality that I admire and with which I can personally identify. He lives his life for today. Judge him by that.

Once, a long time ago, as a foreign correspondent in East Africa under a despotic regime, I came within just five minutes of my own execution. This is not a story that belongs here, but by luck or fate – or both – I talked my way out of it. If I learned anything from that experience, it is that it is foolish to bank all your hopes and dreams on a tomorrow which, by definition, will never come. Savour and appreciate each part of today. That's what Blunty does – and his is a very long day. He rarely sleeps – and never before 6am.

I think that for James there's a deeper and a darker side to the tour that reaches beyond the shallows of the exhausting daily ritual of travel, perform, and party. It's not about dating a different girl each night; it's about stealing a transient moment with another human being.

It's not really about alcohol and the endless pursuit of fun; it's about living each moment as if it were your last – because that's how he views life.

He's someone whose only way of communicating honestly and without fear or caution is to sing. And then, and only then, can we actually hear the voice that he hears in his own head – and it's the same voice that his fans hear in theirs.

Of course, it was never going to be like this. Originally, I set out to chronicle dispassionately the rise of singer-songwriter James Blunt from army captain to superstar. I was going to be the fly on the wall, the bluebottle that dug beneath the official publicity profile, rustled the fabric, and found out what made him tick. It all seemed so easy.

But it didn't work out as planned. Come to think of it, down the decades, not much has. More than my subject, James became my friend. Metaphorically, I should explain, I broke the cardinal rule of objective journalism: I got into bed with the enemy. I suppose I've spent a lot of my life in someone or other's bed, so no surprise there.

Along the way, I've also learned a lot more about myself. It's hugely comforting – or do I mean disturbing? – to discover a generation or two down the line that random sex, drugs, and rock 'n' roll remain largely unchanged from my own Flower Power days in San Francisco in the 1960s. They have the same enduring capacity for survival as cockroaches do in a nuclear conflict. Oh, and Uncle Sam is still at war with guys in pyjamas on the other side of the world. Nothing really fundamentally changes. As Janis Joplin used to say to me: 'It's just the same ol' fuckin' day, man.' But, nevertheless, it *is* today.

Introduction

Just thinking about the journey of *All The Lost Souls* makes me tired. It began in January 2008:

Glasgow . . . Edinburgh . . . Manchester . . . London . . . Bournemouth . . . Plymouth . . . Nottingham . . . Wolverhampton . . . Reading . . . Cannes . . . Belfast . . . Dublin . . . Seattle . . . San Francisco . . . Los Angeles . . . Las Vegas . . . San Diego . . . Denver . . . Berlin . . . Paris . . . Milan . . . London . . . Chicago . . . Toronto . . . Montreal . . . Boston . . . New York . . . Philadelphia . . . Asheville . . . Atlanta . . . Zurich . . . Paris . . . Nantes . . . Strasbourg . . . Lille . . . Brussels . . . Rotterdam . . . Paris . . . Cologne . . . Berlin . . . Copenhagen . . . Stockholm . . . Oslo . . . Hamburg . . . Paris . . . Luxembourg . . . Stuttgart . . . Munich . . . Milan . . . Geneva . . . Verbier . . . Los Angeles . . . Beijing . . . Shanghai . . . Tokyo . . . Nagoya . . . Osaka . . . Seoul . . . Wellington . . . Auckland . . . Brisbane . . . Sydney . . . Canberra . . . Melbourne . . . Adelaide . . . Perth . . . Singapore . . . Hong Kong . . . Taipei . . . Manila . . . Jakarta . . . Johannesburg . . . Durban . . . Cape Town . . . Seville . . . London . . . Reykjavik . . . Sarajevo . . . Tirana . . . Athens . . . Cyprus . . . Glastonbury . . . Nimes . . . Bilbao . . . Lisbon . . . Malaga . . . Madrid . . . Barcelona . . . Antibes . . . St Malo . . . London . . . Werchter . . . Lugano . . . Nashville . . . Uncasville . . . Holmdel . . . Wantagh . . . Boston . . . Saratoga Springs . . . Philadelphia . . . Canandiagua . . . Detroit . . . Green Bay . . . Milwaukee . . . Minneapolis . . . Highland Park . . . Hammond . . . Bossier City . . . Houston . . . Dallas . . . Oklahoma City . . . Albuquerque . . . Tucson . . . San Diego . . . Las Vegas . . . South Lake Tahoe . . . Salt

Lake City . . . San Francisco . . . Saratoga . . . Portland . . . Seattle . . . Amsterdam . . . Paris . . . Cardiff . . . Sheffield . . . Nottingham . . . Birmingham . . . Manchester . . . Glasgow . . . Aberdeen . . . Newcastle . . . London O2 . . . Brussels . . . Bremen . . . Oberhausen . . . Leipzig . . . Mannheim . . . Nuremberg . . . Stuttgart . . . Budapest . . . Bratislava . . . Prague . . . Vienna . . . Treviso . . . Bolzano . . . Basel . . . Marseille . . . Toulouse . . . Bordeaux . . . Dijon . . . London . . . Vancouver . . . Edmonton . . . Calgary . . . Grande Prairie . . . Saskatoon . . . Winnipeg . . . Toronto . . . Montreal . . . Ottawa . . . Québec City . . . New York . . . Halifax . . . St John's . . . Paris . . . London . . . Barbados . . . São Paulo . . . Rio de Janeiro . . . Buenos Aires . . . Santiago . . . Porto Alegre . . . São Paulo . . . Mexico City . . . Lima . . . Mexico City . . . Guadelajara . . . Moscow . . . Helsinki . . . Tallinn . . . Riga . . . Vilnius . . . Warsaw . . . Bucharest . . . Sofia . . . Belgrade . . . Muscat . . . Dubai . . . Lebanon . . . Kiev . . . Kazakhstan . . . and it ended in Athens in March 2009.

Sydney, October 2007

A small group of fans half blocks the entrance ramp to the Intercontinental off Phillip Street. A tall, dark-haired girl is holding up a banner that reads: 'James, I want to spend the night with you.' The look on her face is one of faint hope rather than of expectation. It's the expression you see in the eyes of someone in a supermarket filling out a lottery ticket. In fact, the first night's easy. It's a second night that's difficult.

Four sleek limos with engines running and chauffeurs at the wheel are waiting on the forecourt. It seems I'm just in time. Three camera crews are mechanically recording the empty vehicles. Two power-dressed girls and a guy in jeans with a ponytail are all talking into mobiles. They're circling around the security men complaining about something or nothing. As worker bees they know it's their job to keep on buzzing, even when there's nothing to buzz about. Maybe they don't think the crowd is big enough: 'Hey, Jake, get us some more fans. We need them *now* . . . I don't care where *from* . . . shift their asses over here from the studio if you have to.'

One of the very few advantages indeed of being obviously of mature father-figure age, but at the same time dressed down by a couple of generations, is that I never need ID to go anywhere. Of course, I have it, the current tour laminate around my neck beneath my shirt. This lets me go anywhere, wherever the Blunty show is – arena, backstage, dressing-rooms, and hotel bedrooms. But, like most days, I don't need it today. Rarely does a security guard question my presence. An air of confidence along with my years ('the very fact that you're still alive,' as James is fond of remarking) indicate that I belong.

The band's just assembling in the lobby. I watch them for a moment from the doorway. Karl, the drummer, is just coming out of the lift, smiling as always and looking forward, never back, to what today holds in store for him. Benny, lead guitar, his face almost buried beneath a bush of black hair, looks reassuringly scruffy in his Got Pills? T-shirt. Beardy, the king of keyboard, is talking animatedly to James. Malcolm, bass guitar, looks a bit sad and lost. It's difficult for him – he's made the decision and will be leaving the band at Christmas. A wife, a baby son, and yet another 15-month world tour is not an acceptable combination. Well, not if you want to hang on to both marriage and sanity.

Hugs all round. Clearly no one, not James nor Bobble, the tour manager, has told them that I'm coming. They seem pleased to see me, but it's no real surprise. I come, I go, I come again. We're all used to that, no matter if the meetings are 8,000 miles and a month or two apart. I turn up when the rest of my life permits, join the inner circle of the tour, stay for a week or a month, and then quietly disappear again.

James, too, seems happy to see me. An open grin and squeeze of the arm. As a family friend I've known him since he was a teenager. But I guess we've now quietly become close friends in our own right, despite the age gap,

and we're both a bit astonished by this unlikely and gradually evolving state of affairs. Like two stranger hostages
chained together by chance circumstance to the same radiator for months on end in a dungeon not of our making,
we've been forced to get to know each other. We respect,
and yes, we like what we see. Back in the outside world,
neither of us would ever have necessarily expected that.

They look older – that is, all except James. I'm struck
by this every time we meet. A crease around the eyes, a
weary hand through hair, a new facial expression. It's as
if the constant lurching from country to country and
continent to continent has speeded up time. Somewhere
along the watch face, Karl has abandoned his innocence
in a long-forgotten hotel room. Well, actually, in whole
floors and annexes of hotel rooms. But only the music
matters now. It's the compelling, driving force for all of
them and for Karl in particular. The beat throbs relentlessly on.

But James looks much the same on each of my time
travels. The single difference is the hair on his face, which
varies with dramatic speed from clean shaven, through
designer stubble to a full set within a week. Today, we're
pretty damned hairy.

It's almost as if he lives the lyrics of his own 'Tears and
Rain':

*I guess it's time I run far, far away: find comfort in
    pain.*
All pleasure's the same, it just keeps me from trouble.
Hides my true shape, like Dorian Gray.

PR people and an assortment of minders hover at his elbows. 'Good to see you, Peter. All OK for tomorrow?' he asks me. 'We're just off to do a set at a TV station and then we've been invited to a private dinner.' Introductions to PR people follow.

'This is Peter,' he says by way of explanation, indicating with a casual wave of his hand the unlikely newcomer, who is clearly important to him. Everyone, therefore, with equal clarity thinks that they should know who Peter is. But no one has a clue who Peter is, and no one has the nerve to ask. Actually, I'm just a fly.

The art of being a fly on the wall is to know when to stop buzzing and fade quietly out of sight. If you don't anticipate the timing, you get swatted, in all likelihood, permanently.

'Fine,' I say, burying disappointment beneath an expression of indifference. I've come a long way to be here and sacrificed a chunk of my liver in return for the air fare and now I'm not even going to spend some time with them. 'Maybe I'll give you a call after your dinner and we can catch up later.'

'No, no, I'm sure our hosts would love to have you for dinner – one more will be no problem,' he says, turning to Fran, the chief and pretty minder who is to become my friend. It's a statement, not a question. Fame tends to take the question mark out of asking.

'So come with us to the TV. I'm sure we can squeeze in one more.' Fran looks horrified, but resignedly reaches for her mobile once again.

Then we're in the cars. I see the girl with the banner. Her eyes feast on James as he climbs in behind me. It's never going to be bedtime, but she's managed to get within a metre of him and her sign now hangs limply on her left shoulder cushioned by a quite enormous amount of chestnut-coloured hair. If she wasn't so scarily fixated, I think she'd be almost beautiful. She stares quietly and unblinkingly through the side window at James' profile with an expression I've come to know well over the months – unfettered desire mixed with the almost masochistic thrill of denial that The Song demands:

And I don't know what to do,
'Cause I'll never be with you.

But a girl can dream, can't she? Yes, she can. But in pushing his way through the crush of people around him, the focus of those dreams fails to notice her. Both she and I find that so heart-achingly sad.

In the gathering Australian dusk we've reached a TV studio, James has sung six songs to an invited audience of Sydney thirty-something media people and socialites who down free cocktails with a vengeance and don't listen to any of them.

'Do you like his music?' I ask a girl in a little black dress who is on her third tequila sunrise in the ten minutes I've been talking to her. We're standing side by side at the rail of the balcony bar and down below James is singing 'Annie'.

She looks at me as if the question had never before occurred to her. 'Dunno,' she says, absently stirring her drink with a cocktail umbrella, 'but I'd like to go down on *him*.' Did I hear that right?

'You know,' she says, her voice slightly slurring, 'like this song – *will you go down on me?* Oh, OK, right. Not me, then.

'Annie' is a passionate song about a girl who never quite makes the big time as a singer. The press has widely credited it as a dig at Amanda Ghost who worked with him on 'You're Beautiful'.

But Blunty does not confirm this. 'Is "Annie" about anyone in particular?' I ask him straight, that night.

'Not that I can remember,' comes the reply. Maybe not? Amanda is credited by her publishers with just 10 per cent of the overall writing of 'You're Beautiful', and only a tiny 3.5 per cent of the writing of the whole of *Back To Bedlam*. Yet she is sometimes described in the press as 'James Blunt's songwriter'.

She is not.

At the end of the *Bedlam* world tour and now in the run-up to *All The Lost Souls,* 'Annie' features regularly on the set-list. In the months to come James will sing it regularly at venues across northern Europe. But gradually as winter gives way to warmer weather, 'Annie' is dropped. I guess revenge – if that's what this is all about – is a dish that is truly best served cold.

Personally I like the song, but a poll among fans on his website lists it as the second least popular track on the album. 'I guess it came close to the bottom because it's not a very nice song,' James tells me. '*Annie, you're a star that's not going very far* – I guess it spells it out too much. I wrote it with Jimmy Hogarth and it kind of says what it is, really. We played it a lot on the last tour, but it's not one of my favourites.' Jimmy Hogarth's producing and songwriting credits include Amy Winehouse, Paolo Nutini and James Morrison.

In an interview James has more of a go at explaining the less than gentlemanly lyrics (well, I *think* that's what he does): 'We tell our children now that success is measured by fame and fortune. It's one person's story where they start out on their journey and try to find happiness through fame, and find it eventually through something of greater meaning.'

Backstage, the band drinks the green room dry with a little assistance from me and the night becomes a blur of faces and flashguns.

Long after dinner in a Japanese restaurant, long after a champagne reception in the hotel, long after we stumble into a dirty late-night bar to watch Russia beat England 2–1, I fall into bed with the arch of Sydney Harbour looming both outside my window and in my mind. Last time here it all seemed so much easier. Maybe it was because Blunty was less famous.

Somewhere down the line, we'd been in a karaoke bar – a genuine Oriental-style place, where you have your own private room with lots of drinks and a giant book of songs to choose from. We'd sung away for an hour or so. Then, in a moment of our silence, came the unmistakable strains of a group of office girls on a night out or a hen party clucking in a neighbouring room. Oblivious of us, they were singing 'Goodbye My Lover'. James ran out of our room, burst in on theirs, grabbed a microphone, sang the last chorus, said 'Thank you, and goodnight!' and ran out. For 20 minutes all we could hear were screams.

It's 8am and it's bad. Just how bad, I don't know until

I climb out of bed in the presidential suite of the Shangri-La Hotel and make it to the window.

The contents of my suitcase are scattered around it like the debris of an avalanche.

Adjusting to the daylight, the panorama of Sydney's iconic waterfront fills me with dread. The Opera House has been standing there on Bennelong Point since construction began in 1959 and it's looking today as fresh and as futuristic as when its designer, a Danish bloke called Jorn Utzon, raised a glass of sparkling Pinot Noir at the opening ceremony to what the World Heritage Committee called: 'One of the indisputable masterpieces of human creativity, not only in the twentieth century, but in the history of humankind.' When you've got an accolade like that on your CV, you don't need much else.

My own masterpiece of human creativity is to take place today on the left-hand side of this sensational stage. Sydney Harbour Bridge is where I am to photograph the brochure cover for James Blunt's upcoming *All The Lost Souls* world tour.

Already a lot of work has gone into making this glossy brochure, which will be on sale at 150 venues from Beijing to Birmingham. Back in England I've spent hours creating a still-life montage of all the awards, platinum discs, and gifts from fans around the world. There are quite literally hundreds of them – from a rather tasteful Ivor Novello statuette to coffee mugs and a knitted willy warmer. I've written the introduction and rewritten the copy (twice). Now comes the crowning glory: James and the band standing precariously on the highest girder of the bridge against the backdrop of the Opera House while I perch precariously on a girder opposite and record all this in Canon digital clarity.

When Admiral Arthur Phillip parked his First Fleet here off Bennelong Point outside my window (which of course was absent from the tableau) more than 200 years ago, he couldn't have imagined that bridge, either with or without Blunty perched on top of it. It's the world's largest (but not the longest) steel arch bridge and Sydney residents call it The Coat Hanger. It weighs 39,000 tons, the arch spans 503 metres and the summit is 134 metres above sea level, making it a great spot for snaps and for suicides.

All I have to do this day, with the assistance of a professional Aussie climber, is to shepherd James, Beardy, Malcolm (still the bass player), Karl, and a reluctant bearded and rumpled Benny up 465 steps between the girders to the setting for the photo shoot.

It's not as demanding as it sounds. Lots of people do it – two million of them in the past ten years, including me – yes, even me and one of my teenage sons. It's easy, as long as you don't suffer from a fear of heights. Personally, I thought crossing the first span was ghastly – I felt so sick with vertigo I almost turned back – but I'm not telling *them* that.

It's taken the full two weeks since I arrived in Australia to set it up – and that's not been easy, I can tell you. The project has hardly been aided by the fact that my financial excuse for joining James on the far side of the planet has been a wine-tasting jaunt to Adelaide in the far south of the country. People pay me to write about all sorts of things and, very occasionally, these include *vino*. My late friend John Arlott, the cricket commentator and wine writer, who knew his way with equal passion around Lord's and the great châteaux of Bordeaux, once said that I had a passable palate. 'In 20 years' time it could be a good one,' he told me. In 20 years' time he was dead and because I'm *not* a dedicated wine writer, I'm still (just about) alive.

'Sorry,' I told my editor at the *Daily Mail*, 'there's absolutely no way I can go to Australia for a week at this time of year.' The thought of travelling goat class and breathing in germ-ridden second-hand air in a plane for the best part of four days, there and back, all for the purpose of ruining my liver fills me with dread. It'll take me two weeks to recover.

'It's Qantas Business Class both ways,' he added as an afterthought.

'When do I leave?' I replied.

Killing two birds with one stone is the name of my game as I follow Blunty around the world. I knew that Blunty had a trip to Australia and Japan coming up. A quick check of his diary showed that I wouldn't even have to rearrange the dates for my visit. I'd hit the jackpot. He was going to be in Sydney.

So there I am at a cellar door in the Barossa Valley or Eden Vale or Adelaide Hills, the great wine-growing areas of South Australia. I'm watching kangaroos cavort between the vines and I'm quaffing – and (mostly) spitting out – up to 60 different wines a day while trying to communicate on my mobile with a BridgeClimb PR person a thousand miles away in Sydney. This in itself would be difficult enough, but it is complicated by the fact that my mobile rarely has a signal, and when it does the line has that infuriating echo which means you hear what you've just said after you've just said it. What's more, I've got a glass in my hand, six more lined up on the counter, and I'm surrounded by a case of dedicated Aussie drinkers who've stumbled across a Pommy soulmate also bent on self-destruction and they don't want to waste a drop of him. The windows for any of us to make sense here are limited.

'Yeees, we can do it,' the PR girl enthuses. 'The climb takes three and a half hours to complete.'

'Can we do it in two?'

'*You can do it in one, mate, if you can keep your eyes on the road for 24 hours. Why, last year me and Shane went to Victoria – and back – in a weekend . . . had a few along the way, I can tell you . . . why, in the time it takes to shear a sheep we'd emptied the first . . .*'

'Yes, that should be possible if your guys are fit. James Blunt! He's really big here and I can tell you, Peter, we're very excited about this. We'll get all the TV, radio, and writing press organized.'

'No, that's precisely what I don't want. If that happens he won't do it. It's got to be completely private – the only pictures have to be taken by me.'

'*No problem with pictures, Peter! Where do you want us? Inside or out? Kenny's just opening a bottle of the Majella '04 sparkling Shiraz – I think you'll find it's a real beaut . . . just gone on release . . .*'

Finally, all is agreed. BridgeClimb will waive the fees in exchange for the publicity generated by the brochure. I am to get James and Co. discreetly to the VIP entrance at precisely 11.55am on Saturday, and the fact that we are coming is to be kept secret from Rupert Murdoch and all but our appointed climber.

'Oh, and there's just one more thing, Peter,' she adds. 'There's a legal requirement. Before a climb, everyone has to pass a breathalyzer test.'

'Breathalyzer? If you or me took one now, mate, it'd probably catch fire! Now, a couple of years ago Kenny's brother Michael was coming back from the Crows game in Adelaide . . .'

Football – soccer, not Australian rules – is a warm and constant current that flows through the daily life of the Blunty road show . . . and its occasionally compelling undertow is about to be my undoing.

James either supports the man wearing black, or feigns an interest in Chelsea because he has a house near the ground. Karl – he had to choose between football and the drums as a career – worships Birmingham. Once a year they play against Robbie Williams and his team in LA. Blunty himself knows his way around a pitch and the team made up of band and crew is surprisingly good – they once took on Brazil and won (well, not the national team exactly).

However, Rob's lot are much better. Months of preparation, most of it of the verbal kind, takes place nightly in different bars around the world. Forget David Beckham's famous fractured metatarsal just before the 2002 World Cup. For two weeks on the West Coast during the tour almost the entire conversation of the band centred on whether or not Benny's broken big toe would heal in time for the match. Unlike Beckham's injury, it didn't. In the first one they fielded some really good players. Blunty United was absolutely and completely hammered.

'I'm not sure what the final score was,' Blunty confesses, 'because we sort of lost count. I'm guessing that we had six goals and Rob's team scored 46. The second one was a much better contest. We were hungover, it was a mess, but the scoreline was half that.'

Normally Saturday afternoon is the Holy Hour for the band. But when you're travelling constantly around the world, Saturday afternoon in GMT can – depending on where you find yourself – be mid-morning, early evening, or slap in the darkest hours of the night. Last night, when England faced Russia in a Euro 2008 qualifier, it was the latter.

The phone rings. It's Robert. Actually, when a bedside phone rings in my life, it's nearly always Robert, aka Bobble, the 18-stone, large and lumbering, all-knowing and all-seeing tour manager who, on a diet of chip butties and po-faced humour, keeps this show on the road. Over the next 18 months the Blunty Diet – the stress of touring with James and Co. – is going to reduce his weight by 100 pounds.

He's the one who knows the room numbers, because he's assigned them. He's sometimes cheerful and always brief because he's usually got another 15 numbers to ring with the same message: 'We're leaving at 2pm . . . meet James downstairs in half an hour . . . sound check's delayed to 5pm . . . give me your second passport for the Russian visa.'

This time it's: 'I've ordered the cars . . . 11.45am departure from the Intercontinental. Are you coming with us or do we meet you there?'

'I'm coming,' I tell him and put the phone down. I look

at my watch. It's already 10.50am. I head for the bathroom. My head is spinning. It must have been gone 3am when Rooney scored. James had already scored and left. The goal was the signal for me to head from bar to bed.

I'd looked over at Karl and Benny glued to the screen in the corner of the bar along with a hardened group of Sydney-based ex-pats. 'We've got an important day tomorrow, guys. You will all be OK for half 11, won't you?' I try to say this clearly, but I've got a wad of cotton wool wrapped around my tongue and I'm having trouble seeing straight, let alone walking straight. I put a hand out to a pillar, miss, and nearly take a dive. I've taken my eye off the ball. I'm off the pace and must sleep. How do these guys do it? 'Sure, Uncle Peter,' Beardy smiles, returning from the bar with yet another round of Tooheys. 'We're looking forward to it.'

Now, it's 11.30am. The shower's shown me I'm still alive, and I'm just leaving my room. The telephone rings. It's Robert and he's got only two words, which even by his standards is brief:

'It's off.'

'What do you mean "it's off"?' I splutter. 'They're expecting us in 25 minutes.'

'I've just spoken to James. They can't do it. No one would pass a breathalyzer. James is not prepared for them to try – and if they did you'd never keep that out of the press.' I put the phone down. It immediately rings again. It's Blunty.

'Peter, you've spoken to Robert. It's just not possible. Come on over and we'll do some other pictures instead.' He puts the phone down and avoids further discussion.

Fuck you, James Blunt, fuck the whole lot of you. I can't believe it!

I call the bridge people.

'Can we do this without the blowjob?'

'No way. It's the law.'

Not surprisingly, they're really pissed off with me. Gig here tonight, Brisbane tomorrow – there's no other window. I feel like I should climb the bloody bridge alone and chuck myself off it. 134-metre freefall? Smack. It'd be like hitting concrete.

Deflated, depressed, demoralized and wondering, not for the first time, what the hell I am doing, I stumble through the hotel door and out into the spring sunshine. Other pictures instead? Doesn't James realize that I've spent two weeks setting up the *only* picture for his tour brochure cover? I'm not here to snatch a bloody travel brochure. He doesn't care. Does he care about anything? Why is he putting up with me being here at all?

At a time of life when most of my contemporaries are winding down, here I am hanging on the coat tails of a rock band on the far side of the world. I ought to catch a flight back to London today, go home to Hampshire, to my wife, my family, and muddle through the rest of middle and into old age among my own kind. Instead, just look at me. Wasted and washed up after watching a football match. I don't even *like* football. Just lately I've been noticing that the goalposts in my life are shifting a bit. Right now they're dribbling down the pitch away from me. Time to blow the whistle on this game.

Home truth time. Breathalyzer? If we'd gone ahead, the fact is I'd have been the first to have blown it. I'm not doing what I'm supposed to be doing. Instead of observing, I'm absorbing. I feel I'm being slowly sucked into James' touring treadmill which has no constants; no structure, just 24 hours of travel, music and madness that runs seamlessly into another two dozen of the same. I'm running in mud, I'm sinking into the mire, and painfully I have to admit, I'm loving every single minute of it. I'm enjoying it because I feel I belong. Or maybe I'm imagining I'm enjoying it. Paranoia runs deep today.

I don't really know these people, but strangely I enjoy their company. I'd arrived from Adelaide the previous afternoon. I hadn't seen James and the band for a couple of months. But like a relationship with a close friend whom you only occasionally see, it's surprisingly easy to pick up where you left off.

It's difficult to feel down in Sydney, especially on such a beautiful October morning as this. Groups of tourists are congregating along Circular Quay, the transport hub of the waterfront. I make my way back up Phillip Street to the Intercontinental.

No fans right now, just Bobble in the lobby. He's tour-managed the Northern Ireland alternative rock band Ash and the Oklahoma psychedelic band The Flaming Lips. He got his nickname while travelling with The Libertines and has since run the Strictly Come Dancing Tour, so Bobble's tangoed it all in his time. In those days he looked like Homer Simpson with the kind of belly that demanded serious respect. Now he's half the man he was, but he still looks like a thin version of the cartoon character. However, unlike Homer, Bobble is always quiet and in control on the outside, even if inside he's steamin' fit to burst. During the course of the tour I never saw Bobble lose his temper.

He nods me the London equivalent of 'G'day' with a fixed neutral expression that I've come to know and understand. It's not his job to show any feeling one way or another on this. His job, as a freelance tour manager, is to get James and everybody from place to place around the world on time while squeezing the money out of every local promoter. It's a helluva challenging, 24-hour job, juggling the demands of James' management back in London with whatever crisis has just hit here on the ground. This is just another of these, and for him a pretty unimportant one at that.

'James is on his way down,' he says and bobbles off in his shorts, socks and Chelsea boots to sort out the band's clean laundry, a mountain of which in cellophane wrappers has just been deposited on one end of the reception desk.

I'm still seething with fury. I slump into a chair to wait and to think. But do I have a right to be angry just because I've put so much work into setting up the picture? No, I don't. I'm not an official part of this tour, I'm nothing more than a tolerated gatecrasher. I have no official role to play. I'm not being paid, which must mean that I am either a guest or an ancient groupie. The fact is that I have no right to complain at all. If I make a scene they have every right to tell me to fuck off back to where I came from. How did I ever get to be here? How did a grown-up father of six get to be touring with a rock band? Or, even more surprising, how did a rock band get to be touring with me? Yes, you may well ask. We'll come to that a bit later.

'Sorry, Peter, it's just not possible,' says James breezily, when he finally appears looking fresh as a daisy. 'None of us could have done it. Look at them.' Certainly the other figures gathering in the lobby do look a sorry sight. Benny has a greenish tinge to the patches of skin on his face that are not covered in hair. Karl, usually smiling Karl, looks as if he's missed a penalty. Beardy has the worried look of a man who might at any time, and without warning, throw up all over his fancy shoes.

We set off to get some photos with the Harbour Bridge as a backdrop. I can't really imagine why we need to do this – it won't make a cover.

'It's OK, Peter. It would have been good, but you can still get a great shot of the band with the bridge in the background,' Blunty tells me. That's like Hillary and Tenzing posing on a street corner in Kathmandu instead of the summit of Everest.

'Come on, let's have a go from my roof terrace,' he says, and we troop up to his penthouse balcony. George W. Bush slept here last week but his weapon(s) of mass destruction are nowhere to be seen. I go through the motions of taking a few shots. Then we troop out into the street and down to the Opera House for more.

I'm beginning now to feel a bit better about it all. What the hell! It was only a picture, wasn't it? I really don't know these people and I have to earn their trust, so there's no point in me being pissed off. That would only serve to piss everyone off. So far I've seen them at a dozen random concerts around the world.

Benny was the first, apart from James, to treat me as a friend rather than a father figure who really ought not to be here. Now wariness on all sides has given way to acceptance and genuine warmth. So don't rock the boat.

It's a warm spring morning and I start to relax as James and I walk towards the seafront. I know Sydney well and love it here, largely because of the people and the easy lifestyle. Three times I've come close to leaving England and living here. Now it's too late.

It's lunchtime and office workers are out on the quayside enjoying the sunshine. It seems to me that no one gives a second glance in our direction. James is drifting into one of his long silences. He's on the edge of one of those frequent introspective moods when it's hard to get a word out of him. Once he's actually in it, he's unreachable. Small talk at any time is, for James, a luxury in which he rarely indulges. You can sit beside him on a plane for four hours with barely a word being spoken. He's not being unfriendly, he's just being James.

To the stranger these silences can be, at best, awkward. They can even convey an impression of hostility. But once you get the hang of them they're actually companionable. I can sit in a dressing-room with him all afternoon and the only sound is the hum of the air conditioning and the click of a keyboard. I go about my business, answering emails and writing. He goes about his in a similar way. We listen to a little music on the iPod deck, swap the occasional comment on what's going on in the world, and then return to silence. At the end of it I feel I've enjoyed his company and get the impression – it can only be an impression – that he feels the same way.

One of his long-time girlfriends told me: 'Even in the early days of being together we'd go out to dinner and he'd look at me with those come-to-bed eyes, a small smile on his face, and not speak. I'm a natural chatterer and I'd talk away about my day, my work, my hopes, my dreams, and he'd just sit there in silence, eating, listening but not contributing to the conversation – if you could call it that.

'He'd never ask me anything, anything at all. He'd not even acknowledge what I was telling him. There's be no "really?" or "what did you do next?"'

'Why should I?' he'd say. 'If you want to tell me, you will tell me. If you don't want to talk, you won't. I don't feel a need, or that I have a right to ask you.'

'So I'd just keep talking and talking. Imagine what it would be like if your best friend, your lover, was in a coma after a terrible accident. You'd sit there in the hospital room, holding his hand, talking about familiar, everyday things and all the while praying that he'd respond. But for all the return you get, you might as well be chatting away to the flowers in the vase on the bedside table. What you very quickly end up doing is baring your soul to him. But he doesn't so much as give you a glimpse of his in return. It makes you very vulnerable. Sometimes I got angry at this, but then I just had to accept that that is the way he is.'

She added: 'It's not that he is being unfeeling or unfriendly, far from it. He absorbs what you say. He's a great listener. Sometimes I think it's a kind of shyness and, in a curious way, it's very endearing. The more he doesn't say to you, the more you want to say to him. I think his only way of really responding, his only way of really communicating with people is through his music. He channels all his emotions into chords and lyrics.'

I remember once in Greece I spent a whole day working on a synopsis of this book. At the end of it I went up to the roof-top pool where he was sunbathing and gave it to him on a memory stick. He said: 'Thanks for that, Peter, I'll read it later,' and he put it in his pocket. No one is more polite than James. He has impeccable manners and an absence of self-importance that is alien to the rock star image. When his older sister Emily got married in the village where the family lives, James Blunt was notably absent and in his place was a self-effacing bloke called James Blount. After the service, he stayed at the back, and when locals asked him to pose for pictures with them in the churchyard, he shook his head with a smile. 'It's not my day, it's hers,' he'd say.

The next day in Athens he handed me back the memory stick without a single word. I examined his face, but I could read nothing. I really wanted to know what he'd thought of it. Did he hate it? Did he like it? Was it going in the right direction? But he didn't say anything. We resumed our positions by the roof-top pool with views of the Acropolis and he just carried on treating me in his normal, companionable way. Out of this silence I was left to draw my own conclusions. Curiously, it was easy to do so, although in a rational sense I have no way of explaining that. He liked some of it, he liked the path I was treading, but it wasn't quite right. Keep going, you can do better.

Here, beside the Opera House, no one is bothering us. There're plenty of good sides to being famous – enormous riches being one of them. But the loss of your anonymity is wicked. Some would say – especially those who have never been truly poor – it's too high a price to pay.

Imagine not being able to sneak into a supermarket for a few essentials without drawing a hungry pack of sheep and wolves around you. Dress down, dress up, wear a big hat and shades, the more you hide, the easier the expert celebrity-seeker finds it to spot you. Signing autographs, posing for pictures with every girl and guy in the world who owns a mobile phone becomes second nature. He does all that better than any celebrity I know.

But that's only the paper-thin veneer of fame. There you are at the till, posing with Dave or Doreen for yet another picture. The dozen shoppers who have gathered to stare are now reaching for their phones, but at the same time they're feasting their eyes on what you've got in your shopping basket. Chewing gum, deodorant, shampoo, toothpaste.

James and I are walking along side by side. He's not hiding under a hat, but passers-by don't give him a second glance.

'It must be great,' I say, 'not to be noticed here. For an hour or two you can have your life back.'

'No, I can't,' he replies, quickening his pace. 'Some of them are clocking me. I can always tell. They're just not letting on because until someone makes the first move, they're not absolutely certain . . . just keep walking, Peter.'

I mean, what's with this guy? *He's* got the paranoia now – it must be catching. Here we are strolling along Circular Quay and nobody's even looking at him, let alone staring. That's it. He hates the attention but now that he's not getting any, he's actually missing it. They all protest and they're all the same: a little fame and they're famished for more. Don't you know who I am? Don't you recognize me? No, they don't, Blunty. They're honest Australians along with a smattering of Japanese tourists. To them you're just another bloke walking along the harbourside at lunchtime talking, but mostly not talking, to an older guy who may or may not be your dad. Half the world seems to think I'm his dad.

'Hi, forgive me for asking, but are you James' father?' No, I'm not. 'Oh, I understand. You and your wife must be really proud of him! Wasn't he in the army before he got famous? I seem to have read somewhere that you were in the army, too?'

Look, I'm not his father, I've even got the T-shirt to prove it. Actually, I know his dad. I'm a friend of his dad. 'Oh, I understand. It must be really difficult for you, him being so famous an' all? But we know you *are* his dad.' Fuck off, do I look *that* old?

Yes, I do. But today, I can promise you, no one recognizes him. There's not a single fan out there on Circular Quay. However, he's got it into his head that they are all watching. So maybe I'm completely, devastatingly wrong about him. I thought this was the guy who was refreshingly untouched by fame. A while back when he first hit the big time I wrote in a newspaper that James was unmoved by his new-found wealth. Beyond the bare essentials, he didn't do money. 'So far,' I wrote, 'all he's bought for himself are two pairs of jeans and four T-shirts.'

A couple of days later he rang me from LA to complain that this was simply not true.

'What do you mean?' I asked.

'I was given the T-shirts.'

Suddenly a girl wearing a white cotton dress and

weighed down with what looks like the family's weekly shopping bars the way ahead with her carrier bags.

'James! Could I have a picture of me and you?' she nervously asks. Wordlessly he takes her digital camera, puts a hand around her shoulders, stretches out his own arm, and takes the self-portrait.

That's torn it. Before the shutter's clicked we're surrounded by 50 people pushing and shoving and waving their mobiles and digitals like the feelers on a nest of cockroaches – it's a madhouse. More people join the crowd. Why? Because it's a crowd.

'Who is it?' they whisper in voices loud enough to be heard in Melbourne. 'It's James Blunt . . . Omigod, are you sure?' Fifty soon becomes 100. He stays calm, he signs, he poses, he signs.

Once, in Chicago, a pretty and pushy girl hiked up her T-shirt and wanted her breasts autographed. James happily obliged. The next thing I knew the whole crowd was pushing up their blouses and unclipping oversized bras. He kept on scribbling in black felt-nib. Mostly, after the first girl, it wasn't a pretty sight. 'I won't wash for a week!' squealed a 36D.

Somehow James struggles free. His ability to walk very fast indeed is useful in situations like this. I swear he could win the 20km Olympic Walk, where heel must touch ground before toe lifts. I'm almost running to keep up. Well, I would if I could. I make do with a racing limp.

'So how did you know?' I ask breathlessly when I manage to catch up. 'How did you *know* they were clocking you? I didn't notice a thing.'

'I'm an ex-reconnaissance officer. The army spent a lot of money training me to notice,' he laughs.

Like most people, I guess, I used to think that it might be fun to be famous. Just lately I'm beginning to discover the opposite. Most of the time it's miserable because you can't turn it off when you want to. It's the Midas principle. Everything you touch – including food – turns to gold, so you don't get to eat.

Well, actually we do. Delicious fish and chips. We're sitting on the waterfront in one of the greatest food capitals of the world eating fresh barramundi and fries and drinking Coke. Bobble, as I watch, takes two giant slices of white bread and creates a giant chip butty. James is wolfing his food down at Formula 1 speed. He has only one eating gear. Like Jackson, my chocolate Labrador, he's always anxious when you put food in front him. He looks around hastily in every direction, worrying that someone will take his bowl away before he can lick it clean.

If I didn't know better I'd think that he'd been starved as a child. Contrary to belief, he wasn't born with a proverbial silver spoon in his mouth, or in any other orifice. It was a comfortable childhood, but a far from grand one, living largely in army accommodation around the world like any other Forces family. 'It was the army that taught me to eat fast,' he says, 'so that you're ready to fight when the enemy comes over the hill.'

James' plate is already three-quarters empty. He is showing no sign of slowing. The chequered flag's just a morsel of fish and handful of hand-cut chips away when a random stranger steps into his path. An over-muscled guy in a sweat-stained wife-beater plonks a promo poster and a pen down on the table beside James' plate and grunts: 'Sign this, mate.'

James looks up at him, assesses the intrusion in his usual way, and says in a quiet voice: 'Do you mind if I don't do that right now? I'm just having lunch with these guys. If you're around in half an hour when we've finished . . .'

'What do yer mean, mate, "not right now"? I'm only asking for a fucking signature. I've paid good dollars to see your show. It's not bloody much to ask, is it?'

'Look . . .'

'No, you look, mate, it's people like me what have made you who you are and you can't even be bothered to pay us back with an autograph? You make me sick.' He storms off.

We all look at James. He doesn't say a thing. He doesn't lose his concentration for a second. His eyes are back on his plate and he's coming out of the pit lane with a roar of acceleration into the last bite of barramundi.

It's nearly time to head for the venue, The Forum, a smallish concert hall near Sydney Cricket Ground. We walk back up the hill towards the hotel. James is thinking about the intrusive fan. 'I just try to draw a really clear line. I try not to do autographs at the hotel or when I'm eating, because the hotel's mine and other people's home and the restaurant is mine and other's people's dining room,' he says. 'But I almost always step outside after a gig to meet fans and to sign autographs, because that's a clear place of work, and I'm grateful they came. If someone stops me in the street, I'll pose for a quick snap and sign an autograph. The problem is that some people don't know where this line is drawn. And why should they? They just try to grab whichever moment they can. But if everyone insists on meeting an artist at all times, the artist's life becomes impossible.'

An overtly camp couple of guys sashay down the pavement towards us. I look for any signs of recognition in their faces. I find none. We pass each other. Then, some ten metres later there's a shout from behind. We both turn: 'James Blunt!' one of them cries at the top of his voice. 'You're fuckin' beaut-iful . . . it's true!' James laughs, they laugh. I love Sydney. It seems that this multi-cultural city has taken him to not just their hearts.

Much later that night, long after the show is done, I find myself in a crush of softly scented flesh in a sophisticated nightclub. I don't know what it is called and I have no idea where in the city we are. I'm surrounded by models and I've been introduced to a couple of movie stars who I'd previously never heard of, but pretend that I have. I'm the oldest person in the room by 25 years, but I don't feel it. Actually, I don't think any of us are in a state to feel anything. Beardy is smiling away in deep conversation with two people and I'm talking to my new friend Fran, who's orchestrated this whole segment of the tour and is now in chill-down mode. Karl's curled up on a sofa with his company of the night. Benny and Malcolm are nowhere to be seen. James is at the centre of a male and female rugby-style ruck on the dance floor. Strobe lighting gives his movements a jerky cartoon quality. From his face you can clearly see he's enjoying every minute of it. He's the pedigree party animal, but somewhere under the cloak the real James is in hiding.

I take a slug of vodka and cranberry and look around. Touring with James is an alcoholic's idea of heaven. You don't have to ask for a drink. Fun just appears and is entirely free. On the table beside me there's a couple of frozen bottles of vodka and a magnum of Bollinger in a giant ice bucket. A jug of cranberry and some cans of Red Bull are buried in another dish of ice. Help yourself. I've absolutely no idea who's hosting us and who cares?

I'm learning fast, I can tell you. Touch him, and you come away with traces of stardust on your hand. Once, at the beginning of all this, I was standing in the bar at the Shepherd's Bush Empire in west London. James had just done his first London gig. He moved awkwardly around the stage, his nervousness was obvious, but it hadn't affected his singing. It was the first time I'd seen the impact he could have on a predominantly female audience. James wasn't even in the bar yet. He was still changing, or whatever. I was introduced to this coolly dressed woman in her mid-thirties who'd somehow managed to get backstage through knowing someone who worked in the theatre. We chatted inconsequentially for a couple of minutes and then out of the blue she kissed me firmly on the lips and turned to walk away. 'Hey, what's that for?' I asked.

'That's as close as I'm ever going to get to kissing James,' she replied, and was gone.

San Francisco

Blunty's in his dressing-room backstage at the Fillmore, the city's iconic venue where a lifetime ago the Sound of San Francisco was created – the Grateful Dead, Big Brother and the Holding Company and Jefferson Airplane with the mysteriously beautiful Grace Slick.

James and I have just played Guitar Hero and now he's on his laptop taking a look around the web and at his own website jamesblunt.com. Well, I guess it pays to know what they're saying about you out there in real time, even if some of it is negative. Billy, one of his closest friends, usually acts as moderator.

Is James Blunt gay?

Omigod, nooo! [says Jenny from Miami] You can feel his love for women in his lyrics and the way he sings them, the way he moves. Check out his ass! He's just the sexiest guy that's ever walked and he's got this supermodel girlfriend but I don't think he truly loves her because he kind of plays around with every girl he meets. I guess he's lookin' for true love and that's why he needs to meet me!! Who's goin' to Chicago???? I got my ticket and I just can't waiaiaiait!

Mark, the stage manager, wanders in the door. 'Sound check now, guys,' and wanders straight out again. 'Let's go,' says James. He's in jeans and T-shirt, scuffed cowboy boots, and looking hugely relaxed. The band turn off their laptops and one by one follow him out of the door. Another day, another city, another sound check, and another cheque.

The sound check is my favourite part of the day. Wherever the tour takes them, Mark and his team of roadies spend the whole day assembling the set and wiring up all the electronics. Then at 4pm – it's almost always at 4pm – James and the band wander on stage to sing and play their way through a few numbers while Mike, Gerry and others fine-tune the sound system. Technically, this is an essential part of each day. It's a practice session and a chance to experiment with chords and, just occasionally, for Blunty to air a new song.

What James and Co. wear for this 30-minute performance, watched only by a handful of venue staff and the occasional groupie who has managed to sneak inside, almost entirely reflects the location. Shorts in hot places are the usual order of the day – with Karl always bare-chested. Playing the drums at this level is serious exercise. In the course of a 90-minute concert he will expend as much energy as a Premier League footballer over the same period – and half-time is shorter. The band leaves the stage for only a few minutes while James at the piano plays 'Goodbye My Lover'.

Coats, scarves and plastic coffee cups would normally indicate Canada. Most gigs there take place in ice hockey stadiums. The playing surface has been covered by board, but you still feel you are standing inside a giant freezer.

Weirder places, such as Albania or Beirut, bring out oddball behaviour in the guys. James is quite capable of turning up for the sound check dressed in full Kermit outfit. Johnny and the others dress to the mood. Tonight it's just jeans and T-shirts – San Francisco is that kind of a place.

James breaks into 'Out Of My Mind'. The song echoes from centre stage to the sound desk near the back of the hall.

> *Judging by the look on the organ-grinder,*
> *He'll judge me by the fact that my face don't fit.*
> *It's touching that the monkey sits on my shoulder.*
> *He's waiting for the day when he gets me.*

More bass, less guitar, drum vocals, and let's hear the Wurlitzer once again. Mike The Sound, a guy paid entirely for his ears, is quietly shifting risers behind his desk and calling instructions into the PA and to his sidekick Gerry on the second desk to his right of the stage.

Blunt business is definitely monkey business. The prancing monkey is his now long-established icon. The monkey features on stage in the backdrop and it's even stamped on the packing cases of equipment that are nightly shifted from location to location.

'It's strange,' he tells me, 'that I wrote a song about being a performing monkey before I became a successful musician and then later it has become the public perception of how it all happened for me.

'The monkey symbol came from me not wanting to have my face on my first album. I wanted a logo instead of my ugly mug, and I thought the monkey was a good one. It was freeware. Elvis Costello adopted it later than me on one of his tours and then dropped it when he realized it was already being used by me.

'It's funny how people think that James Blunt and *Back To Bedlam* were created by Atlantic Records and succeeded through a massive marketing drive when, in fact, there wasn't one at all.

'My album was created by me and recorded through a tiny independent record label. No one told me how to dress, how to behave, or what to say. I just did my own thing.

'When Atlantic Records came on board to distribute the album, I was the one who said, "Let's not try and sell this album in massive quantities to begin with. Let's just let it slip out gradually. Don't count my first week's sales, because I can't match anyone else's first-week sales. Don't hope that I'll sell thousands in the first week because I don't know thousands of people. But if I sell 400 the first week maybe those 400 will tell their mates and we'll sell a thousand in the second, and then we can build from there." And that's what happened – it was a slow build.'

For me, being here this afternoon is unbelievably strange. As James sings, I'm hearing a different song but with the same title. It's one I first heard while standing on this very same spot such a long time ago that no one else with me in the room today had even been born.

'Out Of My Mind' was a hit for Buffalo Springfield, the short-lived Sixties band that served as the springboard for Neil Young and Stephen Stills. I had watched them perform it, too. Yes, I've been here to the Fillmore before, a whole 40 years before. It seems that life has gone full circle.

Glen The Lights is looking puzzled. Actually, he often looks puzzled. He cocks his head to one side and gives me a quizzical glance, with the faintest trace of a smile brushing his lips. It's as if Glen can't quite believe the extraordinary inefficiency of the equipment or local staff – or both – that he must contend with in most venues that we hit on a daily basis in the Third World. Sadly America is, for a foreigner, just that these days. I mean, have you ever tried getting IN here lately, even with a work visa?

Today his cynicism is directed at a new lighting desk. 'They tell me it's experimental,' he says, 'and it looks really good with all sorts of bells and whistles that take a little time to get to grips with. The only problem is it doesn't appear to work.'

Glen will make it work. He always does. That's why he's paid to circle the world with the band. I remember he once ran the lighting programme for an entire show in Seoul on his two laptops, which is no mean feat even for a technician of this high calibre.

On another occasion in Hong Kong he manages with two spotlights and an arsenal of real wax candle power. The local electrics were dodgy and only an hour before the show the whole lighting rig suddenly goes live, electrocuting key technician, Jonny G, who is left hanging unconscious in his harness with a hole in his hand. Jonny is lucky to get away with his life and spent the night in hospital. As Mark, the stage manager, told me later: 'The harness Jonny was wearing saved his life that night. He always wore one, but very rarely clipped it on to the rig. I used to moan at him a lot about this, but thankfully he clipped on that night and is still here to tell the tale.'

While the drama is developing, the audience is already in the arena and the whole £200,000 rig is now out of action. Blunty finds Bobble.

'Can you find a runner to pop down to the shops and buy 1,000 candles?' he asks. Quarter of an hour later 1,000 candles are delivered to the venue and the crew set them up all around the stage and start lighting them. The fire officer then arrives on the scene, saying: 'No way am I allowing that. They're a fire hazard.'

James and Bobble drag him into the dressing-room and James quietly explains to him that he has a choice:

'You've nearly killed one of our crew. So, either we're going to sue the fuck out of you, or you watch the show from the side of stage and, as fire officer, if a candle falls over, you can go ahead and do your job . . . and put it out.'

Glen then runs the whole show with just two spotlights, some smoke, a torch to backlight, and by lighting different numbers of candles for different songs. 'It was great,' said James, 'it looked like something out of Vietnam.'

I'd like to tell you about different lights and different artists at the Fillmore. Incredibly, back in the Summer (well, actually, the Winter and Spring) of Love over 40 years ago here in San Francisco I had Glen's job. Yes, I like lights. Ever since that first time here in 1966 they must have lingered in a weed-choked backwater of my bloodstream and today Blunty's brought the memories alive again.

I mean, it's so long ago it's out of sight. I was a hippy with chest-length hair. Harold Wilson was in Downing Street smoking his pipe and Lyndon B. Johnson was in the White House holding up his beagle by its ears and doing his best to napalm North Vietnam off the map.

Back then I was living and loving for a while with a twenty-something, sort-of-unknown blues singer from Austin in Texas called Janis Joplin. The first time I ever came to this theatre with Janis we bumped straightaway into the great Bill Graham, the promoter and owner of the ballroom and the man now largely credited with creating the West Coast sound. We met in the foyer. He loved his new Texan money-maker and he gave her a great big hug.

'Bill, this is Peter, he's British and needs a job,' Janis told him. Bill looked me up and down, a thin, long-haired teenager who appeared to be holding hands with his rising and ever-argumentative star singer of Big Brother and the Holding Company. Humour her, for Chrissakes!

'Hi Peter – go work the lights,' he told me, digging into his jeans pocket and finally coming up with a crumpled 20-dollar bill.

'What's that for?' I asked.

'You'll need more inks,' he replied, already moving away. 'Oh, and keep the change and try to keep her sober enough for the second half,' he added.

'Thanks,' I called after him.

'Don't thank me,' he shouted over his shoulder as he climbed the stairs two at a time, 'that's your pay.'

I found the lights in the gallery, along with a guy whose name was never imprinted upon my memory. He had the thinnest, whitest face I've ever seen. His skin was almost translucent and he was eating macro-biotic rice with ornate red-and-gold lacquered chopsticks from a crumpled sheet of silver foil. He didn't look at all well. In fact, he looked like he might die at any minute. 'You've got to balance the Yin with the Yang or your body and your mind get out of sync,' he explained, 'they go crazy.' To me, it definitely looked like a case of already too much Yin.

Beside him was a curious Heath Robinson contraption. It consisted largely of an ancient, but now electrically powered gramophone turntable, two Pyrex dinner plates, a bunch of multi-coloured poster paints and an old movie projector.

You put dabs of different colours on one of the plates, splodge the other one down on top and wiggle it about according to your mood. If the whole contraption got its Yin and Yang balanced, a kaleidoscope of colour was projected through the dancers and on to the floor and walls. Depending on your state of mind, the air of the ballroom and the figures gyrating in it hung thick with constantly changing patterns that you created with just a splodge and a wiggle.

The shop where we bought the paints is still there on Haight. I stocked up and used some of the change to buy another fifth of Southern Comfort for Janis and food for two. It was all so long ago, but today the memories are as vivid as those psychedelic colours.

'Peter, you look like you've seen a ghost,' says James,

coming off stage and heading towards Catering. 'Take a walk,' he says, 'get some fresh air before the gig.'

In a way I *have* seen a ghost, the spectre of my past. Also, I'm so hungover and messed up once again from last night's after-show that death on this delightfully balmy San Francisco afternoon has a beckoning edge of welcome.

Vague memories from last night of whole litres of Absolut vodka and gallons of cranberry juice, a froth of Californian champagne, and a slick of girls on Golden Tickets grope for the surface of my fevered mind. *I'll take everything*, says the song, prophetically.

Late summer in the city and the last sunshine of the day bathes Golden Gate Park in a soft, swirling haze of nostalgia. I've got this funny, tight feeling in my chest and a faint flutter of butterflies between my ribs. See, it's been one hell of a long time since I last skirted the Panhandle and hung a familiar right homewards on Ashbury.

I almost collide with a blue-haired, bikini-clad skateboarder being pulled along at speed by a foam-flecked German shepherd who looks just as dangerous as his owner. 'The Only Bush I Trust Is My Own' says her T-shirt. I believe her.

Right now it feels like yesterday, but it was a lifetime ago when I lived here with shoulder-length hair on a head peopled by the purple haze of Dr Timothy Leary and this idyllic new world we thought we were creating. I was 19 and hoping to study creative writing down the road at San Francisco State College. Singer-songwriter James Blunt wasn't hoping to do anything at all because he was seven and a half years short of being born.

I'm getting old and I feel history today. I can smell my baggage on the sea breeze, and a distant couple of random riffs from a Fender deep inside a gloomy Victorian house off Oak make me feel that I can almost hear history.

Back in this real time and space I once inhabited three years before Armstrong took his small step for man on the moon there was no Facebook. I mean, like, could the band just imagine a world without PlayStation 3? I read somewhere that Apollo 11 had marginally less computing power than the cheapest Japanese-made digital wristwatch. 'No one will ever need more than 637kb of memory for a personal computer,' said (supposedly) Bill Gates in 1971.

Not for the first time, I ask myself: 'Peter, what in hell are you doing here?'

I'm still trying to convince myself that this was the right thing to do. Going back after 40 years to somewhere you once found happiness and at least a working title on the meaning of your existence is not necessarily a cool move. The journey and the arrival can so easily disturb the fabric of those frail photographs you have clung to for all that time. These are no snapshot digital print-outs from an inkjet; they're Victorian glass plates etched in acid that you've clung to over all the rapids of the river of life. Drop them and they'll smash – and, with them, your perception of those days when you too were young will drift away on the whisper of the breeze now picking up off the bay. But I guess I've done this because of Blunt. Because of him, as history repeated itself, I had to come back.

Janis and I were together for just a few months before

we went our separate ways – she to heroin and a ridiculously early death, me to Fleet Street and now, so strangely, to this life on the road with James.

Yes, I've seen a ghost. Not one but many. I see Jimi Hendrix jamming on the broken sofa. I see Pigpen from the Grateful Dead wielding a pick-axe in the basement to join two houses together. I see Jim Morrison asleep in post-party slumber on the sitting-room floor. Now I see James Blunt and nightly, from a different stage, I listen to 'So Long Jimmy':

I just can't believe that it's over.
We were chilling out on the sofa,
Digging how the guitar goes

'It has references to Jimi Hendrix,' James tell me, 40 years on, 'and the piano line nods to 'Riders On The Storm', The Doors and Jim Morrison. But I wrote it with Jimmy Hogarth and my name is Jimmy – so it's just a JimmyFest. It's really me, having written a whole load of songs with Jimmy Hogarth, saying, "So long, Jimmy, I'm going off now to record my album."

'It was the song I played every day when I was driving along Mulholland Drive in LA to and from Carrie Fisher's house to Tom Rothrock's studio.'

So many memories of the past are now interlaced with the present. Above all, I see Janis walking with me here beside the park and late at night dancing by candlelight, naked save for a home-made necklace of, for God's sake, chicken bones. I see her still, singing at stop-lights, fuelled by a full fifth of Southern Comfort at 5am as I wearily

51

drove us home over the roller-coaster hills in her tiny Austin A35 at the end of an all-night gig.

Now, the first leaves of autumn are falling on to the sidewalk. It's autumn for me in my life, too, and winter will inevitably follow. So I'm living it.

Janis Joplin to James Blunt. It seems such an impossible step, but there it is. How the two of them became entangled in my life is all part of the unfurling mystery. More than four decades later I'm back in San Francisco, travelling with Blunty and his band as they move at breakneck speed from city to city and country to country playing tracks from his *All The Lost Souls* and *Back To Bedlam* albums to packed or not always packed arenas. His critics – and there are many – feel he's got his just reward in being condemned to sing 'You're Beautiful' and 'Goodbye My Lover' on a nightly basis to strangers from Tallinn to Toledo for the rest of his life. My take is different. I've actually grown to love both songs for reasons that may or may not become clear.

Janis and James – they sound like a primary school reader – are two contrastingly different musicians who lived and live a whole generation apart. But to me there are curious parallels. Had they met, I'd like to believe that they would have found much in common, not least a wickedly dry and delightfully perverted sense of humour. Both shag(ged) for their country with honour, but I don't for a moment think they would have fancied each other. James likes his women to be enviably good-looking. Janis wasn't that fussed about her men. After all, they did include me. However, I'd like to think that the two of them would have become friends. Both have truly remarkable voices as well as that almost tangible intensity and single-mindedness that has brought global success. Both are marked by an unhappiness, an intangible void in their lives that sets them apart. Music alone – not people – can help to ease the pain of this solitary existence. To peer once again into that soul-sucking void is why I now feel compelled to make my journey.

Ibiza

'Please come to the launch. It's going to be a big evening and I think it's important that you're there,' says James.

'But I won't be able to walk. I'll be on crutches or, at the very best, hobbling on a stick,' I protest.

'Then, I'll carry you around Ibiza on my back,' he smiles, and adds after a pause, 'You know I mean it.'

I know he does. James and I are sitting drinking large glasses of Australian white wine at lunchtime in a pleasant house in the rural depths of Hampshire and there are quite literally dozens and dozens of people fussing about and using this room simultaneously as a corridor, a kitchen and a conference room.

Outside in the walled garden a giant marquee is being erected. At my feet a small springer spaniel nuzzles my legs in an attempt to block out all this unfamiliar activity. You know what's also refreshingly strange? None of them, not one of these people bustling around us, gives a damn right now about the famous James Blunt. Indeed, it's almost as if, away from the bright lights, you don't really materially exist, James. It's as if you're a ghost in this eighteenth-century room that only I and no one else can see.

Blunty, you're part of the furniture. No, I'll go further than that, the furniture matters, and you don't. For at this moment a handsome, but fierce woman of indeterminate age approaches us with intent. In one hand she is carrying a vacuum cleaner and with the other she firmly grasps the chair you are sitting on. Like a Jack Russell terrier with a rat between its teeth, she shakes it forwards several times in a sudden and brusque emptying gesture. You're caught unawares, but with a nimble bit of well-practised stagecraft, you manage to land on your feet rather than on the floor. You look around, but with not much surprise.

'Off! James,' she says, a bit late and in a rich Hampshire accent. 'Oi've seen mixie rabbits move faster than you. You're in the way and oi need this chair now.'

We *are* in the way. We're in Blunty's family home and far more important events are happening here than any album launch. James' sister, Emily, is getting married to Guy here tomorrow. It's pissing with rain outside and there's lots more promised for tomorrow. We make a hasty retreat into a den dominated by a freshly dusted stag's head that dwarfs the platinum disc hanging on the wall beneath it.

I've just heard the tracks of *All The Lost Souls* for the very first time. We've listened to them twice. Sophomore albums are notoriously treacherous and *Back To Bedlam* and 'You're Beautiful' are such a hard act to follow. *Bedlam*, released in 2004, was officially the bestselling album in the UK of the decade. Beat that.

'What do you think?' he finally asks when the room falls silent. I like it. I'm surprised by how much I like it. I've heard at least four songs here that are potential hit singles and I say so to James.

To my surprise, he looks hugely relieved and pleased by this. Why he should possibly value my amateur opinion is beyond me. What I know about the music industry could largely be written on the palm of one of my hands. A couple of months ago, when we'd last talked seriously, his nervousness about the next stage of his career was apparent, despite a veneer of bravado. I warmed to that. You might think that with millions of sales under his belt and the sudden fame that it had brought him, he could afford a measured level of arrogance about his future. After all, he's now a household name. But James doesn't do arrogance. At times, I think he really doesn't begin to understand the level of stardom he has already attained.

The image of James Blunt At Home in Ibiza is a positive one. At a time when the money has dropped out of the worldwide music industry, he's planning his launch in forgotten style. He's chartered a plane and invited a hundred of the top critics on both sides of the Atlantic to a private concert at sunset and all-night barbecue party at a villa near his cherished home on the Spanish island.

So how about carrying around a middle-aged monkey on your back all evening? What would that do for your international image? The very concept would be enough to cause Todd, his manager, who skilfully steers the course of James' musical career through the reefs of the industry, to seek permanent sanctuary in a remote Tibetan monastery.

But James has no intention of allowing the fact that I am having a hip operation ten days earlier to interfere with his arrangements.

'So come and stay with me. We'll find a room for you on the ground floor – and I'll carry you around,' says James. What can I do but accept?

The surgeon, when I dare to tell him, looks at me with

disbelief. 'Ibiza and James Blunt? You won't be able to walk. Yes, go if you must, but try and avoid waterskiing . . . and don't go clubbing. Get some early nights. The anaesthetic takes a long time to wear off.'

Early nights? Tap, tap, tap. Leaning heavily on a walking stick, I hobble up the stone steps of James' Ibizan farmhouse home.

'You must be Peter,' says a girl who materializes from James' bedroom at the top of the stairs. She's wearing a Panama hat and traces of a bikini. It's a very nice bikini. It's just that there's not much of it.

Blunty's out rehearsing with the band. They recorded the album in a studio in LA earlier in the year. But they don't know the music well enough and they're working against the clock to learn it before the show. Mika, the owner of the micro-bikini, is a newcomer on the scene that I haven't met before, but we quickly become friends and spend the afternoon together in the garden. The sweet scent of bougainvillea fills the air and the sunlight refracts crazily off the spume of spray and skin as Mika powers her sleek body through length after length of the blue-tiled pool.

We lie back side by side on sun loungers. Well, she lies back. Me? I've barely moved or shed a layer since I arrived here in paradise and neither Mika nor the pool is yet ready for the sight of my exposed body. Blunty, I'd just like you to know that she's safe with me. I'm really not going to run off with her, not least because I can hardly walk, let alone run. Anyway, it's therapy time.

Could James have a monogamous relationship with anyone?

Well, in my humble opinion, the eve of an 18-month world tour is probably not the best time to put that idea to the test, is it? Let's just say I wouldn't put all my life's chips on red or black. But I don't say any of that because I'm saved by the bell. Just then Benny comes bounding through the blue gate and down the steps into the garden like a high-spirited boxer dog.

'Uncle Peter? What the hell are you doing here?' he says, giving me a hairy hug. 'I thought you were in hospital?'

I was, Benny, I should be – and in a mental hospital at that. Bedlam, London's eighteenth-century Royal Bethlem lunatic asylum, would fit the bill nicely.

James doesn't want all these strangers in his house. So the show is taking place in a similar-sized hill-top villa a few miles away that's been rented for the occasion. What privacy he has in his over-exposed life is largely here in Ibiza and he guards it with a jealous passion. No sign marks the entrance to the long, steep driveway up to Casa Blunt and it looks like just another pot-holed trail in the virgin woodland that covers much of the island's interior.

Any paparazzi who go orienteering here in search of Blunty at play do so at great personal risk, according to local press and internet reports.

'Singer-songwriter James Blunt has bought a gun which fires rocks to scare away fans who congregate outside his new home on the Spanish island of Ibiza,' says one site.

'Blunt has bought a weapon that fires only rocks to protect himself from stalkers and obsessive fans at his new millionaire's pad in Ibiza', says a newspaper, the source of the story. It is, of course, just another example of the complete bullshit that daily finds its way into print and on to the web. Inventing rubbish like this is how some showbiz writers get their rocks off.

James looks tired and tense, but greets me warmly: 'Like the stick. See, you can walk a bit! Stay sober tomorrow, we don't want you falling over at the party and hurting somebody.'

I awake at dawn to the sound of music and tap my way up the stairs from bedroom to sitting room. James is at his piano, in pyjama bottoms and shirtless, listening intently to '1973' on his laptop. I wait for the track to end. He still looks tired. I can't work out whether he's just got up or is about to go to bed.

'Do you prefer that version, or this?' he says, pressing a button.

'I can't tell any difference between them,' I say. He looks at me in frank astonishment, and then plays a third.

'Are you worried about tonight?' I ask. 'I guess there's a lot riding on it.'

'Not at all,' he smiles. 'I mean, it's only all the biggest names among the world's music press that are coming to listen – no pressure. Yesterday I did a long and kind of strange interview with Austin Scaggs from *Rolling Stone*. But, actually, no, I'm relaxed about it.

'I don't have to prove anything to anybody because I never, ever set out to do that. I made an album that *happened* to be successful. Now I've made another one. It's pretty immaterial whether it is successful or not. There's a lot more to life than worrying about whether a song or collection of songs goes up or down a chart.' I believe him, sort of.

The gig takes place on a stage that, like the infinity

pool on the terrace below it, blends with the sky and the Mediterranean. It's a magnificent setting that the brooding prospect of a thunderstorm fails to spoil.

My kind of fellow travel journalists are blasé about lavish entertainment. Being wined and dined around the world by those who want to get written about is all part of the job. But these music guys are obviously on the wrong side of the scribbling business. What Atlantic Records have done – importing them en masse for 20 hours to James' island home – is bold, cool, and apparently unprecedented.

'Normally my idea of a good night out reviewing music is to pass swiftly through the metal detector at White City,' said one London critic, looking around him in amazement at the liveried staff barbecuing seafood and serving exotic cocktails on the lawn.

Whether they like *All The Lost Souls* or not, Blunty and the band will have to wait to find out. But the outcome is pretty much a foregone conclusion. As one said to me on the night: 'I think the album's not bad at all. I actually really quite like some of it and James seems like a regular good bloke. But am I going to write that? Not bloody likely. It's more than my job's worth. Newspapers have decided for some reason that James is there to be kicked.' Sad and predictable, but boy, do they like the surroundings! Some time much later when the music is done and dusted and the river of vodka, wine, beer and every other drink known to Ibiza – and believe you me, there are a lot of them – is in full spate, Blunty comes looking for me.

I'm in deep reminiscence about Elvis Presley with the

only guy in the garden who is conceivably of my own age.

'I saw him once in concert,' I say proudly.

'I worked with him. He was my first client,' says my drinking companion.

Did he just say that? Jesus, this drink is strong. What's in it?

'Good evening, Frank,' says Blunty, popping up by my side out of nowhere.

'James,' says Frank, with a proprietorial smile and a nod of a job well done.

'Peter,' says Blunty, 'time to go.' He doesn't actually carry me as promised, but he scoops me up into the passenger seat of his car, with Mika in her signature Panama hat in the seat behind him. We roar away down the hill from the music business.

'Did you enjoy it?' asks James.

'I loved it,' I reply. 'Who's Frank? Seems a good bloke.'

'He's God.'

'Right.' What did I say to him?

'How are you feeling, how's the hip?'

'No problem.' I realize with alcohol-fuelled clarity that this must be true. I've left my walking stick behind. I'm sure Frank doesn't need it unless he feels the urge to beat a critic or two over the head.

'Good,' says Blunty, changing gear, 'because now . . . now we're going to party.'

No one, really, should dwell upon the remainder of the night. I remember we went to a roof-top bar with armchairs and sofas in the open air. The worry then was where next? Finding yourself at 5am far from home and in need of being there is a natural hazard of life with James. When you can't walk, it's worse.

We could have headed out to Pacha, Ibiza's iconic club that is synonymous with James. But there are other good places on the island – and much the best one is very private and very good fun. Some people have fairies at the bottom of their garden; Blunty has his own nightclub. 'Blunty's Nightclub Where EVERYBODY'S Beautiful' says the neon sign that formerly graced the wall of every after-show party during the Bedlam world tour.

My shambolic 7am departure from Ibiza together with the band has echoes of Napoleon's retreat from Moscow 195 years earlier, without the cold. We stagger from garden, to taxi, to Ibiza airport, casting belongings aside along the way to lighten our load. If I'd had a musket I would have used it to put myself out of my misery.

'I feel so bad,' says Karl, who's lost his ability to smile, 'that I don't think it's actually possible to feel worse than this and still be alive.'

The months ahead will test this statement to the full. All The Lost Souls are on their way.

Cardiff

'Can someone explain to me,' says James, 'why what is billed as my UK Autumn Tour started in Amsterdam and moved on to Paris before going directly to . . . Cardiff?'

Scampi shakes his head. Stuart Camp is an important and friendly figure in James' management team who puts in an appearance from time to time. Benny is frightened to shake his own head for fear that it will fall off. He's already got the mother and father of a hangover from Amsterdam and that's doubled after Paris. It's a warm late autumn afternoon and we're sitting in a clinical dressing-room in the Cardiff International Arena.

Cardiff doesn't strike many emotional chords with me. I did once interview Shirley Bassey, who was born pre-World War II in the migrant dockland melting pot of Tiger Bay, then a notorious red-light district but renamed and gentrified as Cardiff Bay. But she moved when she was two and couldn't remember a thing about it. The same could probably be said of Robbie Williams, who stayed here more recently at Rocco Forte's swank St David's Hotel. This five-star edifice stands more *in* than *on* the waterfront and looks like a schooner in full sail.

There's not a working girl in sight these days, unless you count the hardcore groupies who hang around the back of the CIA and outside the hotel entrance when a star comes to town. *Condé Nast Traveller* ranked it one of the Top 20 coolest hotels in the world. Williams is said, possibly apocryphally, to have spent his stay trying to hurl TV sets into the bay from his penthouse suite. He made a brave effort, but couldn't quite get one into the water. Room service took it in their stride.

'Another set? Any particular screen size? Full plasma? Certainly sir, our latest model is on its way.'

For me this part of South Wales spells depression: the horror of Aberfan, where a whole generation of school-children died in a rock and mud slide 41 years ago almost to the day. I was there in Ebbw Vale when the coal mines closed and the steel-making furnaces finally cooled. My great-grandfather had been an apprentice here full of hope for the future. But in the borrowed winter warmth of pubs and working men's clubs I saw only despair in the dead eyes of men nursing a single beer and playing dominoes in silence before shuffling out into the cold darkness of permanent unemployment.

I've been to a murder here . . . but that's no surprise. As a young reporter I seemed to have been to a murder almost everywhere in Britain. I used to be able to place them by the red telephone boxes from where I had phoned in my story.

However, Cardiff's looking good these days, with modern clean buildings, bright shops and a positive spring in the step of the people out and about on what's destined to be the last warm and sunlit afternoon of the year. The same can't be said of the acoustics inside.

'The sound's awful,' moans Beardy, appearing from the stage, 'and they've only sold about 5,000 tickets.'

Acoustics are not the only problem. After three weeks

of continuous partying in Ibiza, James has got a heavy cold and his whole body is completely run down like a vintage wind-up gramophone. What he needs right now is a fortnight on a chemical-free health farm with regular meals and eight hours' sleep a night, not a crazy four-month tour of Europe.

I tell him. He grins and croaks. James doesn't do illness. No one on tour is allowed to do illness. No matter how terrible you feel, the show, as they say in the true spirit of showbusiness, goes on.

'What do you do if you've got a cold?' It's a regular question for at least one of the half dozen interviews or press conferences that he gives each day.

'You pass it on to someone else as quick as you can,' he instantly quips.

Today's no joke. His voice box is barely functioning, but he won't accept that. In Paris he felt so bad that he rang his friend Diana Jenkins. Here he was at the start of the tour and unable to sing. Cancellation was simply not a fan-friendly or financial option.

'Diana, what do I do? Have you any ideas?'

Diana, who comes originally from Sarajevo, is not only exceedingly beautiful and stunningly wealthy, she's also a born fixer. If you survived your teens in the bombed ruins of Sarajevo under siege, you learned to be a fixer. Diana seems to have fixed quite a lot since then.

'Don't worry, darling, I know just the thing,' she purrs. 'Tell me where you are and I'll send a doctor over.' Just like that. When she was poor she watched friends die from lack of medical care. Now that she is rich, I expect Diana has a doctor on tap in every port.

I wasn't in Paris, but James explains what happened next: 'Five minutes before show-time, an Eastern European-looking woman in a white coat and with a stethoscope round her neck appears in my dressing-room holding an eight-inch syringe and matching hypodermic needle, wraps a rubber cord round my arm and shoves the needle in.

'At that moment, Bobble pops his head round the door, has a flashback to his time managing The Libertines, and passes out. It's not enough that he's got a packed auditorium out there, we're by now running late and his principal can't sing, but now he's shooting up in his dressing-room with a strange woman who looks like she's an experimental scientist from the KGB.

'I don't know the name of what she gave me, but the next thing I knew I was climbing up on the stage over Karl with a smile on my face and don't remember missing a note.'

But relief was temporary. Tonight this Cardiff dressing-room has taken on the ambience of an A&E after chucking-out time on a Saturday night in any county town in Britain. No glamour here. James is hiding beneath a welter of white towels, inhaling steam and eucalyptus oil. He's downed half a bottle of cough mixture and he's drunk a pint of lemon and honey. Now, with 60 minutes to curtain time, he emerges from the towels and gargles deeply with a mixture of salt and hot water. Gargle, hawk, spit and again gargle, hawk, spit. There's no end to glamour on the road. Blunty passionately believes that he owes it to the audience to give it a try, however bad he feels. 'I think it's better to show up and do your best, rather than to cancel. Touching wood, I've so far never cancelled a performance through illness.'

The rest of us mooch around and check emails and Facebook. Like the real world, life on the road revolves around the net. If the stadium's not wireless on arrival it soon becomes so. One of the real advantages of travelling with a whole crew of pro electronic wizards is that they carry a galaxy of satellite dishes. Even if the terrestrial wires don't work, you are rarely megabyte-less.

Johnny Garrison, the new bass player, is sliding seamlessly into the familiar scene. For a start, he plays Facebook and footie to the same high standard as his guitar. Kicking a ball and social networking are big ways of fighting the boredom, which is a major ingredient of this gypsy existence. Usually between the end of the sound check at 4.30pm and 9pm when James goes on stage there's more than four empty hours to fill in the soulless surroundings of the arsehole of some godforsaken arena or stadium on the outskirts of a city that, unless you make a supreme effort, you never get to see.

The Blunty tour even carries its own goalposts buried in one of the pantechnicons that accompanies the 40-strong group of performers and roadies on the bus legs of the itinerary. The James Blunt show excels at moving goalposts. After the sound check the front section of the empty auditorium is regularly transformed into a football pitch.

The rule of thumb is the bigger the venue, the worse the back-of-house – Cardiff's OK, but London's 02 has all the charm, fixtures and fittings of an Albanian motel room.

If, as now, we're travelling by tour bus, the venue dressing-room is the family abode for at least 12 hours of every day. Blunty insists on giving it all the comforts of home as the tour moves on a crazy 180 times a year. To him, such details are essential methods for holding the band together as a – nearly always – happy family. If the surroundings are good, the mood is good – it's as simple as that.

Usually it's not one, but two dressing-rooms that have been set aside in the rabbit warren of corridors behind the stage. Occasionally, just occasionally, these come sumptuously furnished with soft sofas, subdued lighting and rich pile carpets, and there's a designer bathroom attached. But more often than not, it's a locker room with strip-lights exuding all the ambience of a railway station urinal.

Each day on arrival, these rooms have to be transformed from house to temporary tour home in a well-rehearsed domestic ritual. Sometimes scuffed cream walls are lined with black felt. If the furniture's not up to standard, it's removed and replaced with Blunty sofas and tables stored in one of the trucks. Two large items travel to each venue: the giant wheelie wardrobe of stage clothes and Blunty's entertainment console, an almost-as-big wheelie box of disco sound system complete with mixing decks and every conceivable electronic game from Guitar Hero to PlayStation football.

The daily domestic ritual goes like this: at around dawn the tour bus usually comes to a halt in a car park outside or inside the rear end of another arena in another city. James and the boys in the band sleep on in their bunks until around midday. Then, one by one they stagger from the bus, dump their hand luggage in one of the rooms and move directly on to Catering for a heart-attack breakfast, followed by a shower and change of clothes.

Bobble and Mark, as tour manager and stage/show manager, don't get the luxury of a lie-in. The clock for tonight is already ticking. Among their many other tasks on arrival they will give orders to the arena staff to start licking the dressing-rooms into their acceptable, familiar shape. You've got to keep the boss happy.

Firstly, there's a table, complete with tablecloth, bearing all the essential bits and bobs that keeps his voice in tune: Listerine, Dr Stuart's Extraordinarily Good Teas, Good Earth Organic White Tea Sweet Citrus, Yoga Ayurvedic Herbal Tea, Twinings Pure Peppermint, Earl Grey, Cherry and Cinnamon, Manuka honey, a kettle, cups, salt, fresh lemons, ginger and Marmite.

Marmite? Just before he leaves the dressing-room for the start of each show James swallows a whole spoonful to coat his throat. He says the vitamin B12 that it contains helps protect his voice. Halfway through the tour, he discovered squeezy Marmite. He'd take it on stage with him to eat when the lights went down between songs. However, this practice stopped one night somewhere in the American Bible Belt, when in the darkness he missed his mouth. When the spotlight came back on, his face and right hand were covered in a dubious brown substance that deadened his guitar strings. He's since employed someone to feed him the Marmite from the side of the stage.

Then there's the rest of the bar: a cold cabinet or, in

more primitive venues, trays packed with melting ice cubes. These nightly contain 72 cans of beer – half Peroni, half Corona – along with 12 Cokes, 12 Diet Cokes, 12 mixed soft drinks, eight cans of Red Bull, four litres of orange juice and two litres of cranberry juice. Then there's two bottles of Absolut vodka, a bottle of Jack Daniel's, one bottle of red wine and one bottle of white wine.

While we're on the subject, don't imagine that the crew go thirsty. They consume (before they raid the dressing-room) 48 local beers, 36 litres of mineral water, 12 Diet Cokes, two bottles of red wine and two bottles of white wine. Unlike the musicians, it needs to be fine wine. The crew really appreciate their wine – and they know a lot about it.

Of course the day and night – they tend to blur into one – doesn't end in the dressing-room. Each bus carries an emergency arsenal of 36 local beers, one bottle of vodka, one red wine, one white wine, 24 cans of assorted soft drinks and 12 litres of mineral water. On the band bus there's an extra escalating 'trophy' bar of champagne and fine wines that have been presented by hotels, sponsors and other hosts along the way. It's only fair to drink your share.

The first dressing-room is designated for James alone as the star, and the second is for the band. But that's not how Blunty runs his business. It's one for all and all for one. He always leads from the front. One is where they will live together for the day, while the other is set aside for the after-show. If you want quiet/sleep time, the second one is where you can chill in the afternoon.

In the late morning, Beardy is nearly always the first

of the band out of his bunk and the bus. By this time the main dressing-room should already have reached a reasonable level of readiness. He parks his overnight bag, moves mine for the sake of it, and walks twice around the room examining the furniture and looking behind sofas for the location of electrical plug points. 'This won't do,' he says, shaking his head, 'this won't do at all.'

All the furniture is in the wrong place – in particular, the wardrobe should be over there instead of here, while the disco box should be in the far corner. For five minutes the whole room is given over to Beardy's puffing and shuffling as he switches from musician to interior designer and rearranges the room at least three times to his final satisfaction.

Finally he is happy with his efforts. He fishes around in his bag for the right electrical adapter and cables before going to Production to find out the internet username and password. Then with a sigh of contentment, he sinks into his chosen sofa and opens his laptop.

Enter Blunty (stage right)

James stands in the doorway assessing the scene like Wellington on the eve of Waterloo. Then he starts to move the heavy stage wardrobe back to the far end of the room, where it had been five minutes earlier. Sergeant Beardy snaps shut his laptop and leaps to his feet. Together, under James' instructions, every item of furniture is shifted to a fresh position.

'There, that's much better,' says Beardy with a second sigh of contentment when they've finished. He settles down again on a different sofa at the other end of the room and reopens his laptop.

Tonight there's another piece of furniture in the room. In Paris, Johnny stumbled across a large and mysterious parcel in the corridor addressed to James. He brought it into the dressing-room, and got hell for it. Johnny's been living for yonks in New York and is naively unaware of the daily risks of terrorism we've all learned to accept over here: 'Unaccompanied luggage will be removed and may be destroyed' is the European mantra.

'It could have been a bomb, Johnny,' says Karl.

'There's people out there that don't like Blunty,' says Benny.

'There's people out there that fucking hate Blunty, and the rest of you – and with good reason,' says Brian, the guitar tech, to hoots of laughter. Brian is a Scotsman with a razor-edged sense of humour. His job is to look after all the guitars – mend them, string them, tune them, pack them, unpack them, and then hand them to the guys on stage. In a standard gig James changes guitar around a dozen times.

Johnny looked suitably sheepish. It's opening time. They make him take the paper off. If the thought that the parcel could have been a bomb sent a shiver of fear down the assembled spines, its contents now displayed on the Cardiff dressing-room table are far more frightening.

The package contains a smart oversized briefcase of the type favoured by airline pilots because it's self-standing. Inside this is a glass-fronted display cabinet about the size of a small TV. Inside the cabinet is a room with a fireplace and furniture and it's not just any room. It's James' room – in miniature.

The centrepiece is a piano with its empty stool waiting

for its owner to sit down and start composing. It looks to me dangerously like the grand in the sitting room of his farmhouse home in the hills of Ibiza with a riot of bougainvillea outside the door. Perfect miniature pictures adorn the walls. There's a family portrait, I recognize his sisters, his mother and father. A tiny framed aerial photograph gives a bird's-eye view of the Ibizan villa – you can even make out the terraces and the shape of the swimming pool. Another displays ten golden discs. Yet another shows Elstree prep school and Harrow – with a straw boater on the shelf above. A pair of skis and poles are propped up against the wall. Books are scattered around the place and an open copy of Aldous Huxley's *Brave New World* lies open on the carpet. It's as if someone's been at the soma, Huxley's dream-inducing drug. Fantasy is tripping into reality. Only someone with insider knowledge could have any idea that in recent weeks James has been rereading *Brave New World*. On the table there's a bottle of Corona – his beer of choice – and a jar of Marmite with a doll's-house spoon beside it. Everything, each tiny detail, has been created to scale. Spellbound, we stare in through the glass window pane. It's a work of art that must have taken hundreds of hours to produce, and its detail is scary beyond belief.

'James,' says the short accompanying letter, 'through your music you have changed and enriched my life in so many ways. I wanted to give you a present to say thanks for all that you have done for me and the pleasure you give me. Here it is. Call me.'

James just stares at it, with worried eyes and a nervous smile on his face. We go on to discuss the fact that what this box represents is the ridge between admiration and intrusion, between fan and stalker . . . between a consensual snog and a brutal rape.

'The details are so real,' he says when we talk about it again later, 'that briefly I thought she had somehow actually reached inside my real life. For a moment I thought I saw my own bedside table at home and what only I knew was on it.' It was made with love, but it could be perceived as being a bit frightening as well.

The letter went on: 'I've made it so that you can, if you like, remove the front glass and add to it.'

'I'm just afraid,' says James, 'that all that's missing inside it is me. If I get to look behind the sofa or the piano I'll find my body lying there on the floor.' Mr Blunt, in the library, with a guitar string.

'Maybe there's a remote camera lens in there and right now they are looking at us looking in,' suggests Brian. It's a joke, but somehow not as silly as it sounds.

There're 30 minutes to go and Bobble slips an iPod into the docking station. Time to warm up what voices are left around here. The band moves into a series of repetitive vocal exercises dictated by the girl voice coach who has designed this nightly 20-minute routine. As they sing, they change into stage clothes at the same time. Ben loosens his fingers, playing silent chords on one of his guitars. The exercise track ends and is followed by whatever music one of them chooses on his own iPod. Anything as long as it's fast. Manically, they start to dance, warming muscles and minds. Adrenaline's starting to flow.

I take a peep at the audience. I've got a wad of Golden Tickets burning a hole in my pocket and it's time to start giving them away. Each night James and the band invite – depending on their mood – anywhere from half a dozen to 40 people backstage for the after-show party. The hardcore of those present is made up of local sponsors and organizers, and private guests of the band. For the randomly chosen ones from the audience it does help if you happen to be good-looking. It's a fairy-tale ending to the concert, a chance to meet James along with members of the band and briefly chat to them over a drink. The rules, according to the legend on the printed ticket, are simple: 'no cameras, no autographs, just fun'. To have the possibility of being singled out for a ticket your chances greatly improve if you're not a recognized fan-club member or a groupie.

Suitability as a potential guest highlights the fragile line that James and the band must draw between their public and private lives. The concert is public. Backstage is private. The concert is for fans of the music. Anyone offered the chance to go backstage gets to meet them not as musicians but as guys. For the person – tonight, me – given the task, choosing the guests carries a heavy responsibility. Pick the wrong person, someone who doesn't respect the rules, and the artist's privacy can be seriously breached by consequent newspaper stories and internet blogs. Not just at the party, but throughout each day, getting the balance right between public and private is never far from James' thoughts.

Teddy Thompson, the support act, has finished and the press of hardcore fans at the front is thickening. You can feel the buzz of excitement building. As soon as the doors open they race each other for the front row and now I recognize a familiar handful of boardies among them.

Boardies are the tight-knit bunch of friendly, fanatical, hardcore fans. They are the home crowd who hang out on the notice board of jamesblunt.com and who travel, whenever finances and time permit, from gig to gig. Boardies are not at all to be confused with groupies, although there is an element of crossover here. I mean, is there a female boardie out there who wouldn't take up a no-strings night with James, if it was on offer? That should spark a new thread.

But in general these are the *really* dedicated fans. Their 'need' is not the physical one. What they want to do is gather as much information as possible about James as well as pictures of him and the band. They share these on the web forum with other like-minded boardies. In keeping with the vibrant club atmosphere, they often join up and go to gigs together. Essentially, they're really good people who have James at their hearts.

Mostly it's harmless fun, his truly starry-eyed followers sharing their news and experiences with each other. But just occasionally, in their desire to learn more about him, one of them will cross the line. Affectionately, James calls some of them stalkers, even giving one of the website's most famous boardies the name Steve The Stalker.

They, of course, don't always see it that way. 'It's the other way around,' says a female post on his website, 'he's stalking us.' She may, of course, have a point.

The vast majority of the general audience is made up of local girls and boys who've bought the music and their tickets to see him on stage in their home town or country.

Next come the hardcore of dead-eyed groupies whose ambition is to have sex with him – or one of the band will just about do. Not all of them are girls. The most dedicated and single-minded of these follow him from show to show and sometimes from continent to continent. In the United States they tend to hunt in geographically zoned packs – intense rivalry breaks out if an individual or part of a pack strays outside its own territory. Night after night you see the same faces in the front rows.

Lastly, there are the nutters who have lost all sense of perspective and control over their emotions in relation to this bloke with the high voice who now consumes their dreams. These are the ones who have the potential to be dangerous.

Tonight, the friendly faces of the boardies are here in force, and it's obvious James appreciates them. They all have nicknames like Lonely Dancer, Pookey, Tartan Rainbow, and . . . er . . . Franticfred. One of the most remarkable is a man whose board name is Fentiger. His real name is James Blunt. Not *our* James Blunt. A *real* James Blunt. So amused was he to find a singer impersonating him that he created a website called the Monkey King's Amazing Book of Facts, which documents everything about James' career. James' record label even uses it to reference things that they themselves don't know. On his first encounter with the singer, he told him, 'Hello, I'm the real James Blunt.'

Tonight, there are many more men in the audience than there used to be. Ben blames *Top Gear*. James' interview with Jeremy Clarkson has done wonders for his tarnished image among British men. Blunty should be paying

Clarkson to do all his PR for him. Blokes who've spent the previous couple of years rubbishing him are now thinking, 'Blimey, he's not the posh poofter I thought he was. He knows how to race a car and if he can't actually beat Clarkson on the track, he can beat him with words.'

My theory is that, egged on by the Red Tops and an embittered DJ or two, blokes have been collectively shafting Blunty on three fronts.

One: raw jealousy that their girlfriends/wives go dreamy at the first chords of not just 'You're Beautiful' and 'Goodbye My Lover', but any of his songs.

Two: unlike Chris Martin and other star singers who also went to a fee-paying public school, Blunty's speaking voice remains relatively posh and his singing one has an unusual vocal range. He can hit high notes that other voices can't reach.

Three: he's getting laid and wallowing in it. And they're not getting any of it. Well, just occasionally they're getting it from their girlfriend or wife, and she's lying there imagining that she's being shagged by James Blunt. All in all it's enough to make you want to hate the bastard. And they do. But now, maybe – and it is just a maybe – this Blunt is possibly not quite such a Berkeley Hunt after all. Clarkson quite clearly likes him and he's the original regular bloke, isn't he? *Top Gear* has added a pint of lubricant to the engine of the James Blunt juggernaut.

The backlash against James is solely confined to Britain where his critics like to maintain that his music is only appreciated by women. But I don't think this is true at all.

His online following is 45 per cent women and 55 per cent men. These are people who take an interest in his official website as well as his entries on Facebook, Twitter and other social media. But interestingly a much lower percentage of men are actually prepared to actively respond online. For example if a new picture of him is posted on Facebook, only 30 per cent of comments come from men.

But my own straw poll at half a dozen venues in England, Wales and Scotland puts the mix of concert-goers at almost 50:50. His critics have engineered the idea that cool guys don't like James Blunt – and if secretly they do, it's definitely uncool to say so in public. I guess the problem that James faces in Britain is that men are women when it comes to standing out from men.

Personally I think that most men connect hugely with his music – even if they're afraid to admit it – because the feelings expressed in his songs are written from a male perspective. This is what they'd like to put across to their partners. Women connect in part because these are the sentiments they *hope* their men are struggling to say to them, but mainly because they love his voice.

So what these guys are doing tonight is, in the words of John Lennon, giving peace a chance. Instead of sending their partners off with their girlfriends to see Blunt while they go down the pub and rubbish him some more, they're coming along to take a look for themselves.

The following evening down the boozer over a pint, or in the wine bar with a frosted flute of Veuve Clicquot in hand, there's likely to be more than one attempt at calling, 'Time, gentlemen, please on Blunt is a c**t.' In reality, he's rather proud of his elevation to the pages of the dictionary of rhyming slang.

'I went with Megan to see James Blunt in concert last night.'

'You did what, boyo?'

'Yes, it wasn't what I expected at all. In fact it was really not so bad. See, I've never *listened* to any of his songs before and it's a great stage act. I'll give that bloke one thing, he really knows how to work an audience. Mind you, don't get me wrong, I'm not saying I'm going to go out and buy his albums. But I think Megan was pleased I went with her . . . I can sort of see what she sees in him . . . and when we got home, why you wouldn't believe . . .'

'Never thought I'd live to hear you say that. I did see him on that wotsit with Jeremy Clarkson, and he didn't come across as quite the tosser I heard he was.'

Then the show gets under way with a full-on Welsh roar to which the boardies contribute. Half are fixated on James or their chosen member of the band and singing along – not always in tune – while the rest seem intent on relaying the proceedings by mobile phone to his website and other boardies who couldn't make it.

'Well, we queued up since ten, doors opened and everyone pushed, though we're at the front but right at the side!'

'Oh, well, poo happens!' posts Sweetie Nicola. 'Amazing amazing amazing! James looked ill and he didn't talk much, but it was out of this world! His new song 'Turn Me On' is fecking amazing!'

'James can't be sick! He has the immunity of a Super Hero!!' responds Faith70. 'He's fine . . . nothing a little (or a lot more) booze can't fix,' Jeroncase replies.

Must be nice to know that so many people care about your health.

'Only those people at the front will know this one,' says James into the microphone and launching into 'Love, Love, Love'. The new, about-to-be-released single that he wrote with Eg White has been aired for the boardies before in recent concerts abroad. Here it is in Britain for the first time.

Cause I'll love anybody who's fool enough to believe,
And you're just one of many who broke their heart on
*   me,*
And so I say I don't love you.
Though it kills me, it's a lie that sets you free.

'I guess it's a pretty raw song,' he says later in the tour bus as we head through the night for the north of England. 'I have a bad reputation. It's a song that uses that reputation to escape from a perfectly good relationship.'

This is the first night in Britain with the two stages. It works like this: halfway through the show, when Blunty's at the keyboard singing the Slade cover 'Coz I Luv You', he suddenly jumps into the pit, climbs the crush barrier and launches himself into the crowd down a rehearsed route. The band on stage plays on. The security staff detailed to go with him can never keep up and that's how he likes it: 'If you have a handful of heavies around you, you're giving out the message: "I'm important and I'm vulnerable." I'm not important and I'm not vulnerable.'

Once down in the pit, he moves at high speed with a spotlight trailing his progress. Fans instinctively reach for him, but he pushes through them like a rugby player moving upfield at Twickenham. He stops momentarily to kiss and high five, but it can be brutal. The first time he tried jumping off an eight-foot stage – it's quite a long drop – was at a gig in Chicago, but no one had told the security staff who were standing with their backs to him. 'They saw this guy running along towards the audience and they pounced on me, thinking I was a member of the public and pinned me to the ground. "Let me up," I was yelling, "I'm the fucking singer!"'

Much more recently in Asheville, North Carolina, he slipped and broke the little finger of his right hand.

'My body went one way and my finger went the other.' He played on. That was over a month ago. He waggles his finger for inspection. To me, it looks swollen and still crooked. 'The doctors say I should have it re-broken and reset,' he says with a shrug, 'but I don't have time for that.' Some level of pain goes with the job. The tips of his strumming fingers are often raw and bleeding. He coats broken nails and cut flesh with layer upon layer of nail varnish.

Tonight he's moving fast, making for the gate in the crush barriers surrounding the sound desk and second piano. Sometimes they claw him almost to the ground and you see him disappearing under the weight of bodies. As an ex-soldier he knows about crowd control and tells me how he uses the lessons he learned in the army.

'You need to keep calm and to instil a sense of calmness in them. You have to be in control of them, not let them be in control of you. You want them on your side – they're your friends, not your enemies – and you need to tell them that.

'When I get pinned down, I ask them to help me, quietly and with authority. I don't shout: "Let me through!", I say: "Please help me to get through!" and they always do.'

He reaches the gap in the barrier and a guard slams the gate shut behind him as he leaps on to the already rising hoist supporting the second piano and continues 'Coz I Luv You' with the band still playing on the distant front stage.

The lights are up. The show is over and a scrum of roadies is dismantling the stage and wheeling amplifiers up ramps to the six waiting trucks. Some 14 tons of equipment has to be carefully stowed away, driven through the night to the next venue and then reassembled all over again.

As I walk along the pit to reach the dressing-room, cleaners are sweeping up litter and creating small mountains of discarded plastic glasses and beer cans. A large woman in her thirties grabs me from behind and points to a girl still sitting in a front-row seat at the side of the stage.

'You're with James, right?' With the laminated all-areas pass around my neck, there's no denying it.

'See that girl,' she says. It's a statement, not a question. A rush of words follows. 'She's blind, completely blind, see.

'She's not with us. She's a stranger. Somehow she came

here on her own. We just met her tonight. She can't see his face, but she can hear him – and she loves his voice. It makes her feel funny inside, she says.

'We've been telling her everything that's been happening on the stage and she wants to know more about him. Can you get him to meet her? It's not much for James to do, is it? It won't inconvenience him, like, to do it, will it? Just a minute to shake her hand and give her a kiss on the cheek. It'd mean the world to someone like her who can't see, wouldn't it?'

I look uncomfortable and Ms Large senses it. She's insistent. 'Well, go and talk to her yourself. She's nothing to do with me, mind, but it's not right not to help, like. You don't know what it'd be like to be completely blind, do you?'

She's right, sort of. So I find myself saying 'Hi!' and 'Did you enjoy the show?' to a young girl who can't imagine what it's like to see. She's the only person left sitting in the now almost empty CIA. She's still staring sightlessly in the direction of the rapidly dismantling stage, but cocks her head towards the sound of my voice. She isn't pretty and she isn't plain. She's just an ordinary girl. In my usual nightly quest to provide sightly guest flesh for the after-show, I wouldn't give her a second glance. Already, tonight, I haven't.

But now as I listen to her soft, liquid Welsh voice, water tinkling over polished stones in a brook, I can't imagine for the life of me why not. She has zero idea of who I am, not that I'm anybody. I'm just another stranger who has said barely five words to her and asked if she'd enjoyed being here tonight. But she wants to tell someone – it happens to be me – what she's thinking, what she's dreaming.

She stands up to be closer to where my voice is coming from. She's got a slender figure and I note how her make-up's been applied with enormous care. It's rude to stare, but she's not aware that I'm staring. I find myself wondering how she ever managed to do that on her own.

She's standing very close to me, inside my personal space. She's wearing a perfume that is evocatively sensual to me. I think it's called Ma Griffe and I haven't knowingly sniffed it in over 40 years. I remember the last time I did.

'Do you mind if I touch you?' she says softly in a lilting voice. Without waiting for an answer she reaches out her hand and softly traces the lines of my face. No, I am not James.

'I first heard him in a record shop. It was HMV. I often go in there to listen around, especially when I'm feeling a bit low. That's when I first heard James. It wasn't "You're Beautiful" – I like that, but it's not his best stuff. No, it was "Cry".'

I have seen peace, I have seen pain
Resting on the shoulders of your name

'I'm not a sad person, I'm a happy person. I like all kinds of music – music is my world. But hearing him that first time was a real shock. It was as if . . . it was as if I'd been waiting for him without knowing it . . . it was as if he'd been standing nearby me all my life and I'd been waiting for that moment. I felt strange, confused. My heart was going bumpety-bump. I can't explain and you won't understand. That voice touched me in a way, in a place that I've never been touched. I stood there for a long time, listening. Then I asked them in the shop who it was that was singing and they said James Blunt. I walked out of HMV with *Back To Bedlam* in my hands and a feeling that I can't explain . . . a feeling that here is my best friend . . . that he understands what I feel and that I understand, I truly understand, what he feels. It's not just his words, see, or the music. It's hidden away in the pitch of his voice.

'I was nervous, see, about coming along tonight. I didn't have anyone to go with and it's difficult for me in a crowd and all. I was nervous, too, that, singing live, James wouldn't be the same for me. That it would be a disappointment, I'd lose what he's given me. But it wasn't, he was even better . . .'

Her voice trailed off. She had a faraway, dreamy look on her face. I doubt she'd ever even thought of doing drugs. She didn't need to.

'You all right love?' says Ms Large, turning to her new friend and looking at me as if everything is all my fault.

She's now been joined by a visually frightening pack of fortysomething feral ladies squeezed into impossibly tight jeans and frilly tops. I get the feeling I'm about to defend Mrs Thatcher from an angry picket line of striking miners.

'See,' says the shop steward, prodding me in the chest with an unusually long and ring-encrusted index finger, 'what did I tell you? Go and ask him if he can spare a moment just to shake her hand so that she can hear him speak to her. It's not much to ask Mr Rock Star, is it?'

I have an inkling that this one is beginning not to like James Blunt. But why? Because he won't meet this blind girl? He hasn't even been asked to, yet. Maybe she's already somehow guessed his reply.

'All I can do is ask,' I say, lamely, 'but he'll be really busy right now with interviews and stuff and I don't expect it will be possible. If I'm not back in five minutes, take it that he can't do it.'

'That's not good enough!' she says, viewing me in much the same way as the empty plastic beer glasses and food wrappers that litter the floor. 'You're her only chance, see.'

I nod to the girl, but not surprisingly, she doesn't nod back. I escape and head for the dressing-rooms. The after-show, what there is of it, is already under way. Karl's mum is here from Birmingham with a whole group of friends, so he's behaving. The girls who've been invited from the audience look awkward and bored. In the band's dressing-room James is just out of the shower and Bobble is waiting for him to get dressed before taking him to a conference room next door for Meet and Greet. At each venue there's a nightly auction of a ten-minute private chat with James. In the US it can raise as much as $10,000 a night. It all goes to his favoured charity, Médecins Sans Frontières. War is never far from his thoughts. His experiences in Kosovo continue to shape his life. He once found a man's head in a hedge. Makes you think, doesn't it?

James looks awful. Somehow for 90 minutes he's managed to put his fluey cold and cough aside. Now he's back to full croak. I should ask him to meet her, I really should. But I don't. Why? Because I don't want to hear his answer.

Much later he joins us briefly at the party. He shakes hands, poses for a dozen photos and talks quietly to me over a beer: 'It's good to be touring again in the UK and to see an arena full of smiling faces. If we're playing to a full house all around the country then it's pretty clear that not everyone hates me, just a few journalists who pass on their views to people who have never even seen me or heard me. I don't let the criticism get to me, but I wouldn't be human if I didn't sometimes wonder what it was all about. When you get an enthusiastic audience like tonight, it's pretty reassuring.'

I listen and I agree. The blind girl will long ago have left the arena with or without her new friends, making her way haltingly and disappointed out into her eternal night. I feel wretched.

I have to say it, I have to explain. 'James, I met a blind girl out there tonight. She told me she loved the whole gig and you mean everything to her. She wanted to have a chat with you. She asked me to ask you, and I didn't do so. I didn't ask because I thought you'd say no. Worse than that, I thought you'd resent that I'd asked you.'

He doesn't reply, but simply nods his head at me a couple of times and takes a sip from the beer bottle that he's holding by the neck and turns away to talk to someone else.

Half an hour later when I'm deep in conversation with two couples and discussing Welsh rugby, a subject about which I know absolutely zero, he gives my arm a squeeze as he walks by and says in my ear: 'It's hard, isn't it? I'm off to my bunk.' And he walks out of the room.

Days later in another dressing-room in another city he

brings the subject up again. Clearly, he's been thinking about it.

'It hurts, doesn't it? You feel bad, don't you? There's so much pressure, so many demands to help people less fortunate than me. Look at that lot,' he says, pointing to a whole pile of opened fan mail lying on the table. 'Most of those are from real fans – the majority of them people who want to connect with me. The strength of feeling expressed in these letters is incredibly moving and I'm really grateful for them. It's impossible to pretend that I can give a personal reply to every one. But I enjoy reading them and I appreciate them.

'Then there are those from someone who is, or who knows someone who is, ill or dying or fallen on hard times – or all three. Every charity wants me to perform on their behalf. I'm everyone's potential surprise birthday present.

'I do what I can, but I can't cure people, and I can't be in more than one place at any one time. What they don't understand is that it's not real – none of this world that they have created around me is real. It's all make-believe. I'm just an ordinary guy who can sing a bit.

'When I left the army, all I set out to do was to make an album and play my music to a few people. I wanted them to feel a bit of what I was feeling and the best way I can express my real feelings is through music. When I'd done that I thought I should probably go and do something else. I never imagined that so many people would want to buy that album.

'Of course, it was flattering. At first, I was pretty chuffed being recognized and being invited everywhere. But it's not real. The whole celebrity thing is a dream created by studios, labels, the press and the internet. It all spins on around me. I try not to let it affect me. I don't think I've changed, my family and friends say I haven't changed. I'm still me.'

He's wrong. We are all changing. Today, you are never the person you were yesterday. None of us is. In the beginning it was gradual. When the money started rolling in he might have been tempted to spend, spend, spend. But James doesn't have the vaguest interest in money. He finds it almost amusing that he's paid so much for doing what he wants to do.

Of course, he's not just an individual, he's a multi-national corporation lining the pockets of hundreds of people around the world, from record producers to his team of truck drivers. At the core of the wages bill lies the 40-odd entourage of performers and roadies who travel the world with him making it all happen. Money is paid in from album and ticket sales, merchandising and personal performances. But most of that money has to go out again. It's a multi-million-pound turnover. Get the equation only slightly wrong and you're doing it all for nothing, going bankrupt fast.

Unlike a lot of stars he's been fortunate in having a supportive family behind him. His parents work behind the scenes to guide the Blunt loco through the points and safely down the track.

In the early days, late one night, the phone rang at his parents' home. Jane and Charlie were already in bed. Charlie answered. It was James and he was in London for once. He spoke quietly.

'I'm lying here in the bath and guess what I'm holding in my hand?'

'I'd rather not, actually.'

'It's a cheque.'

'How much for?'

'For . . .'

It took Charlie a moment or two to find his voice: 'OK, James, don't drop it in the bath! Put it carefully on the floor, and I'm on my way to pick it up.'

Sheffield

I awake mid-morning to a grim Saturday in a lorry park adjoining Sheffield Arena. Steel-grey clouds lurk ominously overhead, awaiting their chosen moment to dump a penetratingly slow, cold rain on a city I haven't seen in 35 years. My dad occasionally used to treat his lifetime mistress to a night in the station hotel here and for days afterwards he'd boast about the kippers and what else he'd had for breakfast. She still married him, a classic case of what around here they call 'neither man lost, nor woman thrown away'. His best friend here was a master cutler called Billy, who taught me how to sharpen a carving knife but never him how to behave.

Judging from the level of snoring on the bus, no one else has the immediate intention of checking out their surroundings. I feel I should, if only to pass the empty hours stretching out ahead in the real world which still goes about its daily business even in my absence. Looking around the forlorn Sheffield industrial estate this morning, time spent playing truant with Blunty and his entourage is not such a bad thing. The wind whips through my coat as I head for the bus stop.

For a moment I consider borrowing a bike. Techies Mike and Scott both have racing bikes stowed in the trucks. They use them not just for exercise on days off, but as local transport. More often than not, concert venues are situated on the outskirts of cities and bikes are a useful and economical means of getting around. But it's already spotting with rain and this looks like the kind of neighbourhood where your average teen carries a pair of bolt cutters in his backpack. I suspect that bike theft, like the dole queue, has become a way of life since they flooded the pits and forgot how to make Yorkshire pudding.

Somehow during the night we've been seamlessly transported north from Wales. In the early hours we stopped at a service station. Ben rushed out and bought a handful of movies and raced back in again. We were 20 miles down the road before he realized with a gnashing of teeth that he'd been sold empty boxes. Everybody else finds this hysterically funny. I've no idea what route we took – it's hard enough sometimes to even remember which country we are in. After James heads off to his bunk, the party staggers grimly onwards until the bar runs out. This dovetails with the moment when Bobble, in his usual way, quite literally pulls the plug on the proceedings, thereby switching off the music centre and wheeling it wordlessly out of the room in the direction of one of the trucks. Time to go. And when we go, we go fast. Grab your hand luggage and head for the bus. No need to say goodbye, guys, you'll not see her again.

Bobble occasionally colours this scene with a whole repertoire of monosyllabic 'goodnight' lines aimed at straggling party-goers. 'Right, fuck off' is a favourite for departure from the venue. 'Put out, or get out' is the final instruction to any girls lingering un-certainly on the steps of the bus as it's about to depart. Finally, as he seals the door he mutters: 'You fuck 'em, I chuck 'em.' But, mostly, he just likes to forcefully pull the plug.

The bus is a very smart bus. In fact it's the smartest tour bus in Europe, but it's still a bus. You're never more than 18 inches from one of your mates. We live on it for weeks at a time with every fourth night or so in a hotel. Downstairs it's got a dining and sitting area with two huge TV screens, a better stocked bar than any nightclub, kitchen sink, cooker and fridge. At the front, there's a door to the driver's compartment. Through it, in the real world, sits one of a special breed of drivers who are equally at home in the back streets of Warsaw as Walsall and can overrule the sat-nav to pick a better, personal route from Bratislava to Basel. They take an intense pride in their job.

Sometimes how he manages to do this through the long night, with a full-blown party going on behind him, calls for demonic powers of concentration. There's an unspoken rule here. Don't open the door and talk to him from behind. If you want to say something or look at the view, go and sit beside him.

Then, while sitting there for just a brief interlude, you can pretend that this neon-flashing merry-go-round of sex, drugs and rock 'n' roll is just a dream. You've escaped the Tardis and all its parallel worlds peopled by guitar-playing gods and an ancient one-eyed monster mariner who got his coat caught in the door and came along for the ride. You've escaped Narnia and you're back among the fur coats in the wardrobe with not so much as a rampant faun in sight. Sometimes when I'm tired and it's all got a bit much to handle, I do just that. I plonk myself down in the right-hand seat (it's left-hand drive) for an hour or two, staring through the giant windscreen at the kilometres slipping relentlessly away down *Autobahn, autoroute* or *autostrada* like the dwindling years of my life.

At the back of the bus, by the outside door and the staircase, is the tiny bathroom. Here's another rule – no poo. You only *pee* in the pan. Like small children you learn to go before you get on. If you're caught short during a 12-hour journey, you ask the driver to stop at a service station. You dash inside and make immediate use of whatever facilities, primitive or otherwise, are on offer. Squatting over a stinking hole in the floor off a motorway in Bosnia or perched on a sweet-scented throne in Denmark, you go about your business as rapidly as you can, mentally rerunning that scene in *Almost Famous* when one got left behind – 'I'm only the fucking singer!' he shouts as he chases after the bus. You push and pray that the bus hasn't driven off without you.

Don't ask me why the constipated manufacturers of this sleek duplex apartment on wheels couldn't come up with the full twin-functional Thomas Crapper. I suspect they did it out of spite, just to get their own back on the impossibly privileged bastards who would get to ride in it. There's really no other explanation for a toilet that is allergic to turds. Just one stool – any stool – and it's stuffed. Then the entire Blunty show is temporarily scuppered, shipwrecked by a single shit. A garage, not just any garage, has to be found where mechanics are qualified to dig into the digestive tract of the bathroom and remove the offending item.

It's only ever happened once and, to his horror, it was one of James' guests-for-the-night who supposedly dropped it.

For legal reasons, I can't say whose it was, and admittedly it was hard to identify, so one can never be sure. Either way, you can't polish a turd, no matter how high class, and the cry of 'I'm a celebrity poo, get me out of here!' still echoes around the bus in its memory.

Upstairs there are 14 individually curtained bunks on either side of the aisle and arranged in two tiers. Everyone has their favourite personal billet. Blunty likes to be up front with the Praetorian Guard of the band close by. Bobble favours the top or middle on the right. I get what's left, which is usually by the sound-proofed door to the party room. Sound-proofed, that is, until it's opened by some drunken sod.

Once in your bunk with the curtain drawn and the duvet pulled up to your neck, you can retreat into your own private world. It's much the same size as a coffin, but it has a bedside light and even – in America – a personal airline-style video screen. All these extras give you the impression that you are still alive. Lie on my back and my nose is less than five inches from the ceiling. If I turn over on my side my shoulder touches it. The single-decker North American bus has three tiers of bunks down each side and space is even tighter. Beardy, who's the biggest of us, couldn't turn over at all until he discovered that the marginally less exotic crew bus has mattresses one inch thinner and did a swap. I mean, how did he *discover* that?

On either continent, having sex in your bunk requires

extra-ordinary feats of athleticism and contortion – double joints all round. You've already played to one audience tonight and you're now performing to a hopefully silent, but equally attentive and much more discerning one. They have no alternative but to listen to every grunt and groan as if they were in the same bed with you, which technically they are. Come, it's time we all got some sleep.

The party room offers a degree of privacy – in the US it even has an adjoining shower and lock on the door – and therefore doubles as the executive fucking room. It has soft leather seats down both sides, another overstocked fridge and bar along with giant screens giving access to thousands of movies and TV channels.

So, what do I know about Sheffield? It's got the oldest football club in the world, which was formed in 1857, the year of the Indian Mutiny and the relief of Lucknow when the most Victoria Crosses ever (24) were awarded in a single day.

This morning, you deserve a VC for just venturing out in Sheffield, although it's probably not dangerous as such. The only enemy is the now driving rain, and it's all just dismally depressing. The city that has been putting the knife (and fork) in Britain for seven centuries appears to have lost its edge – and not just because it's about to be Blunted. The cutlery trade is in terminal decline and, judging by the shuttered factories around me, not enough new industry has taken its place. Faces, young and old, at the bus stop, are etched in lines of poverty. They mirror the miserable weather.

Much later, back at the ranch, the mood lifts along

with the clouds. The tour is always this zigzag graph of highs and lows. When the crowds start to gather at the doors to the arena it's impossible not to be infected by their buzz of excitement, while backstage from afternoon sound check onwards the temperature is steadily rising.

When I arrive fresh from a foot tour of downtown Sheffield, James is still oiling his voice with honey and salt while answering fan mail. The letters and cards trickle in, a couple of dozen a day. Everyone who sends a stamped and addressed envelope gets an autograph.

'Dear Mr Blunt, my English isn't that good and I don't know if I can express my thoughts and feelings in a foreign language, but I have to write this letter to you,' one begins.

In the last (few) years you and your music became a very important part of my life. Your songs carried me through dark and painful situations and you brightened up my days.

And so the worst thing for me is, and I really can't stand it, that I'll never get to know the person, the one who stands behind the famous star, the man who has the wonderful gift to touch my soul with his songs like nobody did before.

I'm sure we could have been real close friends, had we met in a world where the gap between 'normal' people and famous people isn't so invincible.

But this is the way it is and I want to send you some wishes from my heart:

Not all women are as pretty and famous as a model

or an actress, but many of them are true hearted and could be a loving wife for a lifetime, if they had the chance to.

Don't ever let the crazy world around you destroy your life!

Don't you destroy your life by yourself! (Just like many musicians did and still do – you are much too important.)

Dear James, I don't know what the future will bring for a man like you. Maybe there'll come a time when you feel lost and lonely and you simply want to escape from it all.

Whenever you need someone to talk to, someone who really listens, someone who's not an artiste, not famous and not rich . . . contact me.

Thank you for giving so much to me. You'll *always* be on my mind, not only as long as you are famous.

PS 'Love, Love, Love' is the saddest song I've ever heard.

Surprisingly, given the vitriol that appears on the internet and regularly in national newspapers, he doesn't get any hate mail at all. None. Maybe those crazies out there just can't be bothered, but it does seem weird that such supposed passion against him should not translate to paper. Maybe they can't afford the stamps or don't know where to buy them. Maybe real people don't hate him at all, just the music and popular press in Britain along with a few bitter webheads. I don't know. I'm not sure I really care. I mean, I'm a fly on the wall, right? I'm not at all involved with these people.

Blunty's feeling and looking much better and there's a manic quality about him tonight. Anything could happen.

'Well, HELLO, SHEFFIELD!' he roars after the first number, and the crowd screams in reply. At least he did that right. He got boos when he muddled Houston with Austin. He got cheers when he did the same with Belfast in Dublin . . . being Irish, they thought it was a joke. I feel his voice is on the edge of cracking. Every high note is an agony for us regular listeners, but he holds it. Tonight, 'Goodbye My Lover' has a quality of desperation about it. Up close from the back stage his face is awash with sweat and tears. It's hard to see where one lot of salt water ends and the other begins – bit like the Thames Estuary. He seems quite suddenly racked with real emotion that goes beyond performance.

Did I disappoint you or let you down? . . . I've kissed your lips and held your head, shared your dreams and shared your bed.

If you take the railway cutting through the rock to the top of the 13,025ft Eiger in the Swiss Bernese Oberland, the train stops for passengers to look out of a window cut into the notorious North Face. This sheer 600ft wall of snow, ice and rock killed the first dozen climbers who tried to conquer it in the 1930s. Occasionally mountain guides are lowered from the window on to the rock face in a desperate and not always successful bid to rescue a stricken climber. From the safety of the tunnel the window gives you a Peeping Tom view of the mountain stripped naked at its most dangerous and enticing point. In storm or sunshine you can see into its soul.

So it is with 'Goodbye My Lover', a window into the real James Blunt. On a daily basis James doesn't outwardly do feelings. I've never seen him angry, I've never seen him openly sad. But just sometimes when he sings this song he loses himself in raw emotion. When I challenge him about this he almost angrily denies it at first and then concedes:

'When I'm on stage I'm inside the song. I'm immersed in the words, the music, its history, its meaning, and its role in my life at that very moment. Beyond the tedium, the travel and, of course, the money there is a truly artistic reward to the tour and that's the complete naked exposure of one's soul on that stage. There's no greater high.

'In those moments I'm elsewhere in my emotions. But what you see on my face is just sweat, never tears,' he protests. Soldiers don't cry. I don't necessarily agree with him.

So who is she, the girl whose memory brings about this change in him? Is she the same girl as in 'You're Beautiful'? Does she really exist? Perhaps I've met her – perhaps I've met her at least five times, girls who are so obsessed and convinced that each one of you, you probably think this song is about you. No, it's not Petra Nemcova, the outrageously beautiful Czech supermodel whose much-publicized relationship with James gave her own career the kind of charge you get when you smack a racehorse on the rump.

'So who *is* she?' I ask him. 'She must be pretty damned important in your life, but you never talk about her.'

'I'll tell you about her when the time is right,' says James after the show, before he leaves in a chauffeured car for a fast ride to London.

He says he has work to do, but I suspect the real reason is to avoid spending the tour day off in . . . Nottingham.

Nottingham

A wet weekend in Robin Hood Land – that's all I need to raise my spirits. Sunday morning and the bus deposits us outside our hotel on Maid Marion Way. The hotel pulls no punches about its location: 'This is the ugliest street in Europe,' boasts the brochure in my room, which from the window proudly offers a grandstand view of it. In 2002, Maid Marion Way won the title of Britain's worst street. But now we're told that £2.5 million has transformed MMW into a pedestrian-friendly area with wide zebra crossings replacing the urine-scented underground tunnels where lurked a glue-sniffing merrye band of men who robbed the rich with no thought whatsoever of giving to the poor.

'The inclusion of wide pedestrian crossings has restored a direct visual and psychological link across the busy road. Large areas of additional public space have been won back in the process, creating generous pavements and areas of planting,' says CABE.

Now, in case you're wondering just who would say something like that, CABE stands for the Commission for Architecture and the Built Environment. I'm sure it's all for the best, but personally I can think of better ways of spending £2.5 million. The cynic in me says that Little John and Co. have simply legged it to other parts of the city, acquiring more knives and guns while upgrading from glue to crack cocaine.

I go for a walk and promptly nearly get run over by a souped-up black Mondeo on the first pedestrian crossing that I come to. City roads and I don't always agree. 'You never look where you're going,' says James, 'limping towards oblivion, lost in thought or conversation – or both – somewhere out in the world there's a car with your name on the bonnet.'

I hope it's a Ferrari and not a white van. Certainly Blunty once saved my life in Buenos Aires. He was walking a few yards ahead of me with his artist girlfriend Tash, Karl, Beardy and Johnny. We were all on our way to a fabled beef restaurant where you could eat a whole cow so delicious that, in the spirit of Desperate Dan, you'd still be hungry for more.

It was a clear, sunny evening in January. I was deep in a heavy conversation with a bad, bad girl called Nicola who was wearing a dress but no knickers. How do I know this? Because the day before, in a clearing in the Brazilian rainforest, she flashed her neatly trimmed Brazilian at a bloke in a helicopter. Anyway, as we were crossing the road, Nicola was telling me that her life is overseen by a pack of guardian angels, nothing to do with Hell's Angels or indeed the *Guardian* newspaper. She said she sees them quite clearly and, yes, they have proper gossamer wings. They appear only at moments of crisis and always look after her.

At that moment Blunty yells from the pavement ahead: 'Peter!' I look right, and all I can see are five lanes of traffic homing in on us. There is no knowing whether all five drivers are just enjoying playing Juan Manuel Fangio or whether they are Falklands veterans with X-ray eyes who have registered the GB plate on my soul, not to mention Nicola's panty-less parts. Whatever, they are bearing down on us at the speed of an Argentinian Exocet locked on to a British warship in San Carlos Bay.

Who says you can't leg it with a limp? Breathless, but alive, Nicola and I hit the pavement, avoiding metal on bone by a whisker, and study James' body for any sign of protruding bumps or feathers. There are none, just the hint of a horn.

This time in angel-absent Nottingham it's not my fault. The driver screeches to a halt inches from my ankles and clearly doesn't give a Friar Tuck that he's nearly murdered me. I look around. I'm bang in the middle of a wonderful new crossing with a full black-and-white herd of Serengeti zebras migrating across the road beneath my stained old trainers. The driver's young, and neatly clad in a black dress shirt with a gold chain around his neck. It's so chunky I think for a moment he might be the mayor – or do they *really* have a Sheriff-of around here, Your Worship? He winds down the window and sticks his head out.

'Wot you tryin' to do, get yourself killed, yer daft old c**t?' he snarls above the roar of rap coming from a bank of speakers that make the whole car vibrate.

Excuse me, less of the 'old', please, I'm with a rock band. Still, at least he doesn't try to rob me. I raise a hand as a gesture of friendship: Peace man! There's no need for violence. Leave the Uzi on the floor where it belongs. In my world a 'drive-by' is a McDonald's where you don't have to get out of the car – or is that a 'drive-in'? Either way, let's be relaxed about this. No harm done, eh? Apart from a centimetre of tyre rubber now embedded in a five-metre stretch of MMW. Poor guy was probably born and raised in one of those dark subterranean underpasses. How was he to know about the spanking new pedestrian crossing up here on the surface?

I give Tales of Robin Hood Function Rooms and Banqueting a wide berth. But, once away from the set of the *Prince of Thieves*, Nottingham shows itself to be a pretty cool university town. I don't know anyone here. Wherever you are, city Sundays on your own are sad in my experience. Around the world, this way and that, I've had my share and more of Sunday sorrows. Back in the Seventies a wet weekend in Ottawa took some beating. Geneva was and probably still is a town that suffers from a disproportionate shortage of men. It's peopled by all those girls who work for the Red Cross, the International Air Transport Association, the European Broadcasting Union or some other bureaucratic or philanthropic organization. Trouble is, as a single man alone, you've no way of meeting them and they've no way of meeting you. So hotel rooms are full of lonely guys all on their own and in apartments across town all these girls are in the same position, sighing.

A friend of mine once claimed that late on any Sunday afternoon in Geneva you can open your hotel window and all you can hear are the sounds of rain softly falling and the distant purr of a thousand vibrators.

When I was going to wars all the time as a reporter, people back at home always asked the same question: 'So, you've never been to Baghdad, Teheran, Jerusalem or wherever before. You arrive at dusk off a plane at an alien, unknown airport stuffed full of stressed and tearful refugees all scrabbling to get out while you're trying to get in. What do you do next? Where do you begin to find out what's going on?'

It's easy. The answer's always been there in the pages of Evelyn Waugh's *Scoop*! You head for the largest and most expensive hotel, where you'll find like-minded others from the international press corps well into their third G&T. Then it all sort of falls into place. Someone, of course, has to be first to the bar. Sefton Delmer, the greatest of pre- and post-World War II foreign correspondents, worked for the *Daily Express* back in those days when the then broadsheet newspaper was the organ of the British Empire. Immaculately dressed in Savile Row suit, with waistcoat and watch chain linked to a gold half-hunter, he'd be shown up to his suite. As soon as the bellboy had parked his bags he'd reach for the telephone and call up HM Ambassador to Iraq, Iran or Israel.

'Delmer from the *Express* here, old boy. I'm at the Angleterre. Would you mind frightfully popping over for a drink and telling me what's going on?' The art of the foreign correspondent has changed a bit down the years, but the rules are the same.

So, Nottingham. Head for the best pub. Ye Olde Trip to Jerusalem claims to be Britain's most ancient inn. It's nowhere near as awful as it sounds and, as far as I could see, entirely free of Kevin Costner look-alikes dressed in robes or rags. Since 1189, which just happens to be the year when Richard the Lionheart headed off on the Third Crusade, this pub, built into the walls of Nottingham Castle, has been serving ale to all-comers.

The Blunty crew know their beers. So it comes as little surprise to find a strong smattering of our 40-strong company raising elbows to at least their second pint of 4.3% alcohol Olde Trip Ale and Old Speckled Hen 5.2%. Bobble and Ben, needless to say, are in the thick of it.

You can learn a lot in a pub like this. King John was a regular and it's possible that Richard wasn't, after all, the hero of the history books that he's been made out to be. He disliked our weather – well, you can't really blame him – and he hated England so much that he spent only six weeks of his ten-year reign in Blighty. He spoke Aquitaine French rather than English and slaughtered unbelievers just as mercilessly as the Saracens. I tell you, you learn a lot over a pint of Olde Trip.

Monday, Monday and it's back to work for James. He arrives refreshed, probably from getting laid in London. Formula 1 cars are powered by petrol. James is fuelled entirely by sizzling, high-octane sex. Put four wheels on the lead driver of Team Blunty, line him up on the grid at Monaco and Jenson Button or Lewis Hamilton eat your hearts out – neither of you would get a look in. A tank of fuel lasts him 12 hours at the most, and then he's into the pits. Any attractive and available pits will do. Then he roars off again, satisfied or despairingly hungry for more sex, more success, or both. I've given up trying to work it out.

Late afternoon at the hotel I strike up a conversation with a girl at the bar, or, rather, she strikes one up with me. I ask her the way to the gig. I don't think I've ever seen her before, but she looks vaguely familiar. There's something about the way she keeps looking at the hotel lift as if she's expecting James to materialize out of it. She could be a regular groupie. If so, she's got a long wait because he's in a TV studio at the other end of town and isn't coming back here until the early hours of tomorrow.

'It's a bit of a walk, love,' she grins, fluttering ridiculously long, false mascara-whipped eyelashes over me. 'If you've got tickets, I could come with you . . . if you fancy a bit of company, like. I know the *real* Nottingham, see.'

I don't know anywhere any more, love, real or otherwise. It's all becoming one in my mind. Sometimes I wake up in the night, what there is of it left, and I can't remember *where* I am. The next stage is *who*?

Basically, there are only three types of hotel bedroom in the world: those where the bathroom is on the left of the door, those where it is on right, and that smaller number of designer establishments where it's up a ladder or down a staircase or in the middle of the bedroom. I once got lost in my complimentary suite in the iconic Hotel Pierre on New York's Fifth Avenue. I found three middle-of-the-night bathrooms – but I couldn't re-find my own bedroom.

Click down a level and there are those hotel rooms where you're sharing the bed, and those where you're on your own. Mostly, you're on your own – and it's dangerously lonely on your own. Maybe I should stop now, go home, quit while there's still a trace of sanity in all this. She's got long dark hair, pretty eyes, too much make-up and a sticky smile. Her bottom teeth aren't quite straight, but that's kind of attractive in a Nottingham sort of way. It used to be meal tickets, now it's concert tickets.

But get real, she's not looking at me. She's looking

through me to James, who's not even here. Sometimes it's hard to remember that I'm not a young man, man. I smile back with a slow shake of the head. It's a 'no' and she knows it. No hard feelings, Pop? No, no hard feelings at all. Thanks for the invitation, but no thanks. I make my way resolutely out into the encroaching dusk.

Everyone's suffering from colds now, but the mood is generally high. Blunty's feeling better – or he would be if the latest bit of bad behaviour wasn't threatening to burst out into the open.

Back in Melbourne he'd met a 19-year-old Sydney model called Kate who went to the gig at the Rod Laver Stadium. She was trying to make it as a singer and managed to slip Blunty a demo. Blunty was impressed, not necessarily by her music.

'Come and stay with me at my home in Ibiza, and let's see if we can work something out for you,' he said, like you do. He hinted – well, she thought he'd hinted – that he just *might* be able to help with her singing career.

But for James, Kate was trouble. Very good-looking trouble, but trouble nevertheless. James can be reckless in this arena. After both occasions they met, word somehow reached the press.

After the first, the *Herald Sun* ran a story: 'If British crooner James Blunt thinks "You're Beautiful" – not to mention loves your voice – it's pretty likely your singing career is going to hit a high note.' Somewhere on the edge of the Never Never, an alarm bell was ringing.

Blunty introduced her to his label. 'We haven't heard Kate's music yet, but James is obviously an exceptional talent and his opinion is held in high regard,' swooned a

Warner Music spokeswoman at the time. As far as I know, they still haven't.

Of course, it wasn't just her music that was on Blunty's mind. The girl was young, beautiful and wild. At the party the next night, Kate dragged James into the loo, produced a colourful but unidentified pill and asked him to help her 'shelve it'.

Don't worry. He was as confused as you. Shelving in this context is a term that seems to have been developed in Australia. It has nothing to do with DIY, and will not enhance your living area. As I understand it, Australian shelving is the equivalent of what the French do with suppositories, but for kicks rather than illness.

Legend now has it that Dave Grohl, the lead singer of the Foo Fighters, was in the next-door cubicle, and that on his return to the party said that all he had heard was a girl's voice saying to James, 'Now your turn.'

'I can't wait to have your naked body lying next to mine,' said the text he'd supposedly sent her along with return plane tickets for her and a mutual friend, Beech. Christ, James, did you really write that or did she or some creative hack make that up? It's so corny, but then it might just be you taking the piss out of taking the piss.

But why did you do it? It's like going on to the floor of the chocolate factory and picking one particular vanilla fudge off a conveyor belt stuffed with vanilla fudges, and having it gift-packed and shipped home by airmail. But what you've forgotten is that you *own* another whole identical chocolate factory back at home. Anyway, you should know by now that vanilla fudge is nearly always at its tastiest in its country of origin. Like those succulent, almost-free, Greek white wines that make taste buds drool when drunk with a platter of seafood in a beach bar in Kefalonia, they don't travel.

Kate, presumably with her eyes fully open, but with a galaxy of stars snuggled up beneath the lids, saw an understandable chance here both to break into showbusiness and to have a bit of celebrity slap 'n' tickle in the Mediterranean sunshine at the same time. Karl warns him, Paul warns him. But no, Blunty's brains have sunk once again beneath the equator and he's not listening. In fact, he seems to be knowingly nosing his way into the lioness's den.

So, understandably thinking that she's just won *Australian X Factor*, Kate pops on a plane Up Over and before you can say 'boomerang' she's landed on the greenest and most beautiful of the Balearic Isles and is all set to boogie with Blunty.

Australian Aborigines invented boomerangs about 10,000 years ago. There are two basic types: the killing stick that comes to a halt when it hits its target; and the recreational sort that flies right back to where it came from. Kate tried for the first, but got the second.

In the early 1980s I bumped into the then Boomerang World Champion on the quayside in Le Havre in Normandy. That's not such a strange place to meet him because he happened to be a 25-year-old Frenchman.

What really impressed me was that he stood by the water's edge and threw one of his home-made missiles down the port side of a cross-Channel ferry. It whizzed around the bow, back down the starboard side, and then he caught it between two flat hands. Catch it with one and you risk losing a finger.

But circumnavigating a trans-Channel ferry is one thing and Qantas Flight 008 Melbourne to London via Singapore and Iberia on to Ibiza is quite another. Kate missed her target and boomeranged unhappily back to Melbourne before you could say: *'James, mai ningú m'ha fet sentir el que ara sento per tú.'* This, if you didn't know it, is the Catalan for, 'I've never felt this way about anyone before.'

For Kate's arrival on the holiday island coincides with that of a new kid on the block – or, to be more exact, on the dance floor of Pacha, the famous Ibizan nightclub favoured by Blunty. She's Sabina, a fiery Catalan with the longest legs on the island, the sexiest of smiles, and a wicked sense of fun. She's got instant appeal, and James can't take his eyes off her.

'I've never felt this way about anyone before!' Before what? Before lunch? says the cynic in me. But no, it's real. She's coming to join us on the bus in Newcastle, which is culturally and climate-wise about as far removed from her native Ibiza as you can get on this planet. Love in a Tyneside lorry park? Truly it must be real.

But back to Kate. Almost the minute she arrives, Blunty realizes he's made a terrible mistake. After 24 hours, it's game over. It's not that there's anything wrong with Kate, it's just that everything is right with Sabina. She speaks very fast and fluently in what at least sounds like English.

'Does he really understand what she's saying to him?' I once asked Karl after she'd just fired two staccato bursts of Englishese machine-gun fire at Blunty before tossing her head in defiance with all the majesty of the *matador de toros* that runs through her bloodline.

'Don't be stupid,' said Karl, 'he doesn't understand a

word. He doesn't need to.' Actually, after a while, this is no longer true. With his musical ear James is so perfectly attuned to this English patois that they develop a whole private language of their own with a bit of Spanish thrown in for good measure.

Sabina also looks a million euros, knows all the right people on Ibiza and in Barcelona. She's financially independent and insists on paying her own way. This is particularly attractive to James. She's got loads of Hispanic pride and, fundamentally, she doesn't see him as a meal ticket.

Kate, of course, speaks Australian, and she's cranky – 'mad as a cut snake', as they say back home – when she figures out by the next day that she's been replaced before she's got what she's come for.

Now Blunty's a great diplomat and he can call on skills learned in Kosovo when trying to separate warring factions. His first major public performance was before a global TV audience of millions – but his guitar was not in hand, it was firmly strapped to his tank. It just so happened that the then Lieutenant James Blount, a troop commander in 'D' Squadron, the Life Guards, found himself to be the first British soldier to enter Kosovo from Macedonia and face down the Serb invaders.

Suddenly he was in a situation alarmingly different to much of his previous soldiering. He'd trotted on horseback down the Mall in gleaming silver breastplate and plumed helmet on the Queen's official birthday for the Trooping of the Colour. He'd guarded the Queen Mother's coffin at her lying-in-state. Now he faced the stark reality of military confrontation on a world stage.

A few fear-tinged moments of international brinkmanship ensued before the Serbs eventually decided that discretion – which, in this case, took the form of a hurried retreat – was the better part of valour. As with all big Blunty moments, this one was not without a moment of light relief. As he faced the enemy from the turret of his tank he was seen by viewers around the world to take a call on his mobile. Instructions from high command?

'James,' came a distant, crackling female voice. 'I just want to tell you how proud of you I am, darling – you look magnificent!' Unwavering, the cavalry commander held the gaze of his Serbian opposite number for a further ten seconds before giving his reply: 'Not now, Granny.' Mobile phones have since been blocked by the British army in all active theatres of war.

This time in Ibiza the threat to world peace is much greater. 'Look, Kate,' he says, 'it's all been a bit of a mistake, hasn't it? You're here for a week – it's not working out. Why don't you just have a great holiday on me? You stay in the house and enjoy yourself. We go out together, but we sort of don't go out *together*. Is that cool?' Yes, says Kate, that's cool. It's all looking as if the full fury of the potential storm has run out of steam before it hit land. But, no, he's just in the eye of it.

Come morning, the emotional weather has changed. It's not just a cold front that's blowing in off Eivissa town and drifting inland towards the Blunty pad, it's a hurricane of Katrina intensity that could result in what the weathermen like to call 'serious structural damage to buildings and property' . . . not to mention people.

Kate wants to go home, or to London, or to a swanky

hotel in Ibiza – with room service. Bobble, at rest in Manchester with his wife and kids, is called in to help. James ends up doing all three: he buys a new ticket and arranges a hotel for her in London and one in Ibiza; plus he gives her €850 for incidental expenses. She'd also like his credit card number.

Now you can ask Blunty for lots of things in this life. You can ask him to fly you across the world and introduce you to people in the music industry, and to do weird stuff in a loo cubicle, but credit card number? He just wouldn't know where to find it. Blunty doesn't properly do cards. Other people shop for him. When he wants a new laptop or a new BlackBerry (which is frequently, because he spends more time on the two than he does on anything else, except possibly singing and sex) they just appear, courtesy of Bobble, who has his hands on James' platinum card on and off tour. Even Blunty is impressed by his remote purchasing power.

'Bobble,' I heard Blunty say one day in a dressing-room in Vancouver, 'I need that new solid state MacBook Air.' Your wish is my command. Just 30 minutes later he's unwrapping a new solid state MacBook Air.

'It's like having a fairy godmother,' he confesses to me with a sheepish grin. I tell you it's not easy being famous and handling money. Well, not if you're James. An old friend from his army days went to stay with him in Ibiza and Blunty picked him up from the airport. 'There's nothing to eat in the house,' says James, who often forgets to eat at all when he's on his own and writing. 'We'd better do a shop before we go back.' He doesn't have any cash on him so first they go to a hole-in-the-wall.

'Blunty fumbled around in his wallet, found a smart-looking piece of plastic and put it in the slot,' the friend told me. 'Back it came with the message: "insufficient funds available". Looking slightly confused, James fumbled around again and came up with an even smarter-looking black card. He put it in the wall and the machine promptly swallowed it, without cash or comment.

'So it was left to me to dig deeper into my own desperate overdraft to buy a loaf and a couple of fishes for my multi-millionaire friend. You know what?' his friend grinned. 'He never even apologized. He thought it was normal.'

No, Blunty doesn't do credit cards. Kate withdraws from Ibiza, but there's the lingering feeling that we haven't seen the last of her.

Now we're out on the town in Nottingham. Next stop is Birmingham. Blunty's in reflective mood as we hit a horrible bar off Maid Marian Way. He's quietly worried, and not just by the spilt beer and broken glass underfoot at 2am in this miserable, overcrowded place. Hell, it seems, indeed hath no fury like a girl desiring publicity. Word has just reached his BlackBerry that Kiss Me Kate has kissed and sold all to an Australian newspaper.

'It was, admittedly, an expensive shag,' he says. His face is shaded by a baseball cap, not that anyone recognizes him in here – they're all so drunk they must be having trouble recognizing their own partners, let alone strangers.

'Same mistake again?' I ask.

He grins ruefully: 'Probably. I really didn't mean to hurt her, but obviously I did.' On cue, Blunty's voice singing just that track blasts from the speakers on the wall above our heads.

I'm not calling for a second chance
I'm screaming at the top of my voice

It's often like that when you're with him – mention his music and you hear his music. I suppose it's a bit like when you're expecting a baby. Suddenly the world is full of pregnant girls and mothers with babes in arms. They've always been there, but you've only now consciously registered them.

Outside in the street as we entered this club the scene resembled a twenty-first-century remake of an eighteenth-century Hogarth engraving of gin-sodden London. A teenage girl is sitting on the edge of the pavement vomiting into her lap, while stumbling friends try to help her and a group of passing guys shouts abuse. I'm seeing the same pathetic and despairing 2am story on streets the length of Britain. The tide of 24-hour drinking has breached the defences and stained the fabric of what were once pleasant county towns in which to work and live. Tony Blair – leave aside Iraq – this may prove to be your worst and most damning legacy of all. But Blunty and the band are high on after-show adrenaline and they don't even notice.

When the government decided to ban smoking in public places, no one thought through the sensory consequences. Take away the scent of stale cigarette smoke from a late-night bar and what are you left with? The overwhelming stench of unwashed bodies, stale beer and vomit.

I make my way across the half-empty dance floor towards

the gents. A girl cannons into me and I only just manage to keep my balance. I put out my arms to steady both of us and she clasps me to her. For a second or two before we break away, we look directly at each other. Her brown eyes are dead, the pupils pin-sized. Her face is entirely without expression. I look down and see she is wearing a broad pink shoulder sash that says on it: 'I'm 18 Today'. For both of us, strangers in the Nottingham night, 19 seems a desperately long way away.

'Get some sleep, Uncle Peter,' says Karl as I finally head towards my hotel room long after dawn. 'Tonight it's Birmingham, and that's my town. Tonight's going to be a big, big party night.' I mean, just where do these guys find the stamina?

Birmingham

It's cold and grey in Birmingham, but Karl can't stop grinning. The local Boy Made Good will be dominating the back of the stage tonight at the NIA, beating the hell out of a drum set of which until only recently he could never even have dreamed.

'Makes a change having you lot,' says the cheerful security guard assigned to keep strangers away from the dressing-rooms. 'Last week there were fish and jellyfish popping in and out of doorways all night long. It was hard to know who to let in or who to keep out.'

'What's he on?' I ask his mate. Both must be nearly my age and look more like staid ex-coppers and family men than the popular image of an acid-head.

'Nemo,' he says, reading my expression, 'it were Nemo – *Finding Nemo on Ice*.'

'Did they?' I ask.

'I suppose so, but no one said. You don't see much of the show, not sitting back here. You have to rely on what people tell you – and they said it were grand.'

Much later that evening, after the concert, I'm talking to the mother of a girl who appears to be friends with the band or some of the crew. She's bright, sparkly and, given another three vodka and cranberries, almost sexy in a mature Mrs Robinson kind of a way.

'You wouldn't believe what those guys got up to with

my daughter and her friends!' she says, almost pleased. Oh yes, I would, honey. Sometimes I hear the acrobatic details. Once there was an overnight visitor on the bus who managed such enterprising contortions in the confines of a bunk that one member of the band feared she'd tie him in a permanent human knot.

'You must have a very interesting time on tour,' she tells me, 'so many places . . . so many people . . . kisses hello and kisses goodbye. The kids are not the only ones who can have fun, right?' Hang about. Where's this heading?

'I just love James,' her voice falling to a seductive whisper. 'When he sings he makes me feel warm inside . . . Peter, do you like to feel warm inside?' Well, I guess it depends on what you're inside.

'Is your husband here tonight?' I ask. Well, I might as well borrow a leaf from the band's chat-up book. Best to establish the facts. No, I don't need to know if she's working tomorrow. She doesn't look, to me, as if she works at all. Question: what would happen if I brought an overnight passenger on to the bus? Answer: the laughter would go on all night.

'Yes, he's over there,' she points to a man who is patting a band member heartily on the back and thanking him loudly for looking after his daughter the night before.

'We'll have to go home soon,' she says. 'Do you want to show me around the place. Is there somewhere like, you know, sort of quiet we could go?'

OK, OK. You can't lay it on the line clearer than that, can you? I mean, she's behaving like some sexual lollipop lady. I glance desperately around for help – and there it is in the ample shape of Bobble. In the moment of crisis Batman always comes to the rescue.

He strides into the room in his white shirt and smart dark suit. In one practised move he rips the plugs of both the music system and disco lights from the wall.

'I'm afraid it looks like we have to go, too,' I smile and down the remainder of my drink. But here's to you, Mrs Robinson. I'm not sure about Jesus' views on loving you, but I'm pretty sure about those of my wife.

Budapest

I've just flown into Budapest and I'm not sure if I'm in Buda or Pest, which depends on which side of the Danube you happen to find yourself. The suburbs are peopled by ancient and crumbling USSR-vintage apartment blocks that are stained with ugliness and age. Welcome back to Eastern Europe, sometimes I feel I've never been away. The taxi driver has a villainous moustache and a murderous look in his eye and is trying his best to kill me on the way from airport to concert hall. 'Can we go a bit slower?' I ask as we miss a truck by inches and swerve dangerously on the inside of a fume-belching Lada driven by a priest.

'Shut the fuck up,' he replies. 'Enjoy the ride.' Seems a bit strange. Maybe I'm being kidnapped like Mrs Muriel McKay, the wife of a *News of the World* executive in 1969 who was supposedly killed and fed to pigs in Hertfordshire. I know she wasn't – because I made that up at the time. But I've got this fear of being kidnapped that must come from the year I spent investigating that case. The guys that did it, brothers Arthur and Nizamodeen Hosein, thought they'd got Rupert Murdoch's wife. A story by me that rival publishing tycoon Robert Maxwell could have been behind the whole thing nearly got me the sack. I was 20 years ahead of my time in exposing the arch-villain.

Then in 1973 when Jean Paul Getty III was kidnapped I went to Italy to try and find the kidnappers. Fortunately, looking back on it, I failed. When his mean old grandpa refused to cough up the ransom, the kidnappers cut off his ear and posted it to a newspaper with the promise of more bits to follow. I sat around in bars in Reggio di Calabria writing improbable rumours and drinking too much shockingly cheap red wine while trying to set up meetings with the local mafia called the Ndrangheta, who were supposedly responsible. I've always been glad they didn't cut off my ear for asking questions.

'1973'? Maybe that's what James' song is all about. Maybe it's got a secret meaning like the *Abbey Road* cover. Paul is dead. No, not Jean Paul, Paul McCartney.

Simone you're getting older
Your journey's been etched on your skin.

My brother's called Simon, which is the same as Peter if you know your Bible. Christ I'm tired. There's no denying the journey is etched on my skin. Petra is the same name as Peter, and it means rock.

And though time goes by, I will always be
In a club with you in 1973 singing
'Here we go again'.

Enough of this shit. Don't let it all get to you. You're in Budapest to see James Blunt. To meet up with him, not to join him in his crazy world. Get a grip. You're not being kidnapped. They might want to kidnap James Blunt; Karl quite often bizarrely thinks he's in the middle of a kidnap; but no one wants to kidnap you.

The driver skids to a halt outside the concert hall. 'Thanks very much,' I say.

'Shut the fuck up,' he replies. 'Enjoy the ride.'

Nine gigs in 12 days in three countries have slipped by since I was last in the Bubble, but hardly anyone seems to have noticed that I've been gone and am now back. Karl gives me a hug: 'Things always happen when you're around, Peter,' he grins, jerking his thumb in the direction of James who is hunched over his laptop. 'In fact, they're happening right now.'

I guess it was always going to be. Blunty's tried to put it out of his mind, hoping she would go away. But she hasn't. Kiss Me Kate has finally got her revenge with a front-page exposé of her boomerang trip to Europe. In Melbourne and Sydney the newspaper story has only just hit the streets, but already it's plastered across the web.

'I just want people to know exactly what type of person he is,' moans Kate. 'I don't think it's right that people are going and buying his CDs and they think they can relate to him. But really everything he says in his songs is bullshit.

'His songs are the opposite of what he's like. He sings about love, yet he obviously has no grasp of it.'

Oh well, it's not the first kiss-and-tell and it won't be the last. In fact, there've been so many in Britain now that, according to Max Clifford, James' 'value', in Sunday newspaper cheque-book terms, has slipped from £8,000 to £800.

'If I keep on sleeping with people who sell their stories to the papers,' James jokes, 'I should be able to get that down to minus figures soon. Maybe these girls will actually have to pay the papers to print their stories!'

He's not wrong. By February 2010, the *Daily Mirror*'s running stories about nights James *didn't* get laid.

On with the newspaper story: 'A spokeswoman for James Blunt said yesterday: "James is very disappointed by these false allegations."'

The phone never stops ringing – management, Mum and Dad, label, and friends. They're all supportive and close ranks around him. Good boy or bad boy, he is their guy. The newspaper's still hot off the press, but already there are 150 comments of support on the net.

'Is this bad for me? What do you really think?' he asks me. Frankly, it doesn't matter a damn – that's what I think.

'What did Kate expect when she accepted your invitation? A vicar's tea party?' I tell him.

One of my only useful functions as part of the inner circle of this tour is that I can say what I think from a no-bias perspective. Because I've known him since before he was famous and because no one's paying me, I don't have to play the 'yes' man. I've got the freedom to tell it the way it is. I think he respects that.

So I tell it to him straight: 'I'm pretty sure that those that like you will continue to like you. Those that don't will read it and say to their friends, "What a c**t."

'Forget it,' I tell him. 'Ruin your reputation? What reputation? Some people at home who read newspapers are convinced you're a c**t because they're constantly being told you're a c**t by c**ts who've never met you and are never likely to do so. The rest of them love what you do and will go on loving you.

'Right now you're in Budapest surrounded by people who love your music and who can't read a single word of

English or, come to that, Australian. The only English they know are the words of your songs, so go out there and sing them to them.'

And he does. The atmosphere in the capacity-crowded arena is crackling with electricity. During my nine-gig absence the performance has gathered a slick veneer that was previously lacking.

'Same Mistake' has a particular poignancy to it tonight. 'It's one of my favourite songs,' James tells me. 'The atmosphere it can create on stage and in an arena is overwhelming. It starts at nothing and explodes, and then disappears again and you're left with the feeling that the room has no more air.

'What's it mean? *Give me reason, but don't give me choice*. Choice means I fuck up. Like I've done before.' I don't understand what he means.

Kate and her poisoned kiss are, for now at least, forgotten. But in the dressing-room, at the after-show and later, there's a new tension in the air that I can't quite put my finger on. The dynamics of the band have undergone a subtle change. I need to find out what's causing this, but right now there's a much more pressing problem. During the gig some hungry Hungarian has done the unspeakable: he's stolen breakfast and half of tomorrow's lunch.

Lisa, our resident caterer who cooks up three square meals a day for the 40 of us on this travelling circus, went to the cupboard and the cupboard was bare. Bastards! She's furious. The band marches on its stomach, with Lisa and her cooks foraging for supplies along the way. Each day she somehow produces a cooked breakfast, lunch and early dinner with a choice of at least three dishes on the menu along with a vegetarian option. Now she's short of a side of beef, ten dozen eggs, and 100 sausages. Has it happened before? 'Not on this tour,' she tells me. But of course. Everything in rock 'n' roll has happened before.

'I can't understand it,' she says. 'It was all there before the gig when we packed up the kitchen, and there was a security guard in the corridor outside the door throughout. Yet, when I went to check on something afterwards, we'd been cleaned out.'

Well, *somebody* wolfed it. Of course, it could have been one of us with an eating disorder. After all, with the frenetic pace of this tour everyone is going slowly mad. Paul suggests a bunk search of both buses. 'Someone's duvet is probably covering a stash of sausages,' he says, and I'm not sure if he's joking. Meals are a fundamental part of the daily routine and are constants in a 24-hour calendar crowded with change.

This time – it's not always like this on tour – the quality of the food served up by Lisa is outstanding. Actually, it's too good; the boys are putting on weight and the occasional 30 minutes of pre-gig footie does no more than slow the piling-on of excess pounds. I suspect it's the same in prison: eating is one of the only available forms of mental escape. We eat four square meals a day – not the standard three. When we hit the bus at 2am for the next leg of the journey there are sandwiches or takeaways for all.

Each night when Blunty waves goodbye to his audience he produces a digital camera and takes a photograph of the fans photographing him. He's smiling and shouting into the mike: 'We'll see you again SOON!' But he's not thinking about them, he's thinking about chicken wings.

There, that proves it, Blunt and Joplin have more than just me in common.

James and Janis, they both love(d) chicken wings. They're obsessed by them. James circles the planet in search of the hottest. So obsessed is he that one day he and Benny fly from Los Angeles to Albuquerque, New Mexico to eat the wings from Wings Basket, and then fly back to LA immediately afterwards. Janis liked to circle her neck with them. First she ate them, the hotter the better, then she'd sit on the floor and make necklaces from the bones. I guess Blunty's not quite as weird as that.

Every now and again the band – Paul in particular – has a collective go at healthy eating. For a day or two, it's all outwardly salads and stuff in the dining room. But behind the curtains of his bunk Paul's always got an alternative larder. He sees nothing contradictory in supporting the diet of lettuce leaves with a couple of life-saving Mars bars between meals. 'As a tour tip,' says James, 'if you can't find food in the fridge, it's best to go and look in Paul's bunk.'

Bratislava

By morning the whole cavalcade of buses and trucks has moved on to Bratislava and we wake up to sunshine and greenery in a park beside a river and the usual stage door of another giant stadium. While we slept, Lisa, who has never before set foot in Slovakia, somehow manages to resupply her army. The smell of frying bacon wafts from Catering as a squadron of roadies with oversized biceps and baggy shorts manhandles a bank of amps out of a truck and up a ramp to the stage.

It's a sunny day in a strange city. Paul and I go exploring. He's the most complex and certainly the most sensitive member of the band. He's been with Blunty since the beginning and when the full band is either not available or required, the two of them perform together all over the world, Blunty on guitar with Beardy on keyboard. I first saw them together a lifetime ago in Beano's mountain restaurant in the super-smart ski resort of Beaver Creek, Colorado. It was a private party, reached by snowcat, for the label at the start of an exhaustive American tour for *Back To Bedlam*.

James and Paul were a team. Their performance was electrifying, more intimate and in some ways more rewarding than with the full band. James' voice and guitar blended to perfection with Paul's keyboard. They belonged.

But afterwards, when you'd have expected them to be

together, chilling out on the wave of adrenaline and adulation that follows such a critical recital, they were not. As we piled into snowcats for the downward rumble across the manicured trails to the village below, Beardy was locked in conversation with a gaggle of sleek executives clad in designer ski jackets that had never come into contact with snow. Meanwhile, Blunty cut a lonely Dylanesque figure as, guitar case in hand, he squeezed unnoticed into the last vehicle and descended in silence towards the valley, lost in his own thoughts.

They've spent thousands of hours together in each other's company and, as the lyrics of 'Goodbye My Lover' say, *I know you well, I know your smell.*

There's history here and it opens a door through which I can travel. Paul and James, James and Paul . . . two unlikely partners, thrown together by music, circumstance and the hard-hearted, hard-headed quest for recognition and fame.

James runs his business with his hand firmly on the tiller at all times. It's his boat and he's the one sailing it. The crew – band and technicians alike – are his employees, not his partners. The hardcore of them love the life at sea, especially under such a fair and competent skipper. Unlike most other celebrities he's down there on the deck with them, raising the sails and getting splashed by the waves breaking over the sides. But they need have no illusions about sharing finance or fame. They're paid a good wage, there'll be the occasional bonus, but they'll be no divvying-up of the gold bullion that's gathering daily in the hold.

Let's get this straight: this is the one-man Blunty show.

Paul is a lovable person and an outstanding musician, ranked in the music business as one of the best keyboard players of the last 30 years – an all-time great. He's been invited and gone to stay with Robbie Williams in LA and to write with him. After this tour Beardy will go on to work with Rob as principal keyboard player and MD of his touring band. In his heart, Paul is full of hope that the future will somehow be more fulfilling than the present, that he will settle down and live happily ever after with his long-term girlfriend, that Blunty will ask him to work on the next album.

I think it sort of hurts that Blunty didn't ask him to work on composing the last album. But he didn't invite any of them to do so. Therefore why would he on the next? Beardy is the nicest guy you'll ever meet: a farmer's son with perfect pitch who's landed on one of the highest haystacks in the music industry. But he can't make up his mind whether he wants to stay on or try falling off in order to see what happens.

Beardy, I can't get the image out of my mind of the look on my Labrador's face if I walk past his bowl on the kitchen floor at 5 o'clock in the afternoon and I don't pick it up. You're so hungry.

His long-term girlfriend is Natalie Clein, the award-winning cellist, and right now as we stroll through the Old Town of Bratislava he's locked into another marathon phone call. You can see the problems. She's in Buenos Aires and he's in Slovakia. Maybe, just maybe, they can grab a day together in London before he leaves for Vancouver and she for Moscow. Maintaining relationships on tour is devastatingly difficult.

We're strolling across Hviezdoslav Square. History was made here 20 years ago, but Beardy is oblivious to this as he chats away into his mobile. In March 1988, 10,000 protesters with candles in their hands held a silent protest in the square and surrounding streets against the dying Communist regime – silent, that is, until riot police charged with batons and water cannon to break it up. In December the following year the Communists were ousted from power in what became known as the Velvet Revolution.

'Will you marry her?' I ask, after he finally puts his phone away.

'That's something I might discuss with her, not you,' he grins. Clearly this relationship has strings attached, but he lives in hope of harmony.

Later, over giant *Wienerschnitzel* and half litres of beer, he says: 'The trouble is that James doesn't do praise, and I guess I need praise for a job well done. Only once after one of the first gigs we ever played did he ever give me anything in the way of a compliment. He put his hand on my shoulder and said: "We need you." That's all.

'But I remember it so well because it was the only time he ever said anything like that to me and it's etched on my mind. I don't blame him – it's the way he is. I blame it on the fact that he was sent away to school at the age of seven. Imagine that, Peter!'

I can because I was eight when I too was bundled off for ten years to the other end of southern England. Best days of your life? I'm still recovering. But, no, I don't think that experience has any serious bearing on Blunty's being. He's just made that way.

Beardy explains: 'I now realize through Nat that to feel love you have to be open, to accept love when it is given. It's a two-way thing. James can't accept love. I talk to him about it, but I don't think he listens.'

And if I can't hear the music and the audience is gone
I'll dance here on my own.

The support act changes for each leg of the tour – I suppose it's a way for Blunty's management to try out different artists. Before fame, Blunty toured as the starter for Elton John's main course and will do so again later, in South America, although this time on marginally more equal terms.

The headline and the support don't necessarily have a lot of contact, although James is always at pains to ask them every night to the after-show. But on this leg of the tour, The Bishops have become part of the family.

Twin brothers Mike and Pete, along with drummer Chris, bring a level of slapstick to the tour, along with beauty in the form of Mike's girlfriend Sophia. They race around like the Keystone Cops. How they manage to keep on track makes me tired just thinking about it. We go from bus, to gig, to party, to bus before waking in the next country at the next arena. Every couple of nights we get to stay in a four- or five-star hotel room. This gives you some needed privacy, sleep, and the chance to do laundry.

By contrast, The Bishops play, pack up, party, and then battle through the night. Taking turns at the driving they eat up exhausting miles in a tired old van before snatching a few hours' sleep in a budget motel. Then it's time to rush to the next venue, set up, and play all over again.

As we recross the bridge over the Danube to the venue, relaxed after a spell of sightseeing and lunch, who do we see? Why, it's The Bishops, hotfoot from Budapest! They scramble out of the van, unload their equipment and make it on stage just in time for their sound check.

Brussels . . . Bremen . . . Oberhausen . . . Leipzig . . . Mannheim . . . Nuremberg . . .

Stuttgart . . . Budapest . . . and now Bratislava – 2,000 miles in 12 days and they're still smiling!

Before the gig I meet up with a cool-looking dude who's somehow got a backstage ticket through the local promoter. But he doesn't have an all-areas pass and he's trying to talk his way past the security staff.

'I'd like to meet James,' he tells me.

'I don't think that's possible right now, but I'll go and ask,' I say, with no intention whatsoever of doing so.

'That's a shame,' he adds. 'I'm just opening my new club here in the centre of town tonight. It's going to be the coolest place in Bratislava and I want to call it the James Blunt Club.

'James and all of you are invited and I'm hoping James will cut the ribbon and officially open it after the show. Obviously all drinks and everything are on me. Do you think he would mind?'

Would he mind? James has a trophy collection that goes with the fame game. Back home he has a studio full of platinum discs, gold discs, statuettes, cups, framed pictures, cut-glass figurines, bronze bollocks, and gongs of every conceivable size. He also has enough T-shirts, hand-knitted gloves, scarves, souvenirs, and knick-knacks to stock a charity shop. On top of this comes the freebie gear – from designer suits to ski jackets – leather luggage, guitars and electronic gadgets.

But for a guy who simply doesn't care a jot about almost all the trappings that super-wealth and fame attract, all this is hugely unimportant. This is the man who travels the world with a small piece of hand luggage and a guitar case.

His own nightclub? Now that's his definition of the perfect accolade. Mind you, he has got his own private one already, complete with strobe lights and dance floor in the gardens of his home in Ibiza. But that wasn't a present, so it doesn't count.

Only once before have I seen him so pleased with a gift. Verbier, where he spent three winters in his regimental ski team when he was in the army, named a ski lift after him. He's not alone – Diana Ross has one, too.

For cutting the tape and smashing a champagne bottle at the opening ceremony they gave him a lifetime ski-lift pass. Assuming he skis on into old age, that's worth around £25,000 at today's prices. Of course, he could afford to pay that without blinking, but that's not the point. When I phoned him to tell him about it he was completely bowled over at the permanent recognition.

'My own chairlift? That's just *the* best thing anyone has given me. Forget industry awards and platinum discs.' Months later, when we're sitting on the chairlift after he's smashed the bottle and unveiled a plaque at the bottom station, he tells me again: 'You know what's good about this? It means these guys are genuinely pleased to have

James takes control. At the helm, aged three, with Cypriot man-of-the-sea Andreas Cariolou

September 2007, live at Koko in Camden, London

Head to head in the ritual pre-show haka. James, the band, and Bobble

The vintage guitars being looked after by Brian, the vintage technician

Beardy holds the keys

Centre stage, Toulouse, France, November 2008

Mike, Front of House Sound, uses alcohol to make the sound better

The band and lone geography teacher (back left), in Nashville

Not long now. Weird Uncle Peter, pictured by James, Saskatoon

An extraordinary board(ie) meeting

Blunty Fans

will always be with

James piano-surfing in Newcastle, October 2008

The Bus of Love, sleeps twelve, sometimes more…

A fan's 1:14 scale model of James' room

YOU'RE BEAUTIFUL
I REALLY LOVE
YOU "♥" I DREAM
TO MEET YOU
AND SPEAK WITH
YOU JUST ONE
TIME!

Musical milestone
mementoes

Bobble-wrapped
in rainy Sao Paulo

Karl and Johnny
sound check
in Cardiff with
technician
Hamish

Mad Hatter's tea-party

Backstage in Geneva
with a friend. Get out
there and sing to them

James has very soft skin.
You just have to touch it

me here. I've been skiing in Verbier for much of my life. To me it's the best resort in the world and I love it enough to have now made a home here. It's recognition of that and it's a gesture like this that means an enormous amount to me.

'But what I have to do now is far more nerve-racking than standing or sitting at a mike in front of the largest audience in the world . . . I have to ski down in front of all those photographers and not under any circumstances fall over.'

The gift didn't end there. Over lunch on the mountain one of the dignitaries of the *commune* approached me: 'Peter, I don't know if you know about fighting cows around here, but it's an ancient tradition in this part of Switzerland and we have breeders and annual contests. We'd like to name a cow after James, only we can't have a male cow – do you think we could name one after his mother?' Sure.

'Hi Jane, it's Peter. Yes, I'm in Verbier with James and you'll never guess what, the locals have named a fighting cow after you. Yes, a cow called Jane Blount. She's a real goer.'

So Blunty's got his ski lift, his mum's got a cow, and now in Bratislava he has the chance to have his own city nightclub.

'I'm sorry, I didn't catch your name,' I tell the guy. 'I'll go and find James this minute. I'm sure he'd love to meet you.'

James is delighted at the idea. However, I get the distinct feeling that Mr Cool Entrepreneur Slovakia is taking advantage of the presence in town of an international star in order to temporarily turn on the street lights in his own galaxy. Somehow, I don't think that a flashing neon sign saying 'James Blunt' is about to be mounted above the front door – and I'm right. Much later in that long night I learn that the club, which is still under construction, is only being opened for the one night before closing and re-launching under a new name. But hell, who cares? Blunty certainly doesn't. He's living for tonight, and rightly so.

Prague

It's 9am in one of the world's most beautiful cities. No doubt Wenceslas Square, where the bravest university students stuck flowers in the barrels of Russian tanks during the Russian invasion in 1968, is looking as serenely beautiful as ever. Quite possibly they're still selling soldiers' fur hats on the Charles Bridge, but I'm in no condition to find out. I'm shaking and I feel like death. I can't work out whether it's the sub-zero temperature here in another desolate coach park, flu, or the king of all hangovers.

Here we are in historic Prague and no one, least of all me, feels like venturing beyond the venue. Nobody partied harder than James last night in the James Blunt Club. Surrounded by the usual bevy of fragrant, long-limbed models he was in overdrive both on and off the floor. We left the club at nearly 4am and partied on board the bus until we'd crossed the border with the Czech Republic and the sun was up. Then at some hidden inner signal Blunty retreated into recharge mode, plugging himself into his bunk like you'd plug a mobile into a socket. His ability to detox and restore his batteries through five hours of unconsciousness never ceases to amaze me. Maggie Thatcher could famously do it in three.

James spent three winters in the ski resort of Verbier training for this existence. Lessons learned in the army form constant positive threads in his current crazy life

139

which actively aid him in holding it all together, while others would melt under the mental pressure. His record in the Swiss resort was 43 party nights in a row – 5am to bed and on the first ski lift at 9am in charge of a group of squaddies taking their first ski lessons.

'We'd ski through the morning, but at lunch I'd sit in a locked cubicle in the gents to snatch 60 minutes' sleep. A bang on the cubicle door from a mate – and back you went up the mountain.'

Later, in the front line in Kosovo, he learned one of the basic rules of survival in a war zone: sleep and eat when you can, because you never know when you are going to do either next – if at all.

Now it's all paying big dividends, and the more important the day/evening ahead, the deeper he manages to sleep. Today he's in a coma. Not only has he got a girlfriend flying out to join him, but his parents and eight of their friends are coming to the gig tonight too.

But what a night to choose. I go back to my bunk in the afternoon, but feel too ill to sleep. Mick, our ever-cheerful bus driver, is fussing about doing the housework. He can see a pair of shoes on the floor and the drawn curtains of my bunk, but he just can't resist a cheerful whistle and a little light vacuuming. I can't blame him for getting his own back. Driving alone through the night, fighting the on-coming headlights through a rain-splashed windscreen in a strange country, is hard on your own, and it's considerably tougher when there's a full-blown drunken party going on behind the back of your neck.

I wake again with a start. I'm alone in the bus and it's already 6pm. What if Jane and Charlie proudly show off the tour bus to their guests and there's their friend Peter lying unconscious, unshaven and underpanted in his bunk, a pathetic old man who really shouldn't be here at all? I cringe with embarrassment at the thought and make a supreme effort to get myself back together. In Catering I grab some food and join the grim-faced band . . . chilli con carne and an encroaching sense of despair.

The tour is always a mood graph of highs and lows . . . but this is a deep depression. If we were looking at a weather map instead of each other around a canteen table in a Prague winter, you'd fear that a storm of cyclonic intensity was about to wash ashore. The contrast with the carefree happiness experienced by all in a club in another country 15 hours ago is quite extraordinary, and not all of it is to do with so many late nights.

'I think I've got flu,' I confess to Johnny.

'No you haven't, mate, you've got the mother of all hangovers. Do you know what we drank last night . . .'

'OK, OK, OK.'

'We all feel just as bad. The difference is you can go back to bed. We have to go back on stage.'

Self-abuse apart, the reasons for these peaks and troughs are complex and they become more so the longer everyone is away from home and the real world. I suppose that, cocooned inside the Bubble, they all feel secure during what is essentially a joint experience littered with in-jokes and remembrances along the line. In each other's well-worn company, they feel safe, unthreatened.

As Beardy told me in Bratislava: 'The secret to James' success is the tour. He's at his happiest – in fact, it's the only time he's happy – when he's away with us. When he's with his other mates from his old life, with a couple of exceptions, it's not the same. Living and breathing music along with the shagging doesn't make him happy, but it does take the edge off his pain.'

Max Lousada, chairman of Atlantic Records UK, sees the results. He told me one time when we were skiing together in Verbier: 'James is unique because of his love of touring and that's what makes him so successful. This guy would tour continuously, if he could. He simply doesn't understand why everyone around him needs to stop from time to time and go back to their lives, because this *is* the life that he loves. He could just go on and on forever.

'Other artists go on the road and after ten days or a few weeks they've got a problem: "I don't feel well, I need to take a break. I have to go see my girlfriend/boyfriend." They need to be somewhere that they are not. They've always got an excuse for not wanting to work. But James is different. He's a workaholic. Occasionally you have to make him stop, or I think he'll self-destruct.'

Self-destruct is what everyone is feeling might happen right now – and the reason for this depression is partly a reaction to four hours at the James Blunt Club, but also because we are about to have a visit from the real world. Get ready to release the seal on the Bubble door and activate the airlock.

Don't get me wrong. It's not so much that outsiders are not welcome. It's good to see friends from home, but sometimes when you've become almost entirely institutionalized over a period of weeks or – in the case of James and the band – months, there's a helpless feeling of intrusion. It's all wonderfully exciting for the newcomers. The more enthusiastic and interested they are, the more difficult it is to cope with that enthusiasm. Almost, you want to shock them.

James and the band begin to feel like animals in a zoo at feeding time. I remember back in the 1970s at the old Chessington Zoo in Surrey, before it became a theme park, there was a particular chimpanzee that suffered from the same syndrome. At 5pm the crowd would gather for the daily and now considered humiliating chimps' tea party, with the animals all dressed up for the occasion. As soon as the groups of schoolchildren and mums and dads were in place, this chimp would adopt a fixed grin, pull down his pants and masturbate furiously. Just to shock.

The band's got better manners – well, some of them, anyway – but I can easily understand the chimp's reaction to rubber-necking. Jane and Charlie are two of my closest friends. However, thanks to Kiss Me Kate, they are understandably deeply concerned about their son's lifestyle and I'm torn between them, with loyalties to both camps. I go off to dinner with the parents and their friends, stumbling along a tightrope from which it's so easy to fall. Maybe I should give up now.

Tash is the girlfriend who has been flown in to join the circus and she brings with her a breath of fresh air. She's small, vibrant and pretty – a successful former swimwear model, and a talented artist in her own right. For months while recovering in hospital from a broken back she continued to 'paint' using what materials came to hand – including pages of the *Financial Times*. With the aid of a mirror and her naked self as a model, she used scraps of pink *FT* newsprint – perfect for flesh tones – to create extraordinary nude montages. Her clients now include the wives and mistresses of some of the richest men in the world. When you have everything, what better present for your partner than a picture of yourself in the altogether that costs $30,000? Yes, she's done James. For Tash, as she admits, there is a troubling confusion between artistic integrity and cash: to earn the latter she needs just occasionally to be economical with the bodily truth and adopt a secondary role as a plastic surgeon specializing in stomach tucks and boob jobs.

James is in defiant mode and appropriately it's 'I Can't Hear The Music' that unites the audience tonight. It's a song about doing your own thing and, of course, this is exactly what he does.

'Benny's guitar makes it sound like Led Zeppelin,' he tells me when I ask him about it later that night.

'I started writing those words at school and didn't do anything with them. Then they became relevant again, because when I started in the music industry it was like going back to the school playground again.

'The song's about that sense of "You know what? I'll just do my own thing". At school people form gangs against others, but I was never into the sheep mentality. People feel safe when they follow in a herd.

'People make friends by being horrid to others. It's what Chris Moyles, the radio DJ, does. He's an insecure man whose popularity has come from being horrible to other people. And it shows the weakness of others who follow him. We aren't really individuals. We talk about freedom in life, but we're not free in the first place. We tend to take our opinion of the world from other people's opinions. We're told what we like and what we don't. So this song is about being an individual and doing your own thing. I kind of like that.' So does Prague.

Now parents and friends are left guiltily behind as Mick drives us through the night towards Vienna. James is in relaxed mood and Tash has a neat line in pyjamas and a bunk beneath James at the front of the bus. James Blunt is a crossword clue in today's *Daily Mail*. This guy *must* be famous.

Vienna

First Prague and now Vienna: two of the most beautiful cities in the world and I don't get a chance to see either. Other writing – the newspaper stuff that pays the bills – has intruded into my world and I spend the day in Austria cobbling together words on lesser-known ski resorts in Switzerland. By the time I'm finished it's already dusk. James and Tash have been away all day seeing the sights. Karl, John and I grab a cab to the Innere Stadt to spend an hour drinking in baroque palaces and beer. Sometimes it's warmly rewarding to discover that beneath the tough veneer of professional and highly creative musicians these guys remain just a lovable bunch of grown-up kids who get along remarkably well with each other and with James. Indeed, a huge component of Blunty's success story is built on the strength of his friendship with the band and the way in which he leads from the front. Like a fresh-faced officer in the trenches of Flanders he's always the first one over the top – pistol in hand. Only difference is that day after day he survives.

Blunty's sold 100,000 tickets in Austria and Germany and the regional promoter's pretty pleased with themselves and with him, and there's an awards ceremony just before the gig. I'm to take the photos.

Tash is sitting in the dressing-room, looking uncertain. She's not sure if she should go or stay.

'Come with me,' Blunty says, taking her firmly by the hand. They look good together, sort of small and neat.

Later, Tash and I watch the show together from the edge of the stage and then from the pit. She's looking at him with sober admiration, and then much less sober admiration after she and I launch a full-frontal assault on the first of the dressing-room vodka bottles.

Back in the pit, we crouch down and watch the last quarter of the set. The audience is screaming so loudly it's difficult to hear yourself think.

'Look over your shoulder,' I shout in her ear. 'There's 9,000 people out there, mostly women, singing their hearts out for this guy. You've only got to look at their faces to see that they worship him, they want to touch him, they want to go to bed with him, right now they'd die for him. Watching your lover on stage, knowing he is yours not theirs, must be the biggest turn-on of all time.'

Tash smiles at me: 'You really don't understand, do you? James is not my lover. We've never kissed – he's never even tried to. We're just very good friends – soulmates, if you like.' Did I hear that right?

I'm shocked. How can this be? James once told me he can tell within ten seconds of meeting a girl whether she will come across. By second No.11, if the answer is negative, he's moved on. So, apart from the shameless shagger, is there another guy hiding inside that compact frame? One that I don't know anything about?

'I think he's in love with Sabina?' she says. It's a question not a statement, and one that goes unanswered. It's not my place to tell her that James these crazy days has not necessarily any sense of being in love with anyone, not even himself, which makes me sad. Carry on playing hard to get, Tash, if that is what you are doing, because it makes you all the more attractive. You all think you can change him, but you can't. It's like trying to convert a gay guy. It's the music that's the driving force.

Tash is going to Paris at dawn with James and I shall miss her. In fact, I'll miss everyone. They're all flying to Paris for a TV show and leaving me to travel southwards alone on the bus from Vienna to Venice.

We reach Vienna airport. I absorb a few swift hugs goodbye and the bus door hisses shut behind them. Shockingly, quite suddenly, it's just me, Uncle Peter, on £300,000 of the smartest tour bus in the world, achingly alone apart from Mick upfront in the driver's cab. So, what shall I do with myself?

Let's see . . . there're 1,100 movies to watch, 9,000 tracks on the music system, 248 TV channels, and two bars stocked with everything from champagne to vintage wines. For half an hour I wander aimlessly from room to room. I've lived in this luxurious, yet confined, space now for weeks on end, but I've not really appreciated it.

In all that time I've never been more than a foot and a half from my fellow human beings who've become my intimate friends. Intimacy isn't a choice – it's thrust upon you. In that time, I realize now that I have only noticed the people, not the gaps between them. I remember once, when I was heliskiing in the Bugaboo mountain range of British Columbia, we skied rhythmically down a long, open bowl of deep powder with not an obstacle in sight. Then we hit the tree line, a forest of pines so close together that at first it seems impossible to maintain that sensual rhythm. 'The secret,' said the guide, 'is not to look at the trees at all, only at the spaces between them.' Now I'm once again looking at the spaces and appreciating them for the first time.

Somewhere between Vienna and Innsbruck, Mick pulls into an *Autobahn* service station. I put my champagne flute down on the party room table and peep out through the Venetian blind. A gaggle of late-night teens drinking coffee, their breath steaming in the cold air, are staring in awe and envy at the sleek tour bus with its blacked-out windows. The movement of the blind brings instant interest.

'I wonder who's in there?' they say. I see them pointing and saying to each other, 'It must be a famous rock star.'

Famous rock star? More like a trashed out nobody. So what do I do? I pour the rest of the champagne down the sink, do the washing up, go to bed alone, and pull the duvet over my head.

Venice

The concert's not in Venice itself, but in the airport town of Treviso, half an hour away on the mainland. Mick dumps me on the roadside and drives off to park at the stadium and catch up on his sleep. Feeling like an ancient Jack Kerouac – I once spent an evening with him in the redwood forest of Big Sur, California – I set off down the road, bag in hand, in search of a taxi to the rail station and the short ride to Venice.

Without the security blanket of the bus and the remnants of the empty Bubble, I feel completely lost and I'm in the middle of nowhere. The taxi driver, not used to foreigners at all, treats me as if I have just landed from Mars until I mention Blunty. 'My wife loves him more than she loves me,' he complains, 'but I have bought tickets for tomorrow night, so now she loves me again, almost as much.'

La Serenissima is sparkling in early Saturday sunlight. A *vaporetto* takes me down the Grand Canal and I meet my wife Felice and Isabella, my 13-year-old daughter, on the steps of the Rialto Bridge. Not, you understand, by chance.

I feel like a convict on weekend release from Wormwood Scrubs. After the isolation of the Bubble, the crowds and cultural feast of Venice are overwhelming. But no sooner am I'm starting to adjust and relax with my family than it's time for us, 24 hours later, to take the train back to Treviso.

James and the band are completely exhausted. Long airport delays both to and from Paris have taken their toll and Blunty's got another sore throat. So why have they come all the way back down Europe to entertain an audience of only 2,500 on a Sunday night in Treviso, better known for its Ryanair flights than its rockability? The answer is that his life is once again at the mercy of booking agents – and counterfeit merchandisers. By late afternoon a whole market place of stalls has sprung up around the stadium selling unlicensed James Blunt T-shirts for €10 instead of €30, the price of the official ones on sale inside.

During the show one blonde and her boyfriend are noticeable from the pit because they shout rather than sing every word of every song.

Afterwards I asked them how they came to learn all that. They give me a puzzled look, turn to each other, and then back to me: 'Sorry, no speak English,' says the girl. But suddenly I'm hemmed in by people who do. 'What's he like? Please tell us what he's really like! Bring him out here, I want to kiss him. Who are you?' Then the inevitable question, 'Are you James' father?'

It's a permanent reminder of the generation gap. No matter how young I might *feel* on a good day, I *look* inescapably my age.

'Is that his daughter?' asks another, indicating my Isabella who is standing beside me.

It's so tempting to say 'yes' and to fuck up the web for weeks to come. 'Blunt's Secret Love Child Unveiled in Venice,' the headline would scream. But I don't. Instead

I wave my family off in a taxi bound for an airport hotel and an early flight home, while I squeeze into the airlock and re-enter the Bubble. The band's tired, but not *that* tired, and the bus is in full swing. The standard of audience talent seemed pretty low to me, but the boys appear to have picked the best of them. James rapidly disappears with a tall brunette. Benny and Johnny are nowhere to be seen, wedded to Skype presumably. Karl asks for pictures of him and the two prettiest and I oblige . . . then without a word he's off into the dressing-room bathroom with one of them, leaving me awkwardly talking to the other.

She keeps looking at the closed door and then worriedly glancing back at me with an unspoken question on her lips. Don't get me wrong, this is no invitation. She just wants an explanation. What's my friend *doing* in there?

Later on the bus, everyone's too tired to party. It's 3am and I call it an early night. Just as I've climbed into my bunk Karl sticks his head through my curtains with his schoolboy grin: 'You dirty, bastard, Uncle Peter,' he says. 'I saw you chatting up that girl.'

'You're the dirty bastard,' I reply, 'and in a toilet, too.'

It's good to be back. We wake up in the mountains in Bolzano and it's pouring with rain.

Basel

I've twice spent Christmas with her – well, dinner in the
same two-family skiing party – and I once spent an evening
with her and Felice, just the three of us, in Verbier and
she doesn't even remember me. This says a lot about Weird
Uncle Peter and maybe a whole lot more about her. At
least my Christmas hangover wasn't so bad that I was sick
into a saucepan.

Miranda was James' five-year live-in girlfriend back in
the warm anonymous days before one song changed his
life forever. Now, on a sunny morning in suburban Basel,
here she is again with her husband and they're planning
to stay on with us into France. James never tells anyone
in advance when he's got friends or girlfriends arriving. I
guess he doesn't see why he should. They just appear, like
I do, without warning. When these two materialize, off
an early London flight, he's asleep. He's only just gone to
bed. Miranda goes upstairs and watches him breathing in
his bunk for a while.

As strong as you were, tender you go
I'm watching you breathing for the last time

Lack of forewarning can't be said of Benny who's been
telling us for weeks that his pregnant Australian girlfriend,
Sam, is arriving today from Perth. Now he's finished

153

counting down the days, turned off Skype, and overcome a vicious hangover after a noisy all-night party on the bus from Bolzano that had driver Mick struggling to concentrate as he manoeuvred our cumbersome wagon through snowdrifts on the mountain pass.

No-sleep Benny has already been out to the airport to meet her and here she is, lovely Sam, the girl he met at her home gig last year in Perth, Western Australia, and a few months later got pregnant in Provence. Funny how these things happen in Provence. I guess that staying in Grasse, perfume capital of the world, and breathing in all that exotic scent can change your take on life. Hello Sam, welcome. As you have already discovered judging by your belly, once you've met Benny nothing is ever going to be quite the same again.

Bobble bobs out of his bunk to say 'Hi' too, before heading off to his in-tray of morning problems, which are already mounting in the show production office inside the stadium. Unlike the band, he has a day job along with the night one. While our lot are following the lead of our queen bee and drinking, shagging and sleeping their way around Europe, James' road manager, along with stage/show manager Mark and his crew, are living in a parallel universe inhabited by a team of heavily muscled workers in hard hats and harnesses. Often before we've even got into our bunks in the grey light of dawn, let alone got out of them, they've unloaded four pantechnicons, powered up the electrics, tuned into a satellite, and half-rigged the stage – and that's all before bacon and eggs for breakfast in the canteen they have first had to create. Blunt's army marches on its stomach – it's no surprise to discover that the collapsible kitchen and the larder are always stowed in the first crates to be wheeled up the ramp into the arena.

Boy, it's busy around here in Basel. No sooner have the newcomers made themselves at home than the electric door hisses open again and there is the long-limbed, fragrant Sabina fresh off the plane from Ibiza, all hair and smiles. She goes upstairs. Is it my imagination, or is this bus getting crowded this morning?

There have been days on this trip when Blunty's become so withdrawn that the only person he seems to communicate with is Archie, a half-sized R2-D2 droid who's escaped from *Star Wars*. Archie travels around the world with us in the band wardrobe, a giant upright trunk that houses all the stage clothes. Archie doesn't do a lot. He wheels around the dressing-room using his sensors to avoid running into chairs, sofas, feet and coffee cups, before dropping off into electronic sleep in a corner. He recognizes voice commands only from Blunty. Any likeness to me here is entirely coincidental.

'Archie, go walkabout,' says his commander, looking up from his laptop just for the briefest of moments. And Archie faithfully does what he's told, like we all do. Sleeping or awake, Blunty is in control.

We're halfway through the concert and Miranda is standing with her husband by the back stage and James is singing 'Goodbye My Lover'. Sabina is watching with a couple of friends in the audience just back from the crush barrier. James is looking at everyone and no one. Miranda has a faraway look in her eyes – you probably think this song is about you – and her husband, as always, has a protective arm around her. Let's face it, his is the biggest love of all around here. Karl understands him well. Miranda's guy gave up a career as a potential professional footballer to go into the City and make money. Karl gave up the City – Birmingham City – to make music.

Then we're off through the night in the tour bus for the nine-hour drive south to Marseille. Blunty's the most energetic we've seen him all tour – one minute he's hanging out upstairs in the party room, the next he's dancing in the downstairs aisle. Benny and Sam have gone to bed early. Miranda's husband drinks beer and assesses the scene. He's a star. Miranda, heart on sleeve, jousts with Blunty:

'Until now you didn't even know my husband's name. You never ask anyone questions about themselves.' Actually, it's the drink that's doing the talking.

Blunty just smiles – he's not going to sing this song.

'That's the way it is,' he tells her. 'Maybe I don't ask questions, but if someone wants to say something, I listen with interest.'

On another day he speaks of the Miranda years with genuine warmth. The beauty of her is that, like a child, she says what she thinks without thinking. Drinking in her surroundings with those huge innocent eyes on arrival in the bus, Miranda, with a look of genuine puzzlement, asks me: 'What's wrong with your legs, why do you walk funny?'

I might mind; she never considers that for a second. But I don't, at all.

'Her husband's a cool guy and she's much better off with him than with me,' says Blunty.

Marseille

Marseille is warm and sticky. There's a big storm on the way and you can feel the electricity in the air. It's a Sunday and a national holiday, and the shops are all closed and heavily shuttered. An air of menace usually hangs over this city of diverse cultures where Africa meets Europe. Down the years the CRS, the French riot police, have been responsible for frequent bloody clashes with students, migrants and anyone else unfortunate enough to have got in the way of their batons. Personally, I've got hit only twice – in Paris back in '68 and in Corsica a few years later. But today they're mercifully absent from the streets and the only menace lies in the weather. We walk down to the port in search of authentic *bouillabaisse*, the ultimate fish stew for which, along with gangsters and drugs, the port is famous.

We find a harbour-side fish restaurant that is open and full of French couples and families making the gastronomic best of their day of rest.

'James Blunt!' screams the waitress. 'I can't believe it!' Then over her shoulder she yells: 'Marianne, get your ass out of that kitchen NOW. We've got James Blunt and he's looking lean and hungry.'

The bad news is that by now virtually the whole of the Midi knows he's here. But fame does have its benefits – an empty table for five materializes before our eyes. We get what we've come for. Bouillabaisse is the perfect marriage of red mullet, mussels, prawns and sea bass, washed down with a couple of bottles of Clos Ste Magdeleine, the flinty white wine from nearby Cassis.

Touring's full of stress; hidden enemies, such as mental and physical exhaustion from constantly being on the move in time and space, are like tree roots waiting to trip you up at every turn on the forest path. But today we can all relax. The only enemy is in the sky – and halfway through lunch the storm strikes with typical Mediterranean vengeance. Umbrellas are ripped from their stands, tables are overturned by the howling wind. Outside diners scurry for shelter as balloon-sized blobs of rain begin to fall upon the open terrace. We retreat indoors. Across the city, half the crew are marooned for two hours in another restaurant by a power cut and a metre of flood water outside the door. Mike The Sound and Scott, another of the techies, have ridden their bikes up into the hills behind the city and are nearly swept away by the weight of water on the road.

Then, in the early evening, comes near disaster. Bobble breaks the news to James and me when we're sitting talking in a bar.

'Benny and Sam have been in a car crash. They've both been taken to hospital. So far, that's all I know.' It turns out that a police van has smashed at high speed into the taxi in which Benny and the pregnant Sam were travelling.

There's a moment of supreme suspense in the bar. How badly are they hurt? For James there's a second inevitable question: What the hell happens if the lead guitarist is out of the game, either temporarily or permanently? There are other musicians who can be flown in, but it takes time to play your way into the tour. Cancelling gigs is financially not an option.

'Well, James?' I ask.

'We'll deal with that one if or when we get to it,' he replies. Like the tank commander he once was, I get the feeling he's already worked out a plan B.

Fortunately for Benny and Sam – and for James – the situation doesn't arise. Word filters through from the hospital that both have escaped with minor bruising. The show must, and now can, go on. But first Beardy, who is locked into a sequence of extraordinarily potent cocktails in the only bar that seems to remain open this Sunday evening, is determined to get rat-assed. It would be unfriendly of me not to join him.

Sometime later, possibly many hours later, a sober Johnny – fresh from a marathon Skype to his girlfriend in Denmark – mercifully appears after a call from Beardy. I guess he could tell from his voice that we might need a little assistance. Like the radio operator in a World War II airfield control tower guiding home a couple of Lancasters crippled by enemy cannon fire, he shepherds us back to the hotel on an erratic zigzag course to a safe landing.

I'm standing in the lobby of the Holiday Inn when Karl, grinning from ear to ear, walks through the door. Who's that girl on his arm? Why it's the brunette from the nightclub in Bratislava. It can't be! But it is. I mean, how does the guy do this? He must have imported her by airmail from Slovakia to the South of France for just 24 hours, unless she's been a stowaway in the bus engine compartment during the past 3,000 miles and six cities. Ah, well, tomorrow is another day and another concert.

The gig's at Le Dome, a futuristic building shaped like the upturned hull of a boat. It holds 8,500 people and it's a sell-out. Ben's a bit bruised and battered from the car crash, but just happy that Sam and the baby appear to be OK. Everyone's up for a good evening, and that's how it goes. Miranda and her husband and everyone have flown home and it's just Sam, Sabina and me as camp followers.

Tonight it's 'Shine On' that brings the house down. Le Dome is ideally suited to the laser show which Glen co-ordinates with James 'encased' on stage in a funnel of light that later in the evening explodes into diffused starbursts that crackle across the ceiling and walls of the arena. It's a spectacular setting for the song, which curiously is not one of James' favourites.

'The lasers certainly help it along,' James tells me, 'but I wonder about that song sometimes. Originally I had some other words for it, but I didn't use them because they were too similar in a way to 'Goodbye My Lover'.

Walk on, Walk on
I don't blame you as you walk from me
You will hold the hand of another man
But it's a lonely walk for me.
So Walk on, my dear, Walk on
And I hope you have a family,
We won't meet again. We have reached the end.
You have been the girl of my dreams. You have been
the girl for me.

Later in the concert, I'm wandering around the audience when I spot a girl in her mid-thirties standing beside the back stage. She is watching James with that familiar doe-eyed acceptance of unrequited desire. She's good-looking with shoulder-length fair hair, but not striking. It's more her daughter who first catches my attention. Children under ten are a rarity at one of his gigs and this angelic little girl couldn't have been more than five or six.

I could see that, for the mother, James and his music mean the world. She knows every word of every song and like most of the rest of the audience she probably didn't speak English. But you don't need another language to see that she really wants her daughter to feel, to share, this intense emotion that is flowering inside her. While James sings, the mother keeps bending down and whispering in her daughter's ear and pointing at James cavorting on the distant front stage. The little girl looks confused and distracted. She can't, for the little life of her, understand at all what the fuss is about.

Then at the appointed moment in the middle of 'Coz I Luv You', James jumps off the main stage and into the crowd. As usual, the whole arena erupts in a roar as he fights his way through the sea of people. A kiss for an astonished girl in his path and then for a moment he almost disappears under the weight of bodies that cling to him. He pushes the half-hearted tackle aside and surges onwards, ruthlessly scything a path to the safety of the back stage. Then he's safely inside the enclosure and fingering the keyboard of the piano as it rises instantly on the hydraulic hoist above the crowd.

'We're going to sing this three times,' he says. 'First

I'm going to sing it, then my band over there is going to sing it, and then you're going to sing it.'

In a single moment, the mother finds that the cheapest two seats in the house have turned into the front row. It's pumpkins to stagecoach and it's all too much. Her eyes lock like a ground-to-air missile on to a tiny patch of sweat darkening the grey of James' suit trousers just above his bum, where shirt meets waistband. Her daughter, the first love of her life, is temporarily forgotten as she sways to the music and sings in a foreign language.

Next on the set-list is 'Goodbye My Lover'. Once again on the mother's face is that now familiar look of overwhelming sexual desire tinged with utterly delicious resignation. 'I love him, I really love him,' it says, 'but I'm never going to actually touch him in the way that he has touched my life.'

Entirely unperturbed by all this grown-up emotion, the little girl turns her eyes away from James and the spotlight, looks up once at her own love who's drifted away for the moment into her private world, and curls up on the beer-sticky floor. Using Mummy's discarded red plastic handbag as a pillow, she falls dreamlessly asleep at her feet.

Sometimes, during the daily doubting moments of uncut paranoia in other cities around the world when I ask myself: 'What does all this mean?'; when I read another vitriolic story in a British newspaper, I replay that scene in my mind. So many people rubbish him and his music, but for all those women like the little girl's mother, for this moment at least, James *is* their world. He provides the dream.

Toulouse

She's in love with him and she hopes he loves her, too – but she's not so sure and Sabina is almost comically angry. There she was, living her life in Ibiza. She had a local boyfriend. He was tall, charming and handsome – he had lots of cash, and he made her sort of happy. Then she saw James across the proverbial crowded room (clubs in Ibiza add a whole new definition to the word 'crowded'). What happened next was *amor a primera vista*, as they say in Catalan – wham! A *coup de foudre*, Cupid's shaft, a lightning bolt, love at first sight. They connected before they even spoke to each other. Sabina's life instantly somersaulted.

Why did she fall for him? Well, for a start, Sabina's no groupie. She loves him, but she most certainly doesn't want to fall into a situation where she could get hurt. This afternoon she wanted him to take her into the town, into Toulouse from the venue. But James said he didn't have time, because of the sound check and all those newspaper and radio interviews.

She told me later:

'I was still waiting for a taxi when he came and found me – I think he felt guilty. "Can I give you some money?" he said.

'"No," I told him, "I have money."

'"Well, can I give you some money to buy a dress?" he said.

'I told him: "Why would I want a dress on a bus?"'

'He said: "For me?"'

'I said, "If I want a dress for myself, then I'll buy a dress for myself."'

'I don't think other girls talk to him like that. But I am not one of his other girls. I don't know where I am. He says: "Come to Rome with me?" I love Rome, but maybe I don't go. Maybe I go home to Ibiza and then to Marrakech with my friends and forget all about James Blunt. Maybe that's best for me.'

I tell her that from now on she is in charge of happiness. 'OK,' she smiles. 'If he is happy, then I am happy, and everyone is happy. Is good. But I'm not in charge of relaxation.'

Then she adds: 'I don't want him too relaxed. Well, not *all* the time, if you see what I mean.'

Sex is the current in which the Blunty show swims and occasionally sinks to new and previously uncharted depths. Love? My God, this is truly terrifying. First we have Beardy in a permanent relationship, then Johnny, then Ben. Is this the beginning of the end of the ultimate rock 'n' roll tour?

Sabina and I are at the back stage with Sam, sitting for once in allocated seats because the show is being televised. My eyes have focused on a slightly plump middle-aged woman who is dancing just behind the front crush barrier and gazing ravenously up at James' crotch, which is around five feet above her face. Apart from this obvious and prurient hunger, she might be the owner of a small bourgeois restaurant, who divides her time between gossiping with the regulars and composing their bills by hand in a neat schoolgirl script behind the frosted, etched glass wall of the cashier's desk.

Quite suddenly, no doubt mindful of the zooming TV camera, she screams out in English: 'James Blunt, I want to fuck you like an ANIMAL!' We're laughing and James is looking at Sabina laughing and you can see that he doesn't get why she's laughing, and just for a moment I glimpse a welcome vulnerability I've never seen before.

We're getting near the end of the European tour, just Bordeaux and Dijon to go. Marathon runners talk about 'the wall' – that virtual barrier you hit at around the 18-mile mark when you're an impossibly long way from the start and the finish is too far away to contemplate. In order to survive, you must fight both the road and yourself. Then, quite suddenly, you're through it and the finishing line starts to winch you in towards it.

While the tour has its exciting moments, the fact is that it majors in tedious and tiring repetition. The crew get some of the worst of it. Each day they must unpack six trucks and assemble the whole stage and set. Each night they must take it all down again, drive somewhere else, and start over.

James' workload is equally heavy. The two-hour sound check and gig are preceded by up to four hours of radio, TV and newspaper interviews, along with press conferences and meetings with sponsors, promoters and public prize-winners.

Every day, he is asked at least ten times by a different interviewer the same set of questions. Only the language changes.

'What do you think about 'You're Beautiful' being the No.1 song played at weddings?'

'Is there a special person in your life right now?'

'How do you like it here in Kazakhstan?'

Standing in studios watching these over and over again in different cities around the world, I sometimes get the overwhelming impression that the interviewers themselves are equally bored by their own questions. After all, all they did was Google 'James Blunt'.

James tries to answer each as if they've been posed for the first time, but if he sounds reserved it's because after the thousandth time it's not boring – it's maddening – and because he's pacing himself.

'My whole day from waking up, washing, getting dressed and eating, to interviews, sound check, warm-up and changing into stage clothes is all done on automatic,' he explains. 'I'm running on an economy programme, functioning with the least amount of emotional output. My daily life on tour is based on conserving energy, like an enormous capacitor.

'While everyone around me is living their normal life, mine's on pause for the 22 hours between shows. I'm re-coiling the spring in such a way that, when I hit the stage that evening, and multiplied by the energy of the audience, I press the "play" button again and explode with all that pent-up energy, and for the best part of two hours I can burn.'

Right now, the circus has moved on to Bordeaux, home to arguably the most famous wine in the world which is known in Britain as 'claret'. These days claret refers to all the heavy red wine that comes from the region, but its derivation is '*clairet*' which means 'pale'. Originally Bordeaux wine was a rosé, an exceptionally dark rosé, much loved by Richard the Lionheart – yes, here's that regal guy again because he sensibly spent a lot more time among the rolling vineyards of south-western France than in rainy Nottingham or in the Holy Land.

However, such a history lesson is apparently lost on Bobble, who is more of a beer than a wine man. To fuel the bar that evening he digs out from his travelling cellar a special bottle of Australian red tooth-stripper.

All would have been well, but for the decision to invite half a dozen influential local wine growers to the after-party. Already they've overseen a wine-tasting session for the crew in Catering. The techies know their wine. As the party gets under way I find myself chatting to the president of the Bordeaux Vintners' Association or some-such, anyway an astonishingly esteemed organization, and I ask him what he would like to drink.

'*Un coup de rouge*,' he replies, putting on his reading glasses. His magnified eyes fall on the label of the single bottle of Dancing Kangaroo Shiraz that is positioned centre stage on the bar.

His expression turns from politeness to puzzled confusion and on to the doormat of anger. But wait, I can see him thinking, '*Quel horreur!* Is this a deliberate insult by James Blunt? Is he taking the piss out of the most famous wine-growing region in the world? No, surely not! No one as charming as he could be that deliberately rude to his hosts.' He recovers his composure.

'*Ah, non*,' he shrugs in that peculiarly dismissive way that is known only to Frenchmen, 'I change my mind, I will take a Jack Daniel's, please, with a little water.' As

Beardy helps himself to a full glass of the Dancing 'Roo, he openly shudders.

It's 7am at Charles de Gaulle airport and another term at Hogwarts is over. The bus has taken us through the night from Dijon to the outskirts of Paris and slowly it dawns on me that I'm going home. The same can't be said for James and an uncertain Sabina – they're going to Rome where James is to be guest editor for the day on *Metro*, the international freesheet. Poor Sabina, you'll never get to Marrakech now.

Sarajevo

The long drive into town is down Sniper Alley, the wide boulevard that is indelibly imprinted on the minds of everyone who had access to a TV set during the Siege of Sarajevo in the early 1990s. Night after night the peace and security of our sitting rooms was invaded by images of the cold and desperate inhabitants of that sad Bosnian city, forced regularly from their cellars and the ruins of their houses by the inescapable necessity of finding food and water. We saw them crouching behind burnt-out cars as they summoned the courage to run the gauntlet of random sniper fire at every crossroads. We saw, lying in the road, the broken rag-doll bodies of those who gambled and lost.

Two survivors have since, in their separate ways, caught the world's imagination. Vedran Smajlovic was one of them. He is a former cellist in the Sarajevo String Quartet, who in that terrible year of 1992 took to emerging from his apartment at different times each day to play Albinoni's Adagio in G Minor on his cello to honour his 22 neighbours, killed by a shell while queuing for bread.

Dijana Catic was another. Dijana, now celebrity socialite Diana Jenkins, was a Communist Muslim Serb and a university student during the siege. She arrived in Brixton in London in 1993 as a penniless refugee.

Now she describes herself as a philanthropist, is married

to a wealthy British banker and is a mother of two with her fingers in so many fashion and showbiz pies that she needs an extra pair of hands. This week these belong to Blunty, whom she has persuaded to perform on guitar and piano – not cello – in her Sarajevo which hardly seems to have recovered at all from the war.

Of course, the ruined cars have long since been bull-dozed away. The traffic lights are working once again and the billboards carry fresh posters of Blunty. But almost every building is still scarred by shrapnel. Our hotel is an exception and brand new. It's been built beside the ruins of a no-vacancy old folks home that was burnt to the ground in 1993. The Serbs, so we're told, locked the doors with the people still inside and set fire to it.

The city's jagged scars are not just physical. It takes just a brief look around to realize that the suppurating mental wounds of the inhabitants have never healed. Benny, Johnny and I take a ride to the Princip Bridge, where a student called Gavrilo Princip shot Archduke Franz Ferdinand and his wife in June 1914, thereby knocking over the first domino in the chain that led to the start of World War I.

Walking around the old town you see people of obviously different ethnic origins displaying a kind of closed hostility as they pass each other on the street. It's one that the passage of half a generation has failed to dispel. You can't help but get the horrible feeling that violence could flare up again here at any moment. Pigeons coo in the square and children play and smile, but not the grown-ups. Lunch in an outdoor café is some kind of local stew with huge dumplings. This was possibly what indirectly killed the Archduke. He was so vain, so the story goes, that each morning he had a small army of tailors sew him into his uniform to disguise the fact that he was putting on weight. After he was shot, efforts to staunch the flow of blood were hampered by the time it took to cut him out of his tunic.

Karl's lost his suitcase between Birmingham and London. By the time it's been found he's already left for Munich and onwards to here.

'Send it home,' he tells an amazed BA baggage person. 'It'll never catch me up over the next two weeks.'

Guitars are a bigger problem – we've lost three of them in Munich en route, but no one seems too worried. We've got 24 hours in which to find them or replacements. James and Paul fly in by private jet with Diana, pausing along the way in Milan to pick up fashion designer Roberto Cavalli, the guy who invented sandblasted jeans, and a truckload of his female models as window-dressing.

Roberto is not sure why he's there or where we're going. He's older than me and ridiculously rich but for some unknown reason our relationship doesn't seem to develop.

'Mr Cavalli, why are you here?' someone asks him at James' airport arrival press conference.

'These Russian girls! So sexy, so beautiful!' he says to no one in particular.

Tonight we're guests at a big dinner given in James' and Ol' Roberto's honour. Bobble, the band and I arrive by car. There's not enough space for us all, so Benny goes into the boot, making doggie noises. Outside the restaurant some 20 paparazzi snap in astonishment as Benny jumps out of the boot still growling and barking. At least they're pointing cameras, not guns.

Talking of guns, the restaurant's surrounded by a small army of tooled-up security men who make no attempt to blend discreetly into the scenery. They're full-on and frightening. By the end of the evening I've counted nearly 20 of them, with matching US Secret Service-style earpieces and dressed in identical sharp, dark suits. You just don't want to tangle with these people. But who are they? Who are they protecting? From what? Well, judging by their shaven heads and the way they move, they're ex-soldiers and part of that international army of private bodyguards that's boomed as an industry since 9/11 and the invasion of Iraq.

Ol' Roberto seems blissfully unaware of all this. He's protected by his own army of slinky models who hang on both his lapels, whispering sycophantically into his ear in *Italiano*, and drinking in through freshly glossed lips every word the great man says.

So it's got to be James, who's no stranger to the violence in this part of the world. After all, Kosovo, where he served as a soldier, is just down the road.

Now I remember that originally he was to have done a gig there on this tour, but it was cancelled when his management discovered that scheming local guys were planning to use his presence there as a political weapon against Serbia. So maybe this security army is being employed by James, who knows a thing or two about security, and rule No.1 is don't discuss it. Maybe they're on the payroll of Diana, who probably knows just as much and, given her survival here as a student, maybe more.

So what are they protecting him from? I mean, there are people out there who say they hate the Blunty voice along with his success. But surely they don't actually want to kill him? Then I guess the vain Archduke could have asked himself the same question, while sitting in a traffic jam a few minutes before his death. His cavalcade took a detour and it was only by purest chance that his assassin found himself in the same street as his target, and pulled the trigger. In Sarajevo, it's clearly still best to err on the side of safety.

Inside the restaurant the main table has place names and some of the guests are already seated, awaiting the arrival of James, Ol' Roberto and, of course, Diana. The band and I are escorted past it to a second table in a corner and well out of the way. For me this is not so much a case of being a fly on the wall of the main dining area, but more a fly on the kitchen door.

White wine is poured, but a gulp or two does little to smooth a few ruffled egos. Let's get this absolutely clear: we've been put in the sergeants' rather than the officers' mess – not that this has anything to do with James. Beardy looks distinctly peeved. All day, he's been sipping champagne while stretched out on the white leather seats in the private plane, looking at bodies of the shape that Berlusconi gets himself into so much bovver about. Beardy's high from inhaling the heady perfume of the global success of the Learjet set. Now he's sitting cross-legged on the bloody wing without a prayer and he's pissed off at this demotion. I can't say I blame him. But it's not James' doing.

Blunty makes his entrance with Diana and takes his

seat with his back to us. Instinctively, he's aware of the unexpected social divide. So, quite deliberately, he spends most of dinner leaning back in his chair, wedging open the door of the sergeants' mess and chatting to us rather than his table companions. I've come to expect nothing less of him. Nominally, he is in charge, but Blunty's army is a bit like the SAS: there's no ceremony between ranks. Well, not outwardly, anyway.

My dad divided men into only two types: those with whom you'd cross the Khyber Pass by night, and those with whom you would not. The first would fight to the last, saving the final two bullets for you and himself. The second would sneak off when you were asleep, taking with him the water bottle and the remaining ammunition, and leaving you to be flayed alive by the Pathans (Russians and Taliban were after his era). It's an acid test that's served me well.

James falls unhesitatingly into the first bracket, but with one modification: when the bullets run out, he'll sing at them until they surrender.

The concert is taking place in the cavernous and hastily rebuilt Olympic stadium originally created for the 1984 Winter Olympics. 'Swifter, Higher, Stronger' is the motto of the Games. Here it was more aptly applied to the trajectory of the mortar shells that rained down on the city in the longest siege of a capital city in modern warfare. Depressingly, it is surrounded by grim graveyards crammed with white crosses that are a constant reminder of the bitter war – as if such a physical memory was either required or desired.

I eat some kind of indigestible meat in the locally

organized Catering and gaze out of the window at parents, teens and small children playing tennis on pot-holed and shrapnel-scarred courts.

Down in the giant hall there's a communications problem between sound desk and stage, but that's why we travel with the likes of Mike and Gerry. They soon sort it.

Karl has just his jeans and no luggage. But he borrows bits off the rest of the band and does a little shopping – fortunately he still has his show clothes which travel in the stage wardrobe. Oh, and the good news is that the guitars have turned up unharmed.

Blunty mouths his welcome in Serbo-Croat and gets a mighty roar of approval from the 3,000-strong crowd.

And I see no bravery,
No bravery in your eyes anymore.
Only sadness.

Here in the Balkans, his performance of 'No Bravery', his anthem against war, is a deeply emotional experience. A moving video of the war in Kosovo, taken by James from the turret of his tank, streams across giant video screens on either side of the stage. We see mass graves and mines being unearthed by the roadside, crowds of half-starved adults and children welcoming the arrival of the NATO troops. Bosnia or Kosovo, the imagery is the same. I notice two guys – definitely ex-soldiers – standing in the crowd to the side of the stage. They have their arms around each other and tears are pouring down both their faces.

'That,' Blunty tells the audience, after a seemingly

endless ovation, 'was the past. Now here's a song about a very naughty girl called Annie . . .' Like a circus ring-master he expertly switches the mood from lions to clowns.

Annie, will you go down on me

There's a lot that would – and not just the girls here tonight. Blunty's got a big gay following, especially in Eastern Europe.

Backstage, the atmosphere's just not the same any more, not since Johnny fell crazily for Pernille in Copenhagen and Benny for Samantha in Perth. They're both wedded to Skype, which has a lot to answer for. As Blunty has decreed to the band, 'Safe sex must be practised at all times – nothing ruins a laptop more quickly than body fluids.'

Tonight James, along with Ol' Roberto, has been spirited away by Diana in a starburst of flashbulbs to hobnob with Sarajevo's finest. Amazingly, the rest of us seem not to have received invitations to the ball.

However, the big advantage of being surrounded by security men linked by earpieces into a radio network is that it takes about ten seconds to find out in which club they are hiding. Goons of this quality are also useful for getting into places. Party-goers part like the Red Sea as we are shown to the VIP table at the back of the dance floor.

Everyone's dressed up in their birthday best, except the band, me and James in jeans. But no one seems to mind. Well, you wouldn't, would you, when you see our frightening minder-in-chief leading the way. As Mae

West, who is presumably missing from Diana's Christmas card list only because she's dead, once said: 'Is that a gun in your pocket or are you just pleased to see me?' It's a gun all right, and, no, he gives the impression that he doesn't seem too pleased to see you or anyone else.

After we successfully gatecrash, I sort of expected the guards to then melt away, but they don't. Our escort joins up with James' and together they actually line the edge of the dance floor looking outwards, eyes probing the dancers.

I mean, who were they expecting to suddenly materialize, Bruce Forsyth brandishing a machete? My mind slips back 30 years to Uganda and a small island in the middle of Lake Victoria where I'd found myself, like you do, on a private picnic with Idi Amin of *King of Scotland* fame. Then, a similar army of security men ringed the entire island, their AK47 assault rifles aimed at the empty convergence of sea and sky. On both occasions the enemy was either in the mind – or the threat was so serious that no one was telling me about it.

I try to ask Ol' Roberto what he thinks of it all, sitting there in his black turtleneck, smiling away at his lissom companions and drinking a *gran reserva* red wine from Rioja.

'Hi Roberto, are you enjoying yourself? You're an old friend of Diana's, right?' I ask him. But he just looks through me as if I don't exist at all. Maybe I don't. Maybe he's even deafer than me. It *is* kind of hard to make yourself heard in this sea of sound. Maybe he thinks I'm a waiter. Maybe – a ring of truth here – he doesn't like the cut of my TK Maxx black velvet jacket. Whatever, he remains as silent to me as a stone Caesar.

When I take to the dance floor, a guard comes too. It's definitely difficult to strut your stuff and look cool, when there's a younger, fitter, and altogether cooler goon standing hands on hips between you and your dancing partner. She – the girl not the goon – proves to be a small alternative poet, or maybe that's a poet-ess, who's unilaterally decided she is going to collaborate with James on a misty project called The Common Moment.

Like Ol' Roberto she does not speak to me either, so how could I possibly know this? I know this because later she wrote me a letter. Actually, she wrote several letters to me, and to James and the band a whole lot more. At the moment of writing, she's still sending me letters.

This first one begins: 'I am the poet you met at the night club in Sarajevo. I am not quite sure what to think of that whole night, except that it made me see even more how beautiful my life is.'

Now, I can appreciate a bit of flattery and flirtery as much as the next guy – especially after getting the silent treatment, being sent to Coventry Sarajevo-style with a twist of Milano. But hang on, you're jumping to the wrong conclusion about me and this girl. Ours is a meeting of minds, not bodies. Remember there's a second guy packing something hard in his pocket who's in the middle of this relationship. Of course it's James, not me, she's interested in.

As we dance, she puts her mouth close to my ear and finally speaks: 'Can you introduce me to James?' On the wrong end of a bottle of wine or two and a female tongue almost in my ear, sure I can. I can do just about anything, legal or otherwise, if I get the chance. After all, Blunty is dancing right behind me in the middle of the usual bevy of beauty.

'James,' I say, between gyrations, 'you haven't met . . .'

'No,' he smiles, 'Peter, no, I haven't met. Do you want to get fired?' and turns quite politely away.

'I must say that I was slightly disappointed,' she wrote to me some weeks later, 'that I did not get to speak to James about things that matter, like making a change in this world and how we can best do this in a combined effort. It seems absurd that James does not have 30 minutes to hear about something that could make a great difference in this world, but there is time for nights, which suck your soul right out of you.

'James is always talking about how we should focus on real issues and I think if he heard me out, he'd see my real motives and they are pure. Pure love and the need to heal this world.'

Well, I guess was slightly disappointed too. I mean, did I do wrong in trying to help a fellow artist, even if she was a bit alternative? She's right. There is indeed 'a time for nights, which suck the soul right out of you'.

But, My God, she wasn't finished yet: 'I thought not only was it quite disturbing to see all these women throwing themselves at James, but just the whole being/personality and structure of the event all together: body-guards, barricades as if James and Co. are some kind of objects put on show. This is by no means the first time I am exposed to something like this, but I will never accept it as part of a healthy society.

'I think the whole celebrity culture/obsession is a joke and a reflection of a very empty and vacant society that seriously needs to rethink their focus, values and priorities. Where is the people's sense of perspective and sense of self, even?'

You've got it – or maybe you haven't. I read on: 'The project that I am doing is called The Common Moment. It is intellectual and with passion and meaning. Nothing like what I saw at the club that night. James is always saying he wants this – this is his chance.'

I'm not calling for a second chance, I'm screaming at the top of my voice.

This night he's screaming all the way to bed and alone without model or poet-ess. Not, of course, that either was interested in his body.

The band and me – the drink flows free – party on. I was really enjoying myself while not talking to Ol' Roberto. Then, quite suddenly, it's time to go. We know this because the head honcho comes up to me. He thinks that because of my age I must be in charge. He gets very close to my face and orders: 'We go now.'

The temptation was either to say: 'OK then, mate. See you. Thanks for your help,' or 'Your place or mine?' But I got the impression that either line might earn me a pistol-whipping.

The still partying Red Sea parted once again as we made our way in double time out of the building. Karl, always ready for any emergency, has the foresight to bring his companion with him on his arm. Like bringing a packed lunch from the breakfast table, you never know when you might get hungry and it's always best to be prepared.

Outside in the cold air, a ring of guards once again face outwards, flexing their fingers. I tell you the meanest gunslinger in the Wild West wouldn't have stood a chance against this lot. I had the briefest flashback to Arizona 40 years ago and a Victorian tombstone in the Arizona town of Tombstone. It said simply: 'Here lies Lester Moore. Four slugs from a .44. No Les, No More.'

Karl's about to bundle his girl into the back seat of the waiting people carrier – the third in a three-car convoy – when the head honcho speaks to her rapidly in what I take to be Serbo-Croat. Desire drains from her face like water down a storm drain. Immediately, she frees her hand from Karl's and starts to walk sadly away alone into a night which has suddenly got much colder. Karl starts after her, but feels a gentle restraining hand on his shoulder that does not allow argument. He never knew her name.

The front two carloads of goons roar off ahead of us. In what is clearly a well-thumbed manoeuvre, the lead bunch secure the first and second intersections on Sniper Alley before we even leave the safety of the club surround. Then as soon as we've passed them, they leapfrog us to secure the next – and so on. This allows our driver to maintain a steady 70mph through all the red lights. But in the hour before dawn there's not another soul or a single car to be seen on the streets of Sarajevo. Perhaps they've witnessed so much bloodshed that they don't need mine.

By the time our car skids to a halt on the forecourt of

our hotel, the first squad has already taken up defensive positions around the perimeter. I go to bed feeling fully protected, but I've absolutely no idea from what except, perhaps, myself. We've got an hour before we leave for the airport.

Albania

'Albania is a safe haven for tourists and you can travel everywhere, provided that you take the usual precautions against bandits.' Well, that's what the room brochure says at my five-star hotel in the centre of the capital Tirana. Just what are the 'usual precautions'? Wear body armour and carry a sub-machine gun? The Foreign Office is also careful in its advice to travellers here:

> Albanians are very hospitable to visitors, but crime and violence still represent a serious problem in some areas . . . you should bear in mind the widespread ownership of firearms.

Outside my window it all looks sunny and benign. Never for a moment do I have reason to think otherwise. Nevertheless, like everyone else, I take Bobble's advice and leave my watch hidden away in my room before I make my way to the stadium. After all, you don't want a wrist job as George Bush got just a year previously. The US president went walkabout among the 'folk' – as he likes to call them – and one of the folk successfully relieved him of his watch in what for him (or her – there's no sex discrimination among pickpockets around here) was the greatest golden handshake of all time.

Strangely, there appear to be a lot of British cars with

UK licence plates on the roads around the city. Surely, it's a long way to drive for a holiday in a country that is so relatively new to tourism? Then it's explained: this is one of Europe's sinkholes for stolen cars. The last time you saw your BMW was when you parked it that night on a side road in Fulham. Here it is again stuck in a jam on an unmarked detour off a dual carriageway on the road in from the airport. The thief often doesn't even bother to change the plates.

Tirana is hot, dusty and looks half-built. This is – or was, before recession brought construction to a halt – a great place to be in the ready-mixed concrete business. You can buy a house on the nearby Adriatic coast for a snip compared to the Greek island of Corfu, which lies just offshore. Of course, you don't have to be an Albanian pirate to own one, but then you don't have to be a tailor to work in Savile Row. However, it sure helps.

Warning: you are entering Norman Wisdom country. The British comedian is the icon of Albania. When a visit by Sir Norm coincided with an England v Albania football match in 2001 the comedian was mobbed by an enormous crowd at the training ground, leaving David Beckham and visiting footie fans open-mouthed in amazement.

In fact our home-grown comedian – long before your time unless you're older than me but remember him in *Last of the Summer Wine*? – is the perfect victim of the cult of celebrity. Back in the days when Albania was the most hard-line Communist state in Europe, he was the only foreign actor whose films were allowed to be shown in the country.

In a place where daily hardship meant that humour

was in miserably short supply, a whole generation grew up worshipping the little guy who seemed to have stepped straight off the catwalk of Tirana Fashion Week – tweed cap askew with the peak turned up, crumpled collar and tie, and jacket so tight that it was obviously second-hand.

'You fan of seagulls?' says the waiter in the open-air café where we grab a sandwich. I scan the sky for any incoming marauders. The coast is barely 20 miles away. In these hungry times of economic downturn fearless Cornish birds are known to nick chips and even ice-cream cones from unguarded hands. God knows what an Albanian one on the wing might do – open up with a burst of .50mm cannon?

'No, no, football!' he says. I get it, when it's finally explained to me. Seagulls – Brighton and Hove Albion. Norm, it transpires, managed to get a whole nation to follow his team. 'Well,' I tell him, 'I've got a daughter who lives in Brighton.'

'You *know* Brighton?' the smile's so big I fear for a moment that the beer's going to be free. But don't worry. This *is* Albania. Nothing is free, except, of course, George's watch.

The open-air Qemal Stafa stadium – Albania's Wembley – is just a short watch-free walk from the hotel and stage manager Mark is having a little local trouble. The trucks have arrived late and he's way behind schedule with the rigging. At the Albanian frontier the carnet was not in order – well, not until unexpected palms had been greased beyond the normal quota – and it's taken 17 hours to clear the frontier controls and get here. The drivers are back at the hotel and, with their overnight job successfully completed, they're relaxing by the pool.

The thermometer's risen to the high 30s and the Albanian riggers seem more interested in sheltering in the shade thrown by one of the trucks than in humping oversized wheelie boxes up a steep ramp on to the stage.

Mark's red in the face and not just from the heat. 'Come on you lazy bastards, you're here to WORK, not sit around on your arses.'

However, in a place where forced labour camps under Enver Hoxha's regime rivalled Stalin's Gulags for physical and psychological brutality, Mark's shouts fall on deaf ears.

Meanwhile Blunty's also lying by the hotel pool and he's not alone. This one's a tall and cool Scandinavian blonde who's just flown in from Stockholm with a bikini, a gorgeous suntan, and a sex toy. I'm not absolutely certain that you're allowed under current customs regulations to import jumbo-sized dildos into Albania. I guess I could ask the exhausted drivers who are flat-out in their deckchairs. After unpacking and repacking 14 tons of imports they know all about what is and what is not allowed into Albania.

Maybe you are. Maybe it's 'one, for the personal use of'. Anyway, Blunty's imported its scrumptious-looking owner because, as he says, he'd been worrying for weeks about the quality of the local talent. They'd met at the concert in Stockholm and she and a surprisingly close friend of hers had travelled the 18-hour trek to Hamburg on the tour bus. She and James had got on so well together on board that they'd decided on a rematch. It now remains to be seen whether he's bitten off more than he can chew.

'I'd got this picture in my mind that Albanian women might be small, dark, and look like their mothers,' he tells me. 'Wrong, as it turns out. But when you've seen a few Eastern European middle-aged mothers, you can't be too careful.'

Seems a long way for a two-night stand, a big distance to come. But there you go. She's delightful, sweetly shy, and appears to be out of her depth here. However, still waters run deep, and we're not just talking about the swimming pool.

Later, she and I have a long chat together. For some reason or other I get the impression that Blunty doesn't seem especially comfortable with this. He doesn't say anything, but I can tell. What's he think I'm going to do? Is that old bastard going to steal the dildo?

She works on a cancer ward, which I suppose fashions you with a useful mindset for dealing with a rock star. 'I can handle it now,' she says, 'but not for much longer. Some of my patients are only 20, like me, the difference between us is that they are going to die. There is no hope for them.'

I ask her what she truthfully feels about James. She looks down at the ground and doesn't reply immediately. Then she glances up again and goes all serious: 'When I met him, he was just leaving. I guess the trouble with James is that he's always either arriving or just leaving. He said he'd contact me sometime and would I maybe go and spend a weekend with him somewhere? And that's what he did. That's why I'm here.

'To answer your question, it's very simple. I love his music and I love him,' and then she smiles and I think she feels she must explain:

'In my job you have to live for the "now". I'm happy to be here now, and tomorrow I shall be gone. It doesn't really matter if James loves me a lot, a little bit, or not at all. I'm happy just to be with him for while.'

There's an unforeseen problem with the show tonight. It's Euro '08 and Italy are playing France to see who will go through to the quarter-finals. It's an evening game that clashes with the concert. No one's told us until now that when not supporting the Seagulls, all red-blooded Albanians are rooting for Italy. The chances of anyone turning up to watch Blunty seem slim.

'No problem,' he tells Mark and Bobble. 'We'll open the gates two hours early and put up a couple of giant screens. They get to watch the match and then watch us. I just hope Italy wins.'

Later we all go to the show together. Every night, just a couple of moments before they go on stage, James and the band link arms in a circle and put their heads together – it's their equivalent of the All Blacks' haka war dance. It ends with a collective shout, usually involving the word 'fuck'. Occasionally a tour guest gets invited into the circle – tonight Miss Sweden makes the grade. James asks her what 'fuck' is in Swedish. She says a word and then adds: 'Actually that means "fuck in the ear".'

'Fuck in the ear?' says James . . . and there's us thinking that *we* were the perverted ones!

It's 11pm when they get on stage and the Curse of the Qemal Stafa has struck again – albeit by proxy. Albania always wins its home games and the national team went unbeaten here against foreign opposition from 2001 to 2004. Tonight Italy, the honorary 'home' team, has provided James with the best possible warm-up with a 2–0 win over France. The atmosphere is electric.

There's a moment of high tension when James jumps off the stage and the girls lining the pit try to drag him over the barrier. No friendly boardies here to help him. But he keeps his cool and waves off the security men who start to act like pit bull terriers that haven't been fed for a week.

'No Bravery' and the video that accompanies it, showing the plight of the Kosovar Albanians, is greeted by repeated bursts of cheering. They're watching it on the two giant screens on either side of the stage that were rigged for the football. It's difficult to work out who they're rooting for – the army, you would think. In Albania you're never absolutely sure who is the baddie and who is the goodie.

It's way after midnight in downtown Tirana and several thousand Albanians are singing 'Wisemen' at the top of their voices and apparently taking every word to their hearts. Norman, this is pure comedy, you would have loved it.

Look who's alone now,
It's not me. It's not me.
Those three Wise Men,
They've got a semi by the sea.

I mean, what's with this semi by the sea? When I first heard it, I thought by its title that it was a Christmas song – I'm sure lots of DJs think that – but then I hadn't listened to the lyrics. What does it all mean? 'You tell me,' James tells me. 'I'm still trying to find out what this song is all about. I really have no idea. I just wrote it down as it came to me. I really pushed the American record label to use 'High' as a single. In hindsight I would have gone with 'Wisemen' because it was a massive radio hit around the rest of the world. Truth is, it's not one of my favourites, probably because I just can't work out what it's about.'

As the crowds clear and the dismantling of the stage gets under way, a lone, smartly dressed guy in his forties pleads with me almost aggressively from the far side of the crush barrier. 'Please, *poleese* could you get me a souvenir, an autograph, a programme, a set-list– anything that James has touched? I really need to have something personal from him.'

'Sorry, it's just not possible,' I say firmly as I walk away across the football pitch towards the dressing-room.

'A piece of used toilet paper would do!' he shouts after me.

I mean, is this guy serious? Or is he just taking the mickey? You never know, but there are some weird people out there. I tell Blunty, and then rather wish I hadn't. Just talking about it seems like an invasion of privacy.

In the dressing-room they're on a high and playing with paper – silver, not toilet. For reasons that no one can explain Johnny is being wrapped in baking foil from head to toe. He's then led out on to the pitch to screams of amusement from the large group of fans who've gathered to catch a glimpse of James leaving.

'Mr Pitkin, Mr Pitkin,' they shout, some of them rolling on the ground with laughter. We're at a disadvantage here:

we've not all seen Sir Norm playing Pitkin in *Follow a Star* (1959).

It's rumoured that somewhere in Tirana there's a statue of Norm like there is in Sir Norman's Bar in the Sefton Hotel in Douglas, Isle of Man. But I couldn't find it. I do discover a university called Wisdom. But sadly it transpires that this has more to do with knowledge than Norm.

Athens

It's 8am and another airport immigration queue. A look at the posters on the wall tells me it's Athens. The blonde's gone back to Sweden and we've gone on to Greece. Judging by the state of the landing party it's been a hell of a last night in Tirana. I remember watching football on an open-air screen at the hotel and nothing much after that until some animal instinct sent me scuttling from unconsciousness to airport transfer, suitcase and travel bag in hand.

There's a ritual to departures. When you reach the lobby Bobble is already there, bright but not breezy. Johnny and Karl come next, followed by the bedraggled figure of Benny. Blunty arrives exactly on time – never early, never late – and quietly focused. I guess he's pleased because he's moving on. He's got to keep moving. But whether he's sad or secretly relieved to see the back of that giant dildo is anybody's guess.

'Mornin', Peter' . . . 'Mornin', James.' Well, that's the end of that conversation then.

After we've landed in Greece, I'm standing behind James as we shuffle forward to the glass-walled immigration booth. Its occupant is an unsmiling woman of about 35 with short dark hair and heavy black-framed glasses. For her, it's just another morning at the mill checking entry permits, her demeanour a delicate balance between diligence and boredom.

She stretches out her hand from the window for the next passport, places it on the desk in front of her and studies name and picture. Then her forehead creases in a frown. Her finger goes from photo back to name, back to photo. Finally she looks up at James – and screams. Mercifully, it's more of a shrill squeak than a scream because it does not reach the two policemen standing 20 metres away, fingers on the trigger guards of their sub-machine guns. Yelling at international airports in these terrorist times can have fatal consequences. But it's scream enough for the other immigration officers to turn their heads. Now pink with embarrassment, she struggles to stop smiling as she fumbles with the rubber stamp. 'Sign here, please,' she says, in a hopeless attempt at authority, as she produces a blank piece of paper. An autograph at immigration? It's got to be a first.

Centuries have passed since I last came to Athens. I remember dirty, traffic-clogged streets, and a crumbling Parthenon eaten away by pollution. It's great to be greeted by a modern vibrant metropolis topped by a painstakingly restored Acropolis.

However, while the city may have changed, the scheming bureaucracy that underpins Athenian business life clearly has not.

We've got two gigs on consecutive nights here and, after the Wild West atmosphere of Albania, James and the band are looking forward to playing to sell-out crowds in a major European capital. But it's not to be.

On the way into the city Bobble points out the stadium, the Lycabettus Amphitheatre, on a green hill above the city. That's the closest we ever get to it.

By the following afternoon the crew have already rigged the stage, the refreshment stands are being stocked and there are three hours to go before the doors open for the first of the two concerts.

We've spent a hot couple of hours climbing the Acropolis before chilling out around the roof-top pool of our hotel. Now I'm in my room, dithering over the usual problem: how secure is the dressing-room going to be? Do I take laptop and cameras, or just cameras? A change of clothes? Will we stay at the venue after the 4pm sound check, or come back here? When you live in an institution where 99 per cent of decisions are made for you, the other one per cent is pure hell.

The phone rings. It's Bobble. 'No concert tonight and most likely not tomorrow. It's off,' he says, 'no one's telling us exactly why. There is, apparently, a "health and safety issue".'

The doors of the municipal-owned stadium have been locked – with the trucks and all the set inside – and police are barring the entrances. Safety inspection? It quickly transpires that some 'necessary paperwork' has been 'misplaced'.

Digging a little deeper I discover that the giant local promoters are unhappy that the concert is being staged by a much smaller outsider. Could this be the reason, or is there a more sinister one?

'In the best case it's carelessness and in the worst case corruption,' an angry Blunt tells *Ta Nea*, the Athens daily paper. Back in 1999, when Blunty was a tank commander with the NATO peace-keeping force in Kosovo, it's worth remembering that the Greeks openly sided with Slobodan

Milosevic's Serbia against the Albanian population. To me it sounds suspiciously like politics interfering with music.

Whatever the reasons, someone needs to have a serious chat with the mayor – he's the guy who has sanctioned the lock-out for no explicable reason. There's going to be 12,000 very angry ticket-holders out there tonight.

Back in Hampshire, Charlie Blount gets on the blower to the British Embassy in Athens. But all he gets is an answering machine: 'Can't you sort this out?' he asks the Foreign Office in London. 'This is bad for the Greeks and bad for an important British export.' No one rings him back. I could have told him that this was a complete waste of time. Early on during my 20 years as a foreign correspondent I learned a valuable lesson: when the chips are down and you desperately need help, always avoid the British Embassy – usually they can't even help themselves. If you want something done, go to the Swedes.

We didn't. We went instead to the hotel's roof-top swimming pool to drink mojitos and beer. Blunty's quietly furious at having to spend the best part of 72 hours in a city where he's not being allowed to perform. Karl, deprived of his drum kit, is actually having withdrawal symptoms. His hands are starting to twitch.

Once it's been decided that not one but both concerts are irrevocably cancelled, Blunty makes every effort to relax. Fortunately he has had the sense to have imported Penny, a pretty French–Canadian girl with a Jaffa spray-tan, to help him do this.

Blunty and Bobble spend hours on the phone sorting out insurance and exploring compensation for the fans. Even if it were possible to find an alternative venue, there's no way to fit another performance into the tour schedule. I ask him how he feels about the concerts being cancelled.

'I feel bad for all the people who bought tickets, booked flights, trains and hotels. Inevitably they are going to blame me for what's happened, but it's completely beyond my control.

'The fact is that I've come to Athens to give two concerts that were organized months ago and now, for whatever dark reason, I'm not being allowed to perform.

'There's nothing whatsoever I can do about this. But what I can do is to move on very quickly and not worry about it and go on to Cyprus, and never, ever come back to Athens.' In fact, his anger is short-lived. Just nine months later he will be back in the Greek capital for the final gig of the world tour.

The concerts are off, but the party goes on. Late evening on the second day finds us seated at open-air tables in a sumptuous private club and restaurant on the seaside at Piraeus. The all-too-temporary orange glow of Penny has faded away and Blunty's ready for action.

We're spread across two tables on the terrace with fabulous food and the ocean as a backdrop. As usual I've really no idea who are our hosts. Women and drink just keep on coming – well, the drink does anyway.

Much later I'm sitting there chilling out to the music, James and most of the guys are on the dance floor. These are lonely, wallflower moments for me, ones when I question why I'm here. Then, this attractive woman with long blonde hair plonks herself down beside me and starts asking me about who I am and what I'm doing here.

It's kind of flattering to have someone interested in me

for me's sake and an hour slips by as we chat. I notice that there are lots of camera flashes. Around Blunty you get so used to white blinks that you don't even register them after a while. A couple of times the girl puts her hand on my upper arm when she's making a point, not so much in a flirtatious as in a demonstrative way. She's Greek and she's clearly a touchy-feely kind of person. We're getting along famously – she's fascinating. The flashguns keep flashing and I don't really notice that they're aimed my way.

She gets up to go – presumably to the loo. 'Don't go away, Peter. I want to talk some more,' she says. I'm happy to do just that. Being a fly on the wall can get downright boring at times in a place like this, where James and the band are on the dance floor and I'm left fiddling with my mobile. As soon as she's threading her way between the tables and skirting the dance floor in search of the ladies, a guy sitting opposite me, who I haven't really clocked all evening, leans across and asks me:

'How old do you think she is?'

'Who?' I say.

'Anna, of course.'

'Is that her name?'

'Come on, guess! 30, 35?'

'I expect so.'

'She's 50. I tell you this, my friend, because in a minute, when she comes back, she's going to ask you, "How old do you think I am?" and you are going to say 30.' Crumbs, this all sounds a bit confusing.

'You really don't know *who* she is, do you?' he adds conspiratorially. 'You are the only person in this room who doesn't know and they are all watching you. She's Anna Vissi – she's a singer, she's the Madonna of Greece, the most famous woman in the whole country. No?'

'No. I've never heard of her,' I say truthfully (I've only heard of Nana Mouskouri and I never did fancy her), 'but Anna does seem very charming.'

'She is very charming and she is very beautiful and very famous. That's why the photographers are taking pictures of her – and of you.'

Anna comes back to the table and sits down beside me. She puts her hand on my shoulder. 'Peter, look at me,' she says, staring deeply into my eyes. 'How old do you think I am?' I take a long time considering the question before answering.

'30,' I say. 'I've got a daughter your age and she is also called Anna.' Karl's chat-up manual states that it's always a good move to tell a girl you know her name.

'No,' she smiles, 'if I am 30, you are 40.'

Out of the corner of my eye I see the guy opposite nodding approvingly. 'Anna, I'm sorry, I've only just clicked who you are and that you kindly invited me to dinner along with James and the band.'

'Don't be,' she interrupts, 'he says what I think also – that you're a very interesting person. I could see that you didn't know me and that you like talking to me because you like me, not because I am Anna Vissi. In Greece, for me, it is very refreshing not to be known. I like talking to you, too – and, by the way, I am 50.' Never.

Hmm. It's 4am, the hour when my judgement and resolve are at their most putty-like. Maybe I like talking to you, Anna, a bit too much. The situation is resolved by Chris, Anna's thirty- something companion, and Blunty who come and sit with us.

'Where are you playing next?' asks Anna.

'Limassol, Cyprus,' Blunty replies.

'When?' asks Anna. 'Cyprus is where I was born.'

Blunty looks at his cheap, pink, plastic watch. Don't ask me why he has a cheap, pink, plastic watch when he's turned down offers to promote a whole range of the finest Swiss gold timepieces. I did once ask him, but the only reply I could get was: 'This does me fine.'

'Tomorrow night,' Blunty replies. 'Why don't you come over there with us and sing a number with me on stage?'

Anna's eyes light up. She looks across at Chris and he nods.

'Take me home Chris, we're going to Cyprus on the midday flight. But first I need my bed.'

Blunty, of course, doesn't believe in beds for sleep's sake. We party on until finally, with dawn long broken, we grab a taxi back to Athens and the hotel. The minibus booked to take us to the airport is already waiting outside with the engine running. An outwardly calm, but internally ruffled Bobble is standing in the lobby with a faint smile on his face as we stagger through the swing doors.

'You're late, James,' he says.

'No,' says Blunty, looking at that watch again as he heads for the lift, 'it's late, but we're exactly ten minutes early!'

'Sorry, Bobble!' the rest of us chorus. Bobble shakes his head in resignation and wheels his cases to the waiting bus.

Cyprus

The birthplace of Aphrodite's got a lot to answer for this morning, as with sleep deprivation and raging hangovers we make for the magnificent five-star Aphrodite Hills Resort. Quite why we are staying here near Paphos when the gig is in Limassol at the other end of the island is beyond me, but that's the way it is. Ours is not to reason why.

Snatching moments of sleep on plane and bus, I'm plagued by confused dreams of Anna, Aphrodite, and me. The hotel is magnificent. I take a look around my room and bathroom. That's all I'm going to get to see of it.

Sometime in Greek mythology the Goddess of Love popped up out of the sea about a couple of hundred metres from my window and I've decided that Aphro is now to be adopted as the resident deity of the *All The Lost Souls* tour. Her cult, which was big across Cyprus and the Middle East, required all women, regardless of rank, to take part once in their lifetime in ritual, sacred prostitution. 'Only once?' I hear Blunty say.

According to the historian Herodotus it went like this: all the girls in the land make their way to Aphrodite's temple (Blunty's gig).

There is a great multitude of women coming and going; passages marked by lines run every way through the crowd, by which the men pass and make their choice.

Once a woman has taken her place there, she does not go away to her home before some stranger has cast money [a Golden Ticket] into her lap, and had intercourse with her outside the temple [venue]. It does not matter what the sum is, the woman will never refuse, for that would be a sin. So she follows the first man who casts it and rejects no one.

Herodotus wrote this in the fifth century BC, but it all sounds a bit familiar. He adds: 'So then the women that are fair and tall are soon free to depart, but the uncomely have long to wait because they cannot fulfil the law; for some of them remain for three years, or four. There is a custom like this in some parts of Cyprus.'

I've been travelling so long and partying so hard that it's become impossible to take an objective view of what I am actually doing here. I'm coming apart at the seams. It's time to go home and detox, not just from alcohol, which I can probably handle, but from the tour which is in itself a hugely addictive drug that I'm finding hard to cope with. Like it or not, I've become part of it.

For Blunty, Cyprus has special significance – it's not just another gig in another country, but the place where he spent the first few years of his life. His father was flying helicopters as a young officer in the Army Air Corps and was part of the United Nations peace-keeping force. His soldier grandfather was once the British garrison commander at Dhekelia. Strangely, Blunty's early memories here as a toddler are not of beaches and lukewarm seas but of skiing – well, driving to the ski area with his father – in the Troodos Mountains.

'I actually put on skis. It was a fairly strange place to start. But I'm pretty sure I have a vision of it, the sense of trees going past – just a scrap of memory.'

Right now it's nearly 40°C and an ice cream is about as near as anyone's getting to snow today. The crowd at the Palais des Sports is capacity and includes a substantial number of British soldiers. I guess they feel strongly that Blunty is the guy who made it, the one that got away. He's a rare creature to them: an entertainer and international icon who is one of their own, a bloke who understands war and peace and who without fanfare raises hundreds of thousands of pounds for Médecins Sans Frontières and later for Help for Heroes.

However, how much he or anyone else around him understands about anything this afternoon is debatable, but we're on a roll because this is the last gig of this leg of the tour. Tomorrow, we're going home for a brief break before Canada.

Anna Vissi shows up in the dressing-room with Chris, her much younger and super-cool partner, and greets me warmly. Her arrival sends shockwaves through the huge crowd already gathering outside. Rumours echo around the island in minutes. Blunt and Vissi going out together? Can this be true?

No. She's too old for Blunty. 'She's more your sort,' says Blunty to me. 'You seem to get on well with her?' I leave the question unanswered. Too old, for Blunty, is about 25. It's quite crowded in the dressing-room. I sit talking to Anna who looks remarkably none the worse for having had only marginally more sleep than the rest of us.

'Peter, we're going to rehearse now,' says James coming over to us, 'so why don't you leave us for a while?'

I do what I'm told and wander out into the corridor. That's strange, that's really strange. Just when I feel that I've been integrated into the tour, I suddenly feel excluded. I'm really uncomfortable about this and yet I've no reason to be. I'm not a musician, I'm not part of the band. I've got my own job to do. Yet I've been through so much with them, shared the highs and lows. But it's a reminder that I'm here on sufferance as an observer. I'm an onlooker who's just been told not to look.

Is James telling me that it'll be easier on Anna Vissi to practise without an audience, or is he telling me just to fuck off? I don't know. The more I think get to know him, the less I actually know him. Did I get too close to Anna? Have I just been disciplined? Am I making all this up? I just don't know.

I grab my cameras and wander aimlessly into the arena. At times like this I wear my cameras as a personal prop. Like a smoker lights a cigarette because he doesn't know what to do with his hands, I carry a camera with a long lens on my shoulder. It gives me substance. It gives me an identity, a reason for my presence. It explains who I am to security staff, to fans – and sometimes, like now, to myself.

Almost immediately I run into Jill, who is also carrying cameras and whom I've already met briefly over lunch back in Aphrodite Hills. She's wearing white jeans and I couldn't help but notice that she's strikingly pretty. What's with this island? What's with me? Take me out all night to a club in Piraeus and suddenly I'm behaving like Blunty on heat. Time for home. Relax, I'm so spaced out. Then there's smaller, darker Anna, another Anna, who's also a photographer accredited for the evening who becomes my immediate friend. I'm sort of thinking of moving to Cyprus.

'Tell me about James,' says Jill, who comes from Newcastle and is an apparently extraordinarily successful wedding photographer when she's not snapping showbiz. I guess when you work on Aphrodite's isle you've got to be versatile. 'What kind of a guy is he?'

What kind of a guy is he? Frankly, right now, I haven't got a clue. What I can say is that he's very polite, Jill, and would most definitely be into ritual sacred prostitution. If we were to turn the clock back 26 centuries he's the guy in the dressing gown who'd be walking through the roped cattle grid of your local Temple of Aphrodite. He'd toss his coins and definitely choose you – all young, blonde, suntanned, and fit as they come. Provided, of course, that smiling Karl hadn't come along first. That's the correct answer, but not the one I give.

Heat and lack of sleep give the whole evening a surreal tinge. I feel I'm walking a couple of inches above the ground. Rehearsal over, I'm back in my comfort zone with James. Did I just imagine that? Anna Vissi leaves Chris chatting to the band, takes me by the arm, and leads me to the privacy of the party room. There are two hours left before James goes on stage. 'Peter, I want to hear all about you,' she says, sitting back fragrantly and patting the sofa beside her. 'Tell me where you've come from and where you're going.' I think I'm going home, pretty damn quick.

Anna lives between LA, Athens and her mother here in Cyprus. 'Don't go away tomorrow,' she says, 'come and have lunch. Stay a while. I need to talk to you some more.' Aphrodite, get your ass out of here and back into the sea.

The show starts with a truly awful local support act that the crowd seems to love. James hits the stage with a couple of moves taken straight from Guitar Hero, although whether anyone notices that is always hard to fathom.

The strong army contingent roars their approval as he starts into 'One Of The Brightest Stars'.

One day your story will be told.
One of the lucky ones who's made his name.

This is Blunty's personal story and clearly he enjoys singing it. No harm in blowing your own trumpet, even if it is on a guitar. But like all his songs there's a dark side to the lyrics. Despite his outward dismissal of the stinging criticism he gets from some music critics back home, I suspect the wounds run deep.

One day you'll hope to make the grave,
Before the papers choose to send you there.

'For its story, "One Of The Brightest Stars" is my favourite song,' he tells me. 'Anyone in the film industry or music business can in some way relate to the roller-coaster ride of popularity, the claims people make in explaining your successes, and the speed at which the highs can become lows, and then highs again.'

Cameras in hand I take my turn in the pit in the front of the stage. Quite why I would want to take yet another picture of James in full vocal onslaught is beyond me, but I do so anyway. Mainly I like to check out who's in the front row. James himself can't necessarily see them. This can create unexpected problems. One night in Orlando he jumped down from the stage and threw himself at what he judged, through the footlights, to be the prettiest girl in the front row – there was no crush barrier. What he couldn't see was that she was on crutches, and she immediately fell backwards. Her boyfriend looked like he was going to punch him, but by the time he'd eaten the spinach and pumped up his biceps, James was fortunately up and running halfway across the room.

The true bodysurf is a wholly different thing that requires collective energy and massive faith. If you've ever sat around a heavy table in a restaurant, linked hands one on top of another to supposedly concentrate the energy, and lifted up the table using just one finger each, you get the same idea. I did this once in a seventeenth-century cellar in the old part of Innsbruck and the table bounced off the ceiling. In reality it's more about the even distribution of mass than some hidden source of kinetic energy – but timing, faith and a skinful of liquor seem to be essential ingredients.

'I thought stage diving would be kind of fun, but I'd never seen anyone do it, so I didn't know the first thing about it. The first time I tried it was in Barcelona, and while I was in midair, the crowd parted below me, like

Moses and the Red Sea. I managed to get a hand to the shoulder of someone in the sixth row to stop my face piling into the floor. With hindsight, I now realize that you kind of egg your crowd into an expectation that you are about to jump. But not knowing that, I thought the whole thing should be spontaneous, so I just played, ran and jumped. Their reaction was to get the hell out of the way.

'But I still think it's more entertaining to do it spontaneously rather than to prepare the audience. Surprise is the key element!'

Back to basics: the first stage of learning is the bar dive – a favourite of James' and a speciality of the Farinet bar and Casbah nightclub in the Swiss ski resort of Verbier, where James spends as much time as he can in the winter. This is positively the best après-ski joint in the whole resort and rocks from 4pm to 4am. James and the band once even did an impromptu gig there. Rob, its South African-based owner, is a close friend of James, and runs it with a spirit that quite literally blows people away. Rob's favourite trick of the evening is to take one of the cylinders of CO_2 used for pumping the beer to the bar, and blasting overheated dancers on the floor with sweat-drying jets of gas.

If you're a friend you then, as a rite of passage, get to ride in the hotel's industrial-sized tumble-dryer. I once saw a girlfriend and ex-wife of a ski guide friend of mine taking a slightly reluctant spin together while he watched. It's a great way to get to know people – or to get rid of them.

Rob's hospitality is legendary. After an evening upstairs

on sofas in the Farinet with the strawberry mojitos, magnums of champagne, and frozen bottles of vodka flying around, you head down into the Casbah Club beneath and a VIP area packed with more alcoholic goodies than should rightfully be allowed.

On this occasion, James hadn't been there since he got famous, and Blunty being Blunty figured he could just party with Rob as usual in a fairly anonymous way. It didn't quite work out like that. Every chalet girl and female guest within a five-kilometre radius of the resort homed in on the club in the hope of spotting the newest celebrity in town. But by 3am it all looked slightly demeaning for the flower of mainly British womanhood. Half-pissed, over-bred and overheated, they were all pushing and shoving on the dance floor to grind their groin closest to his.

I particularly admired the smiley brunette chalet girl who went up to him and said: 'Do you want to just cut all this shit? Take me home now and shag me rotten until I have to go and cook breakfast for my clients?' But she wasn't quite pretty or sober enough to get a positive answer.

Outside the bar area, a sea of predominantly drunken people rock on. Pick your way, if you can, through the over-capacity crowd and you come to the DJ booth. One night Rob and I tried to get in here through the rear locked door that leads down into the bowels of the hotel's service area. The DJ wasn't hearing us or wasn't letting us in, so Rob tried to smash his way through, using his usual drum of CO_2 as a battering ram. No response. Later, I learned the DJ piled another load of gas canisters against the splintering door as a countermeasure. When Rob came around the conventional way and complained, the DJ shrugged his shoulders and replied: 'How the hell was I to know it was you, man, it could have been green monster reptiles coming up from the sewers to sabotage the decks?' Come to think of it, he was spot on.

Anyway, the booth is the setting for the bar dive. You climb on top of it to a height of 12 feet above the dance floor and launch yourself face forward onto the people below. Hopefully, they catch you.

It's 3am when James breaks off from the groin-grinding and turns to me: 'Peter, I want you to do it.'

'Do what? Groin-grind?'

'I want you to dive off the bar.'

I looked up at the bar and at the sea of people dancing below.

'No way, James, I'll die. As you keep telling me, I'm not exactly in peak physical condition and the stress of touring with you has already aged me an extra ten years.'

'That doesn't matter. Do it,' he says, looking into my eyes. 'I'll catch you. Believe me.'

If Blunty says he will do something, he always does . . . eventually. However, *prompt* attention to the job in hand seemed of crucial importance here. The fact that he is standing alongside Big Nick, a former forward in the England rugby team, gives me just a little confidence.

What the hell, you only die once. I climb up. The DJ announces me as the oldest guy ever to bar dive in the club. I look down at the crowd, they look up at me, and I sail out into them. James is at the front of a phalanx of outstretched arms that catch me. It is a surprisingly soft landing. They pass my body hand-over-hand like a human stretcher and lay me out like a corpse on the bar. Glasses scatter in all directions, as the barman pours tequila down my throat direct from the bottle. I am soaked, unhurt, and the new owner of some quite considerable cred that follows me to this day.

The full bodysurf is the gig extension of the bar dive. Firstly, the artist has to whip the crowd up into a frenzy of adoration. Then he has to pluck up the courage to plunge. Get it right and you 'float' on a platform of dozens of hands that pass you on to the people behind. You become a human Mexican Wave . . . until they lose the momentum and drop you, hopefully feet and not face first.

I've seen James do ten metres. 'Not enough,' he says. 'One day I want to surf all the way from the stage to the back of the hall, land on my feet and run out of the front entrance. I'll grab a taxi, head for the airport and fly straight home to Ibiza, while the band plays on.'

Feet back on the ground in Cyprus, Anna Vissi is chilling out before her curtain call and James is on stage. As usual after the first three numbers, the security guys clear the photographers from the pit. I stay on for a little while, largely just to prove that I have the right to do so. As I leave I meet Fit Jill, face flushed with excitement. We watch the show together from the side of the stage, her eyes locked on to James, her hand locked on to my shoulder. Boy, Aphro's isle is all fired up tonight . . . and here comes Anna Vissi, wafting from the dressing-room to the back of the stage in a Union Jack-inspired top.

Older people on Cyprus remember 1973 as the final year of the *ancien régime* when life – if you were a Greek

Cypriot – was full and happy on a united Greece-oriented island. In July 1974 the Turks invaded and annexed the north. So I guess if you're a dispossessed Greek Cypriot and come from around Kyrenia you will always in your dreams want to be in a club in 1973, not least because you could not have been after the midsummer of 1974.

Anyway, Anna gets an enormous cheer when she enters stage left and joins James at the microphone for the final verses of the song. The fact that she forgets almost all her lines immediately is entirely forgiven or not even noticed by a crowd pitched to nationalistic hysteria.

Backstage is awash with invited guests from the British army, a scattering of Golden Ticket holders for the band, not to mention photographers Anna and Fit Jill. Three generations of descendants of Andreas Cariolou are waiting to see James. Man-of-the-sea Andreas was a Cypriot, a national hero who died trying to save the life of an injured UN Canadian diver suffering from the bends 100 feet below the surface. Charlie Blount describes him as 'the greatest man I ever knew – and I wouldn't say that lightly'. James personally doesn't know any of them, but I notice he takes particular care to talk to them all and poses for endless pictures.

They've been waiting a long time to see him and he doesn't disappoint. Andreas' son, Glafkos, a man of my age, tells me:

'The Blount family have been very good friends to us over a long, long time. It seems incredible that when I last saw James he was a small boy learning to walk. Now he is an international star, but he's still finding time to talk to all my family tonight. He has wonderful charm, just like his father. James behaves like a true English gentleman.' Well, if you'd seen him in some of the situations in which I've seen him over the past year, I wouldn't put it *exactly* like that, my friend.

The after-party's in full swing when Bobble confirms the worst: 'Hotel lobby at 3am for the airport,' he tells Johnny, Benny and me.

James, Karl and Paul get a 90-minute reprieve. It seems that Ol' Roberto Cavalli has been on the blower:

'James, come to my fashion show in Milano. I'll send a private jet to pick you up and then take you afterwards on to London. Do bring the band [but don't bring Peter].' Despite the lateness of the hour, visions of all that toned flesh on and off the runway sends shivers down their spines and beyond. What they don't know – yes, the last laugh is on Johnny, Benny and me – is that it is a male fashion show.

But hang about. It's 1am right now and neither James nor the rest of us have been to bed in 41 hours. Right now we're at the other end of the island to the hotel where the only relationship I've developed as yet with the inviting-looking double bed in my room is to open my suitcase on it. I haven't been between sheets for two nights and now you're telling me I'm not going to bed at all?

'That's right,' says Bobble. He's clearly on the cloven-footed Pan's team rather than Aphrodite's, and in grand style pushes his way past two groups of dancing girls, surveys the music system, yanks the plug from the wall and wheels the whole caboodle out of the room, leaving the door swinging behind him. This European leg of the tour is over.

Well, not quite. We head back across the island to Aphrodite Hills. It's a magical starlit night and Blunty has an amazing private villa in the grounds with its own swimming pool. We lounge by candlelight with Fit Jill and others in the cool of the terrace, with the heady scents of mimosa, bougainvillea and other sweet plants filling our nostrils. In rich red wine we toast the tour and hug our goodbyes. Hearts are full, but the words are as empty as the wine bottles standing sentinel on the terrace. We'll not see you again. Goodbyes are for 'All The Lost Souls'. Time, not for bed, but for home.

Vancouver

It's mid-November and 10pm in Vancouver, home to the 2010 Winter Olympics and one heck of a lot of rain. In winter it rains here on the north-west coast of Canada on average every other day and I've picked the wet one. It's coming in off the sea and blasting down Robson Street as I walk from downtown to the hotel near the venue at General Motors Place for tomorrow night's concert.

The crew's already here and James and the band should also by now have arrived after their short break in England. I flew in six hours earlier, alone from London. I've forced myself to stay awake, lingered over dinner in a seafood restaurant, and now I'm heading home to bed. What I desperately need is eight hours' sleep to conquer jet lag and stock up z-time for the lean nights ahead. But, of course, it's not to be.

At the junction with Beatty Street I look right, left . . . left again and almost bump into them. James, Paul, Benny, Karl and Johnny are already in town – and out on it.

'Uncle Peter!' Benny cries, folding me up in a hairy hug. 'No one told us you were coming.' James and the others, too, look genuinely pleased to see me, but not remotely surprised. It's as if you always expect to run into a friend while walking in a rain-drenched back street in a country on the other side of the world which is different to the one you woke up in earlier that day.

James and Karl don't say much beyond, 'Hi, good to see you, Peter,' because they are concentrating deeply. It's a Sunday night in the quietest month of the year and almost nothing is open. Earlier, when I left the almost deserted restaurant where I'd had my supper, they'd turned out the lights and bolted the door behind me. But James wants chicken wings and Karl – after all, he's been cloistered in a plane for nine hours – wants to at least talk to a girl.

At the next street corner they pause, signalling us to wait. They look around them, sniffing the breeze like a couple of Squamish Native American trackers might have done on this very spot before the first houses of Vancouver were built in the 1860s.

James and Karl both have the uncanny ability to smell out the action, wherever or whatever it might be.

'Let's hang a right here,' I suggest. After all, I know this city moderately well and it must make sense to head back towards the centre. They shake their heads in unison and hang a left instead – and then a right. Five minutes later we're being shown to a table in a smart, modern bar, crowded with casually dressed, thirtysomething affluent-looking men and women.

It turns out that the bar only opened two weeks earlier. Neither of them had any inside information. They navigated here entirely on instinct. Karl wastes no time at all. He pulls as he walks through the door. Before he has even taken off his coat he has a date for the following night – tickets to the show, of course, do help.

We're sitting drinking our beers. A guy comes over and says a friendly 'Hi' to James.

'I saw you a few weeks ago in Budapest. The show was unbelievable. In fact, I enjoyed it so much I've got tickets for tomorrow night and I'm really looking forward to it.'

'That's good!' says James, glancing up briefly at him before returning to his second plate of extra-hot chicken wings. The guy walks away, looking distinctly deflated.

'Good wings, too, though not as good as in Albuquerque,' he says. Here we go, here we go. This is a well-grooved vinyl route of his.

'Wings Basket, that's the place – it's a chain. They've got three restaurants there and they don't come any hotter than that.' For the amount of advertising time he's given them, on and off air, he should be entitled to free wings for life. What he doesn't know is that rival Wings & Things, also in Albuquerque, wins awards for its triple X-rated Killer Q sauce. Reputedly, I'm assured, it's even hotter. Curiously, when I hitched from San Bernardino, California to Philadelphia 40 years ago, getting my kicks on Route 66, I remember blistering my mouth on chillies at a lean-to Mexican takeaway on the outskirts of Albuquerque with a girl called Phil Handtusch. Phil, where are you now? But we're in wet Vancouver, not parched New Mexico.

'Maybe I was a bit short with that guy,' Blunty ruefully admits to me after another couple of wings and a beer go down the hatch. 'Do you think I should have been more friendly? Trouble is that everyone wants time. Sometimes when I'm tired like now I feel I have nothing to give.'

Just at that moment, the same guy comes back for an autograph. It's willingly given and with a smile. For a moment I think James is going to apologize and offer him a drink, but he thinks better of it.

'You good, Uncle Peter?' says Benny. 'You coming the whole way across Canada with us?' Yes, I'm good, but no . . . if I stay the full 5,000-mile distance I won't be alive by Christmas.

Much later still, we stagger – all except Bobble – homewards. Bobble strides out towards his bed . . . he's given up all alcohol for the duration of the tour. Why? 'Because I've seriously got to lose weight.'

'Bobble, is this going to make you utterly miserable to be with?' asks Benny.

'Yes,' he scowls. No one is going to disagree with that. Outside the hotel the two largest tour buses I have ever seen have their engines and all systems running in the chilled night air. But that's tomorrow. Tonight we get to sleep in real beds.

General Motors Place is home to the Vancouver Canucks and official ice hockey venue for the 2010 Winter Olympics. Consequently, despite the ice being covered, the atmosphere before the concert is chilly.

'Hi, are you two here on your own?' says the old man. Even at twentysomething, when they're all dolled up for the night out and in a crowded place like the lobby of a giant arena, it's a question that merits suspicion, coming as it does straight out of mother's promise-me-you'll-never-talk-to-strangers textbook. But a hopefully disarming smile and the oversized cameras on my shoulder take the initial sting out of it.

Is he a talent scout? The cover of *Vogue* flits for a micro-second between mascara-ed lashes. Then the boring old voice of common sense kicks in with a resounding 'no'. But, heh? What's the harm in finding out more?

'Yeees,' comes the cautious reply. If it's 'no' the stranger's moved on before they can blink – or at least before a quarter-back-sized jock returns with drinks from the bar and plumps a massive hand on his shoulder.

'Have you seen James in concert before?'

'No, first time.' (If 'yes', could well be a stalker, swift exit as above.)

Supplementary question when Karl is doing the asking: 'Are you working tomorrow?'

'You're going to enjoy it. Would you like to come backstage and meet James after the show? We usually have a bit of a party with 20 or 30 people, very relaxed, music, a drink, no cameras, no autographs, a chance for him and the band to meet people in whatever city we're in, and for you to get to know him.'

Eyes narrow. 'You're kiddin', right?' Suspicion starts to slowly give ground to a look of utter delight and astonishment that is spreading across their faces.

'No, really, I'm with the tour. Here's a couple of tickets for the after-show. Just stay behind at the end. Someone will come and find you and take you back.' If you're pretty enough, I'll come myself.

'OMIGOD!!!'

Sometimes, handing out the Golden Tickets can be a rewarding job. You get a hug, a kiss, and even tears of joy. Why, they've been known to ask my name and what I'm doing here. Then it's ego-stroking time.

'Peter, can you tell me, why us? Why did you ask us?'

'That's easy . . . look around you! You're much the most beautiful girls in the whole stadium.'

'Oh, wow! You really mean that?' Course I do. Another kiss.

'Enjoy the show, see you later.'

Yet sometimes, like tonight in Vancouver, it sucks. I've got instructions to invite at least 20 girls.

'Big night, Uncle Peter . . . none of your older stuff,' says Karl.

'Think about who we'd like to party with, not who you'd like,' says James. Bloody cheek! I swear one night I'm going to invite 20 grannies, shepherd them all from arena to dressing-room and then do a runner for home. That'll teach them.

But here I am, hanging around the entrance to GM Place with a fistful of Golden Tickets in my pocket – but I can't find a single girl that fits the bill.

It's not that they're plain or anything. The Canadian girl standard, taken from the detached stance of a middle-aged procurer of young, firm flesh, is pretty high in the world league. Not Brazil or Argentina, mark you. But then, again, not Borneo or Siberia. They're all nice, fresh-faced, clean-cut Canadian girls who are mainly out with their equally well-groomed boyfriends for the evening.

The first two I approach are good-lookers. Hmm . . . maybe a bit on the young side, but they're decorative garnish for the main course, if I can find it.

'Hi,' I say, blocking their path with my best jet-lag smile, 'is this the first time you've seen James in concert?' They gaze at me in utter wild-eyed horror. I look down at myself to see if I am really wearing a dirty raincoat smeared with marmalade on the inside and nothing else. One screams – a short, high-pitched wail of terror – and they both run off down the corridor in a clatter of impossibly high heels.

For an awful moment I think they're going to call a security guard. Either I've aged overnight like the vampire in a horror movie impaled on a stake at midnight, or during my ten-day stopover at home my technique's got a bit rusty. In rural Hampshire, there's not a great deal of demand for this kind of propositioning.

Strangely, it's an experience I had many years ago with – or rather because of – Anna Wintour, editor-in-chief of American *Vogue* and the dominating fashion diva on whom *The Devil Wears Prada* was supposedly themed.

If she is the frightening figure to her staff that she's said to be, her father Charles Wintour was even more so. He was editor of the London *Evening Standard* and my boss when I was a young reporter and occasional stand-in for the news editor. One morning in September 1968, during the daily 8am editorial conference to decide what should be in the later editions of the paper, he asked: 'Why won't my daughter, Anna, eat a proper breakfast? Don't teenagers eat breakfast any more?'

Never having met the then 19-year-old Anna, I had no idea. But because I was the only person in the room within two years of her age, all eyes turned to the terrified me. But I wasn't going to get caught out twice.

Only the week before, Wintour had been to the West End opening night of *Hair*, the musical. He'd clearly been shocked by the ground-breaking nudity and the richness of the language. At the meeting the following morning he asked in all sincerity: 'Can someone tell me please what is "cunnilingus"?' Again, all eyes focused on me. My face went beetroot.

This time I managed to actually speak. 'I'll find out,' I mumbled.

Half an hour later found me out on the streets of London carrying out a vox pop, asking teenagers as they came out of a tube station what they'd had for breakfast. The idea was to get a quote – and a picture profile – of ten random pretty girls. Despite the fact that it was a dark and particularly wet morning, it would have been easy . . . but for Billy B.

Billy was a diminutive crime photographer in his sixties whose brain had long since been rotted by alcohol to the point of dementia. He looked to have – and almost certainly had – slept in his beer-stained clothes for some days, if not weeks. His overall appearance was not helped by some kind of unfortunate suppurating skin condition that covered his face. 'Am I right, or am I wrong?' was his catchphrase. He'd been a great crime photographer in his day, but in his latter soaked years he was mostly wrong.

'Hi, I'm from the *Evening Standard*. Would you mind telling me what you ate for breakfast today?' I'd say, holding my umbrella over the young victim outside Chancery Lane tube station.

But just as she was about to reply, Grinning Billy would jump out from the crevice in the pavement where he had been sheltering and fire a flashbulb in her face. She'd run screaming down the road. Anna Wintour, I've never forgiven you for not eating your Cornflakes.

Back in Vancouver, I don't have Billy so I persevere

and meet some good ones already in the audience, along with a helicopter pilot who served with Charlie Blount in the Army Air Corps and now lives in Vancouver. He and his teenage daughter – I don't ask what she had for breakfast – get two of my remaining Golden Tickets.

Backstage before the show, it's clear that Blunty's pleased to be on the road again. We've only been home for ten days but for him that was ten days too long. As I've said before, he's only happy when he's travelling, although where he is going I'm not necessarily sure and neither is he. Maybe he's just avoiding some home truths.

He's glad to be back in North America and I get the distinct impression he's glad to be freelance for a few weeks – this time, no regular girlfriend has been imported. For me, in a selfish way, that's all for the best: he spends more time with the band and therefore with me. On his own he's more talkative, crazier, and better company.

Together, we sneak out of a back door, circle around the queuing crowds and take a walk downtown. Blunty's wearing a smart new black parka with a huge outsized hood that leaves his face unrecognizable in the shadows. However, the overall cool effect is somewhat ruined by bits of contrasting grey gaffer tape across the chest.

'Why the tape?' I ask.

'My promoter in Germany gave me the jacket to keep me warm and hide me from the world,' he replies. 'But beneath the tape it says "James Blunt" in giant red letters, which kind of defeats the object of the second half of the exercise.'

We go in search of a camera shop. I need a lens and he needs a new pocket digital. At the end of every gig, as part of the act, he produces his camera from his trouser pocket and takes a picture of the audience taking a picture of him.

Freedom is being able to walk around a city like this in complete anonymity. But it doesn't last. An eagle-eyed Chinese guy spots him at an intersection and asks for a photograph. Within seconds we're swamped by shoppers and office workers rubber-necking. They don't necessarily know who he is, but everyone else seems to – so it's compulsory to stop and have a gawk. To be famous in the twenty-first century, to become a so-called celebrity – even a minor one – appears to be the driving ambition of everyone under the age of 40. I think there's a sort of innate belief that if you touch his or her robes you'll catch the Midas effect and turn to gold yourself. No one, I note, is touching me.

We throw off our followers by Blunty walking and me limping away very fast indeed. Back at GM Place no one notices as we slip inside again. In a recent survey on the quality of life in cities around the world, Vancouver was ranked third. It tied with Vienna, behind Zurich and Geneva. But it seems to me pretty sad that the only way in which James or someone like him can appreciate this city and its standard of living is if he stays inside a cordon of security men. So that's the price of fame? Maybe, and he's not whingeing about it. After all, the income from it paid for the camera and, I guess, indirectly for my lens too. There ain't no such thing as a free lunch, although you really wouldn't believe that if you saw the amount of chilli con carne that Beardy is consuming in Catering right now.

In the dressing-room there's talk of the financial down-turn. Banks and money markets around the world are spiralling out of control. But on the multi-million world tour of a rock star, world recession – for the moment as far as the players are concerned – still takes the cheapest back seat so far up in the gods that it's almost out on the roof of the arena.

The band is completely cushioned against it. When big money is landing in your bank account each month, when your only day-to-day expenses are your mobile and the occasional restaurant meal on a day off, it's impossible to relate to factory closures and growing dole queues back home.

The dressing-room talk turns to buying flats and houses. The band, led by Blunty, is buying into bricks and mortar. Johnny is selling his flat in Leamington and looking to buy in London or in New York, which is his spiritual home. Benny has already bought a love nest in Perth for him and Sam and yet-to-be-born baby. Even Karl is talking of deserting his beloved Brum for a two-bedroom flat in Notting Hill.

'When will the recession hit pop stars?' quips Blunty, looking up from the keyboard of his laptop.

Well, actually James, right now. Only half the tickets for tonight have sold – and that's got little or nothing to do with your current popularity. In truth, James already knew this. Before the journey from England, he'd sat down to discuss the tour projections, and for something that would turn over £1.5 million, the likely profit, if he was lucky and nothing went wrong, was under £50,000. With money tight, concert tickets and downloads tend to be among the first items slashed from personal budgets in countries around the world – and Canada is no exception.

However, those fans that do turn up – all 4,700 of them – are out to have fun and bugger the expense. James and the band rise to the occasion. It's a good performance that attracts great reviews – just what's needed at the start of a nationwide tour.

The buses in which we are to travel across Canada have now moved from hotel to stage door. Ours is reputedly the smartest bus on the continent and the crew bus only marginally less so. Unlike the European model, it's a glitzy Greyhound rather than the sophisticated reincarnation of a London double-decker.

It's all on one level with a spacious sitting room behind the driver's cab. At the press of a button when stationary, the width expands by around a third. Back from this is the sleeping area, a dozen bunks in triple tiers down either side.

At first glance this looks a bit like a scene from a German POW camp, with officers resting on their over-crowded pallets while their pipe-smoking leader outlines the plans for the tunnel and where to hide the loose earth. In fact, each curtained bunk has lights, ventilation and personal video screen. The only thing lacking is enough room to turn over. At the back there's a bathroom with an electric sliding door, a separate shower, and another door leading to the party room. This, Blunty and others note with satisfaction, has a lock on it.

As the show ends and I turn to leave my viewpoint at the stage-right corner of the pit I'm approached by a girl in her mid-twenties. She's wearing tight jeans and a rather demure top, as if she's come straight here from work.

'Hey, Mr Photographer, would you do something for me that would really make my day?' I look warily and wearily at her. Jet lag's kicking in. What would make *my* day would be a good night's sleep in a bed – alone, well, maybe alone – not a few hours snatched in a bunk on a bus.

'Could you get me a set-list off the stage?' she asks.

'Sure,' I say. Benny and James both usually have these sheets showing the song order taped to the floor by the guitar microphones. I climb up on to the stage. But the crew are working extra fast tonight. They've stripped the carpet and the lists have already been junked.

When I come back down and tell her, she looks so crestfallen. Originally, she said, she'd been coming with a whole group of friends, but one by one they'd dropped out because of the price of the tickets.

'When you work in Subway as I do, $60 or $70 is a lotta money for a night out. But I had to come because I love his music so much. You know what? I wasn't disappointed. I can't afford a T-shirt or any merchandising like that, so I thought maybe I could get a song sheet as a memento. Never mind, thanks for trying, Mr Photographer,' and she turns for the exit.

The room is emptying fast. She isn't what the band would consider after-show material. But she's what we are about to find all over Canada – a really genuine and easily likeable person who loves James' music.

'Hey, maybe I can do something,' I call after her. She turns, surprised, and walks back.

'You could get me a set-list?'

I dig into my jeans pocket and find the last crumpled Golden Ticket.

'I could do better than that. If you like James' music so much, maybe you'd like to come backstage with me now and meet him?' Her face lights up like what used to be a 150-watt light bulb before they banned them.

'You mean it? You really mean it?' she says, her eyes scanning and rescanning the ticket like Charlie Bucket after he's just opened the wrapper of his Wonka bar and found the ticket. I've never meant it more. She reaches up and kisses me softly on the cheek.

'This is *absolutely* the best moment of my life,' she says. And she means it, too.

Power tends to corrupt, absolute power corrupts absolutely. I don't know what Victorian moralist Lord Acton, who originally coined this quote, would have said of me if he'd been present in GM Place tonight. Certainly, his beard would have gone instantaneously white at the sight of all that willing flesh wanting James.

Also, here's what Lord A had to say to the Archbishop of Canterbury in 1887: 'If a thing is criminal . . . if, for instance, it is a licence to commit adultery, the person who authorises the act shares the guilt of the person who commits it.'

Pretty clear, huh? This leaves Weird Uncle Peter rightfully to be stoned to death as the arch-shagger by proxy, a wicked love bite on the body of Canadian womanhood. I say this because as Miss Subway and I make it backstage through the ring of roadies and security guards to the packed party room and pour ourselves a much-needed vodka and cranberry, more kisses come my way. This time they're from three pretty and enthusiastic girls from the front row who were clearly having such a good time that I gave them passes.

'Peter, how can we ever thank you?' they chorus. Well, now you mention it . . . But, no, my role is sadly supervisory. Such nice girls, too.

'Come and see my tour bus' is the rock star version of 'Do you want to come up for a coffee?' And rarely does it fail. No, make that a 'never'.

In this case an extremely content James ('it's great to be back in North America') decides to invite not just the fittest of the three front-row girls, but half a dozen others to have a look around.

When James gets to the bus with his group he finds he's not alone. Benny's already there with a beer, settling down to a sensual marathon Skype session with Sam in Australia. Blunty shows them around, listening to the squeaks and squeals of excitement . . . and that's just Benny.

As a novice groupie you don't get a bigger turn-on than this. A few hours ago you dressed up in your birthday best and headed out to watch in concert, along with 4,699 other people, this guy who for months you've secretly been getting off with on your own.

Now, you just can't believe what happened. You've seen the show and you somehow got talking to this older guy who could have been his father, but said he wasn't. He gave you a ticket and you've got backstage to meet him! And, what's more, he's just as gob-smackingly gorgeous as in your fantasy. You've had three glasses of wine, which is two too many, and now you're on the tour bus with James! He's so polite, such an English gentleman – and that lovely lead guitarist is with you, too. He may be small and hairy, but he's perfectly formed. I just wish he would get his d**k out of that laptop.

And then the un-be-lievable happens! While he's showing you all the party room on the bus, he takes your hand and gives it a little squeeze, just for a moment. He looks you straight in the eyes and you can see that he only has eyes for you! I tell you, these are the original come-to-bunk eyes.

Back in the bus sitting room it could be kinda awkward, but James takes the initiative. Maybe, you think, he's done this before. The thought does cross your mind, but, no, of course not.

He's looked at the goods, made his approval, and the rest need to be returned to the shop.

'Ben,' says Blunty, picking up a bottle of Absolut vodka from the bar, 'the party's run out of alcohol. Could you take these girls back and give them all a drink? I'll be over in a minute.' Benny absorbs the situation, sighs, and closes his laptop. In a house in central Perth, Western Australia, the broadband's just gone down. Atmospherics, I expect.

Five out of six girls dutifully troop off the bus behind Ben. In the Blunty tour version of *X Factor*, only one act, with deep vocal chords as it turns out, has made it through to the next round.

Back at the party Miss Subway and I grab the vodka bottle before it's wasted on the rejects. It's a good party with a carnival – or rather, carnal – undercurrent to it.

'Do you know where my friends have gone?' says the third of the front-row trio, coming up rather than on to me with a worried look on her face. 'We belong to the same church. I'm a bit worried about them and we ought to be going home soon. They're kinda innocent and they've never been to a party with guys like this before.'

Well, I guess it depends on your dictionary definition of 'kinda innocent'. And 'guys like this' – they're a lovable bunch. Your dark-haired friend is probably, at this very moment, down on her knees and I shouldn't imagine she's praying.

The other one I saw disappearing with Karl into James' dressing-room bathroom. I guess they were going to freshen up.

'Oh, I wouldn't worry about them,' I reassure her, 'James and the band are really nice people. Someone's probably just showing them around. I'm sure they'll be back in a minute. Can I get you another drink?' In the eyes of Lord A, I am truly a dead man walking.

Now she's starting to search around for her mates. She does actually know what's happening, but she can't quite believe the evidence of her own eyes. I guess the three of them are going to have a lot to talk about over cookies and cocoa when – if – they all make it home tonight.

Eventually the party starts to thin. Miss Subway gives me another kiss and a hug goodbye and fades away from Wonderland, clutching a Blunty-signed poster, into the reality of serving chicken mayonnaise sandwiches and coffee at 6am to dock workers on the other side of town.

'Hey, Peter, I want you to know that it really has been the best night of my life and it's all thanks to meeting you. Have a great tour, have a great life.' Another kiss, and she was gone. I feel warm inside.

The remaining skittle from the front row is still standing and getting even more worried. Bobble's pulled the plug on the sound system and the rest of the band and the remaining guests are all heading for the bus.

'Can you help me?' she says, tugging at my sleeve. Tonight I seem to be cast in the role of Sir Lancelot. I guess it's time to rescue a couple of (no longer) maidens who are more likely to be in a state of undress than of distress.

But look! Here's one of her missing companions. She's calmly seated beside Blunty on one of the sitting-room sofas and she doesn't look lost or unhappy at all! In a discreet, but distinctively possessive gesture, he has his hand parked casually on her left thigh, just above the knee. The solitary standing skittle gives her pal the kind of glare she normally reserves for someone who's just sworn in church. What she gets in return is a Jezebel grin of deed done.

Easy, the driver, has got the engine ticking over. In fact, it's just to keep the air control system running, but Skittle is worried sick we're about to depart and there's still no sign of her other friend. Gently I explain that she and Karl are possibly having a good time together exploring the arena. I tell her not to worry, we're not going anywhere just yet. James would leave me behind. He would leave many of us behind. But he won't leave without his drummer.

She's got the picture now. In fact, she's actually starting to enjoy herself. 'If my friends can behave this badly, what's to say that I can't too?' she says to herself, and gingerly tries out one of the bunks for size. Someone who shouldn't suggests she might like to stay in it with him through the night to Edmonton.

'No,' she says, 'but it's nice of you to ask.' Isn't that just too polite? I love these Canadian girls.

'Peter, have you seen Karl?' asks James.

'No, I thought he was doing whatever you were doing,' I reply. I get an 'OK, wise guy' look.

'What time will you get to Edmonton?' says Skittle, mentally measuring the width of the bunk. She's wobbling. Looks like she's about to topple. It could be a full strike.

But no. It's a brave last bowl, but her timing's way off. She should have come across earlier. For at that moment Karl comes aboard holding hands with her 'missing' friend. They both look like cats that have been at the cream. Karl's wearing an even bigger smile than normal.

The three friends say their goodbyes and leave, but the party's not quite over yet.

Up the steps behind them comes a camp gay couple as well as a crazy girl and her – judging by the way they are holding hands and hugging – close female friend. She tells me all about the tattoo on her breast and how she had acupuncture to ease the pain.

'Would you like to see it?' she asks.

Well, you can't really refuse an offer to see a work of art like that without causing offence, can you? But just at that moment James brushes against her shoulder as he reaches to the bar for his drink. Instantly I'm upstaged. In the flick of a blouse button, I've disappeared from her line of vision. She's just switched channels. I no

James demands to have a pink pop-shield for recording. It makes him more sensitive

Vocal support act from The Hoosiers

Benny, inappropriately dressed to meet the Queen, Santiago

Blunty's
NIGHTCLUB
WHERE
EVERYBODY'S
BEAUTIFUL

Gerry, Stage Sound, spends his time playing with lots of little knobs

A sea of fans

Down Mexico way, in Guadalajara

Flying high, in Canada

Animal behaviour on the tour bus in BC. James swaps his laptop for Uncle Peter

Connecticut, the homecoming queen

Japan, Kung Fu fighter

It takes three people to dress James in his intricate stage outfit

Two perks of being the drummer

And will the winner of the Best Male Body competition please step forward! Uncle Peter and the band, Barbados

In the bath, with James Blunt

Basel, Switzerland. Miranda and husband, Ben

James and Anna Vissi in Cyprus

My name is Blunt, James Blunt

Smiling Sabina,
in Marseilles

The band feast on a strange man
picked up somewhere in France

Uncle Peter. DNR – Do Not Resuscitate

Lost love? 'If time is all I had, I'd waste it all on you'

Stand on it? No, I'm going to sit this one out. Blunty meets his first boardie

longer exist, nor indeed does the girlfriend who's obviously used to this. She turns away in search of a new interest – Johnny. He's chilling out charmingly in the corner.

'Time, please, ladies and gentlemen.' Bobble, rather gracefully for such a big man who hasn't had a drink all day and wants one, shepherds the remaining guests towards the door. We've a 12-hour drive ahead of us. It's 2am and it's definitely time to go.

'Come with us,' says James to the girls. I can see he is saying it just for the hell of it, to see how she'll reply. Miss Tattoo plays the hard-to-get card, which hardly becomes her.

'OK, I'll go to Edmonton with you. Why not? I'll share your bunk, James, but I won't sleep with you. I never put out on a first date.'

'In that case, you should stay here,' replies James. 'I *only* put out on the first date.'

'OK, so I'll sleep with you,' she says.

But James laughs and escorts her and her friend to the steps where Bobble is clucking to close the door.

The giant tour bus is like a transatlantic liner leaving port: two blasts on the horn, 'All shore passengers to leave the ship immediately!' A couple of the girls still look a bit undecided, but they're not getting much encouragement now and the last stragglers finally leave. 'You fuck 'em, I chuck 'em,' Bobble likes to repeat as he shoos out the last of them and seals the door. He gives Easy, the driver, the nod, and we're on our way.

Goodbye Vancouver, but sleep is a long way off yet. The praise heaped on me for the standard of girls tonight is lavish. 'You've got the job of party organizer for the whole trip,' says James.

'We've got to give him something to do, because he doesn't have any other job. Exactly why *are* you here, Peter?' asks Beardy.

But now, as we clear the city suburbs and Easy settles down in his cab for the long night drive, the conversation in the party room turns to a much more serious issue than either sex or music.

When Karl finally got home to his flat in Birmingham last week, he hadn't been to bed in around 65 hours and could hardly see straight. He managed to get the key in the door, dropped his suitcases unopened on the floor of his bedroom and crashed into a dreamless sleep.

'It's good to be home,' he thought, when he finally awoke with afternoon sunlight streaming through the window.

'But wait. What's that disgusting smell in here?' He threw open the window and started to unpack. When he reached into a side pocket of his main suitcase his hand closed around . . . a rotting German sausage.

Who put it there? Who would *do* that?

'It was you Beardy, wasn't it? You bastard,' says Karl. 'You're the only person around here who would do such a terrible thing.'

'I never,' Beardy vehemently protests. But the more he does, the more Karl thinks he's the culprit. Whoever did it, what presumably started as a joke now pongs malevolently.

'What do you think, Uncle Peter? Who did it? Maybe you?' No, I'm not playing Hercule Poirot with this one. If we don't drop the sausage and bury it, this is in danger of getting out of hand. They're all good friends. They watch each other's backs as closely as squaddies in Helmand. But constant exposure – on the bus you're never much more than a foot and a half from one another – gives these intimate relationships a frailty that occasionally becomes starkly apparent.

I once saw Karl hit Benny quite hard on the jaw. He just shook his head and carried on with what he was doing. 'Good, I feel much better for that. I haven't hit you since that time in Australia months back,' said Karl.

'Glad about that, mate,' said Benny, 'feel free, any time.'

Edmonton

I can sleep surprisingly well on this bus as long as it's moving and going in a straight line, which in North America is more often than not. I guess it's like being in the womb. Here you are, floating in the security of your bunk. I've got Mike The Sound, who makes not a sound, above me and the daily diminishing shape of Bobble opposite, and no one beneath.

Getting in and getting out of bed requires a reasonable feat of athleticism. Taking up tenancy of the bottom one might be easier, but to me it would feel like sleeping on the floor. James, as always, gets to his bunk and slips immediately into a self-induced coma.

When I awake we're already pulling into the outskirts of Edmonton on the North Saskatchewan River, which is home to North America's largest shopping mall, the Oilers hockey team and, as far as I can initially see, not a lot else. Home tonight is a downtown hotel that everyone but me knows well.

It's 3am – isn't it always? – and I'm standing (just) in Oil City Roadhouse on Jasper Avenue talking to a pretty young girl who says she comes from Alaska. Sarah Palin's the only female I know who comes from Alaska. This one's kind of younger and much slinkier.

'I need to go to bed with you,' she says. 'Right now.' Now, that's the kind of opening gambit guaranteed to get anyone's full attention. I may be conscious that I have lots more years than her, but right now I'm all ears.

I've no idea how she got from Juneau – that's the state capital, if you didn't know it – to Edmonton. I mean, how does *anyone* get from Juneau to Edmonton? If you're a salmon – and, if my memory serves me right, there's a helluva lot more salmon in Juneau than girls who look like this – I guess you head upriver and keep hanging a right. But then I'm not absolutely sure how we got here from the Sherlock Holmes pub in downtown via the Black Dog. The last twentysomething all-American girl who said something like that to me was Janis Joplin – and she's been dead for 40 years.

Up until now, Tuesday in Edmonton has seemed pretty dull. Makes you wonder about Wednesday and Thursday. We head for a place called Dirty Pretty, which sounds promising, but – you've guessed it – it's closed. We settle instead on dinner in the Steak House and I guess that's where the real damage was done. It's been a slow alcoholic wind-up – and it's all been caused by Ben's Sam 9,593 miles away in Perth.

While we're having lunch in the Sherlock Holmes, the scanning department of her local hospital maternity unit is doing a little detective work of their own. Boy or girl? Anxious moments. Ben's pacing up and down here in Edmonton, breathing urgently into his mobile.

Blunty's not saying much. All this family activity on the other side of the world's making him wonder about the future of his band. I mean, how can Benny live in Western Australia and tour? He can't. So after the birth he and Sam and the baby plan to decamp to London. Nothing stays the same, Blunty. You really can't expect it to.

'Well?' comes the collective question when he returns to the table. 'The baby's got its legs crossed. Sam has to go back later.' Frustration calls for full glasses.

It's bitterly cold and back at the hotel shop James has everyone buy silly woolly animal hats that become our uniform for the rest of the Canadian tour and beyond. James wants Bobble to have the pink pig, but settles for the pirate. His own is, naturally, a mad monkey. I get the wise owl, which is soon promoted to Weird Owl. We settle down to dinner in the Steak House where the waitresses seem completely oblivious to James' presence, which of course is an illusion. Ben arrives late and bursts in with a grin a mile wide on his face. 'Well?'

'It's a boy!' he shouts.

Shots of tequila all round and an immediate competition for the most suitable name. With Castle for a surname there's plenty of scope. I favour Windsor and Elephant-and-. More tequila. Johnny goes for Windsor or Warwick. The blonde waitress gets very excited at serving a celebrity, but not as excited as Karl and Blunty who both fancy her. Karl strikes first. He goes off and has a chat with her and invites her to the show. Blunty bides his time and then makes a clearly more successful move.

'What did you say to her, you bastard?' Karl asks later.

'Oh, I just told her that you were my drummer and that you weren't entitled to ask anyone to the show . . .' Sometimes it's hard to tell where the kidding stops.

So here we are in this cowboy-themed club where in

getting through the door Blunty cuts a fine line between hilarious and humiliating.

'Five dollars,' says the very pregnant girl at the entrance booth. Blunty digs in his pocket and pays.

'How much for this old guy?' says Blunty, indicating me beside him.

'Same price for everyone,' says the girl.

'You can't be serious?' he protests. 'He's a senior. You can't charge full price for an old bloke like this. He might not even last the evening – he might die at any time.'

'OK, half price, then,' she says, and Blunty counts out another $2.50.

Of course, he could have just said who he was, or got me to say who he was, and we'd all have got in free and been ushered through to the VIP area, if there is one – but that's not Blunty's style.

At the bar we order shots of truly disgusting tequila, but the Stetson-wearing owner has spotted us now – the pregnant girl at the door proves to be his wife.

'You don't want to drink that stuff,' he says, 'it's bad for you,' and promptly orders a fresh round.

James is up dancing behind a display of beer bottles with the go-go hostess who is wearing jeans, a Stetson, and not much in between. I'm locked in conversation with this girl from the state they call the Last Frontier, a conversation that is now so deep that I'm in danger of drowning. I've become the lead and about-to-be-laid character in an erotic Jack London novel. 'North to the Future' is Alaska's state motto. I'm going south, fast.

'You see,' she confides, in an accent that, just for a moment, conjures up thoughts of a vice-presidential candidate – fully dressed, of course, in twin set and pearls – skinning a moose with a nail file.

'You see,' she repeats, 'I've been chaste these past three years.'

'Who's been doing the chasing?' I ask. She reminds me of a girl I once shared a house with in San Bernardino in California. I can't for the life of me remember her name, but she couldn't say 'spaghetti'. No matter how hard she tried, it always came out as 'pussghetti'.

'No, I mean "chaste", like a virgin – like no sex,' she says. This is interesting.

'I haven't been to bed with any guy in three years, and now I am going to make out with you.'

Hang on, did I hear that right? Yes, I thought that's what she said. Now, hold your horses, sober up and think about what's going on here. Peter, you're in a Wild West club in Edmonton, Alberta, with James Blunt and an Alaskan girl – not even a Canadian girl – who wants to go to bed with you. Right now I feel like a cross between a guy who's picked a winning lottery ticket up off the street and a guy who's been randomly stopped in the green channel at customs.

'Why me?' I croak. I'm not trying to be sexy, I'm just losing my voice.

'Because the Lord wishes it,' she replies firmly. I admire her faith. Some 42 per cent of Americans (but only 22 per cent of Alaskans) go to church once a week. I guess this is one of them. There's nothing like a bit of religious zeal for spicing up a night out in Edmonton.

I try to focus on her and the situation at hand, but all that tequila and beer's giving the situation a rosy hue around the edges. I have to say that she's looking pretty damned pretty, and pretty damned determined about this, staring into my eyes and licking her lips like she's been eating ice cream – or is just about to.

Now, my kids don't own a pet rabbit. But if they did, I don't think I'd leave it lolloping around in the kitchen at present, not until we've got a clearer grasp of what's going on here. I glance across at James – he's having a fine old time with his cowgirl. Spotting me he gives a half-wave that could only be construed as encouragement.

'Have you considered the possibility, Marie,' I venture, for I think that's her name, 'that the Lord, just this once, might have got it wrong?'

'Nope,' she replies with a shake of her head. She gives a big smile, puts her arms around my neck and briefly kisses me.

'Every time in three years that I've thought about going with a guy who's kind of cute, the Lord's said, "No, honey. This man is not for you."

'But tonight I am getting a message loud and clear. The Lord tells me: "Honey, it is written that you will sleep with James Blunt's daddy!"'

Oh, it's that old chestnut. Time to tell the truth, I will never be with you.

'There's just one problem here,' I reply. 'I'm not James' daddy.'

Marie's mouth falls open. She looks me up and down in a new light that is not necessarily a celestial one.

'You're not his daddy?' she looks genuinely disappointed. Well, that's what I'd like to think. For one awful moment,

I think she's going to cry. The hotline to Heaven in her head is ordering a rapid rethink – 'recalculating route, turn around where possible' says her spiritual sat-nav.

'Maybe we should get another drink and talk about this?' she said brightly.

I'm positive that we shouldn't. Let's not give the Lord the chance to come up with some alternative programming.

Grande Prairie

'Are you *really* going to Grand Prairie?' is the question we've been asked ever since we arrived in Canada.

'James, why *are* we going to Grand Prairie?' I ask him as the tour bus eats through the 500 miles from Calgary in the early hours of the morning.

'We're going to Grand Prairie for the same reason that we go to lots and lots of places that other bands don't bother with – like Kazakhstan, Bosnia and Albania. We go because they're weird and wonderful places. We get looked after really well and it's a good excuse to keep touring. I won't make any money out of it – in fact it might even cost me – but we're going because it'll be fun,' he replies.

'If people are good enough to buy my albums, but they live in the back of beyond, I'll still go and sing to them. Touring's not about the money. If people like it in Grand Prairie, then we should go to Grand Prairie.'

Maybe, but first impressions aren't good. As we come into town we pass a giant store called Liquidation World. Further investigation reveals a hoard of superannuated golf-ball typewriters, power drills and fishing tackle. You can buy anything in GP as long as you don't mind it being second-hand. Only the sex toys – this place seems to be abundant in sex toys – are new.

It does make you wonder what happened to all the

first-time owners of these golf clubs and filing cabinets, hockey sticks and coffee machines. Did they just move on, or did they die of boredom or bankruptcy, or both?

Did they shag themselves to death with all these plastic vibrating sex toys on the shelves of the five 'adult' shops. What's with a town that's got five sex shops – one per 10,000 men, women and children? Oh, and 18 escort agencies from Barely Legal to Abby's Elegant Older Ladies. Quite possibly, of course, Grand Prairie rocks. We'll just have to find out.

GP is known as Swan City because its official emblem is the trumpeter swan. These giant birds – they've got a wing span of up to three metres – possibly get it right. They don't actually visit the city, they just fly overhead on their migration route.

The venue's at the Crystal Centre. Monster Madness and the Backstreet Boys were here early this month, and Kenny Rogers is coming for Christmas . . . CHRISTMAS? Kid Rock goes to visit soldiers in Afghanistan at Christmas. Kenny comes to Grand Prairie.

We take a look around town. There's not much to see beyond Liquidation World and the window display in the Afterhours Loveshop, unless you count the Grande Prairie Animal Hospital. The band in their animal woolly hats get some funny looks as they pose by the window.

We go into a Wendy's burger bar and several small children and their mums can't take their eyes off the hats. I guess frivolity is in short supply around here. Later, as we're walking down the road an attractive, but tired-looking young mother comes running after us with two kids in tow. Autograph time? No.

'Guys . . . I don't know who you are, but my kids have had a whole lot more fun laughing at you in Wendy's in your crazy hats than they had at the whole City Christmas Fair this morning. I just wanted to say thank you. You should be on the stage!'

'Well,' says Johnny, 'we sort of are.'

Encouraged by this and by the fact that it's Friday night and the average age in Grand Prairie is supposed to be 29 ('Does that mean half of them are 29-year-old girls?' – Karl, our resident mathematician), James decides that we should have a gala after-show tonight.

The dressing-rooms are small and dreary, so we go across the road to BJ's Q Club and Sports Lounge, a giant pub which boasts that it has 'Grande Prairie's Best Live Entertainment'. Bring it on.

Byron, the friendly owner, pretty soon gets the picture. 'I can print some tickets for you and block off the gallery area for your party,' he says.

At BJ's it's a big night, even without us – they've got a live trio of girl country singers and they're auctioning a special basket of 69 sex toys. This is a strange town. They seem to have plenty of money for vibrators, but not for much else. Each night in Canada, James is having his own auction for a chat in private with him after the show. In Edmonton this raised Can$1,600 for Médecins Sans Frontières. In Calgary fans forked out $500. But in Grand Prairie there are no takers at all.

Money may be tight, but I've got a party to organize – and the first thing you need for a party are guests. It may be a strange town on the edge of the earth, but the people are extremely friendly. I hand out 45 tickets for what may or may not be the greatest of all after-shows.

The gig itself is a riot, with girls trying to climb onto the stage. Whatever else they do in Grande Prairie, they know how to let their hair down. *I really want you,* he sings, and judging by the decibel level of the screams, they really do.

'I started writing the song at university in 1995,' James tells me, 'but it didn't go on the first album because it's a really tough one to record. It's best sung live; it needs an audience. Record it and it loses its magic. That said, I think we've got it 80 per cent on the album *All The Lost Souls.* I think we've got it 90 per cent when we made it into a single and we re-recorded it with Jimmy Hogarth. But I still don't think we've ever captured it the way I play it live.'

At the end of the show in the usual ice hockey stadium a small crowd, despite the bitter cold, has gathered where the tour buses are parked. James comes out of the bus and is making his way across an abandoned railway track to the pub for the party when he sees a little girl aged about ten. She's standing beside a jolly-looking housewife in the front row of the crowd and holding up a banner that reads: 'James, please marry my mother.'

He stops and signs her outstretched programme, and while chatting to the little girl he glances up at the banner and the woman and smiles: 'I'm really sorry, but I can't do that.'

The little girl looks from woman to banner to James and then pulls him by the arm and whispers: 'No, no, *that's* not my mother. *That's* my mother,' pointing in the direction of a tall and strikingly elegant girl standing on her own a few feet away.

'Ah, maybe I should reconsider.'

Much later on the bus there's a bit of an inquest and I find myself at the centre of it, in the witness box and under cross-examination. OK, so the party didn't quite go exactly as I'd anticipated.

'Peter, I think you just got fired,' says James.

I have an explanation. 'When you hand out 45 tickets, you can't *just* pick the prettiest girls in town. Sometimes they're with their friends,' I protest. 'You can't invite one without the other. That's hardly diplomatic – and if you do she'll be unlikely to turn up at all.'

Indeed, Karl has honed this to a fine art: he approaches a couple of girls of whom one is good-looking and the other not so fit. He then asks the plainer one to the after-show and adds as an afterthought: 'And do bring along your friend.' The reverse whammy approach never fails.

OK, OK, so I've got to admit that there were some kind of strange people at the party – but not all of them were invited and, anyway, Grande Prairie never pretended to be a cold version of Copacabana.

The mistake I made was that, as man-in-charge of the party, I had positioned myself at the bottom of the stairs, checking people had tickets. What soon became evident is that I'm no match for a herd of rabid women. At one point I found myself trampled to the floor and looking up skirts as the stampede of excited guests – invited and otherwise – flowed over me in their rush to catch a glimpse of James up close. They showed no mercy.

As a result of the breakdown in the vetting system,

many of them were just a little bit – well, actually, a lot – older than that average of 29 and, no, they weren't exactly 'fit' in either sense of the word.

I suppose the rot set in when I got talking to this girl called Karen at the show. She fitted the guest list perfectly, so I offered her a ticket.

'Hey! You're really cool and sweet!' she said. Hey, I like being told that – even if it's only in a kind of not-so-bad-for-a-dad kind of way.

'Yes, I'd love to come and meet James, but can I bring my friend? You'll really, really like her.' Sure you can, Karen.

The trouble was that Karen's 'friend' turned out to be her aunt. Karen, bless her, when given an inch took the proverbial mile, or kilometre as it is here in Canada. She also brought along a load of friends . . . her aunt's friends. For a while back there it looked like a Women's Institute pre-calendar-shoot meeting.

'I really, really like James, but . . .' Karen's aunt tells me, snuggling up too close to me at the bar. I'm sure she's a nice person, but she's definitely invading my space and I'm pretty sure that Karen gets her looks from her late uncle's side of the family.

'That's great,' I say, worrying whether this is going where I think it's going.

'I also really like you, Peter . . .' Across the room I catch Karl looking in my direction in open-mouthed disbelief. Time for an emergency exit strategy.

'I think,' says James later on the bus, 'that Peter was using the wrong eye when he picked those girls. Peter, you've got to stop thinking of what you, rather than we, would like.' This gets a grand laugh. The old jokes are always the best.

248

Saskatoon

Saskatoon sits on the banks of the South Saskatchewan River. It has four times the population of Grand Prairie, which is good. It was founded by the Temperance Colonization Society, which is bad. The good news is that Victorian liquor laws have since largely relaxed. Just don't try smoking in Saskatoon, indoors or out.

'It *can't* be. This is *unbelievable!*' says the loud whisperer in the row behind us.

'I tell you, it *is* him,' says his companion. 'Why can't he watch a movie like anyone else?'

'Man, where's the bodyguards and all?' says a third voice. 'Do you think that's his father with him? James Bond and James Blunt – I tell you that's weird!'

'Hey, man, check this out,' says another into a mobile phone. 'I'm sitting watching a movie with that "You're Beautiful" guy James Blunt . . . yeah, man, I'm right behind him . . . I could reach out and touch him . . . you wanna what? [laughter] You'd better come down here and do that yourself.'

If Blunty hears, he doesn't react. He and I are sitting in the best seats of a multi-screen movie theatre. *Quantum of Solace* has just gone on release and this is Blunty's treat. Earlier in the evening he bought tickets for us. Sometimes he finds it relaxing on a day off like today to get completely away from the tour for a couple of hours and just relax

249

in front of a movie – as the girl behind us says – 'like anyone else'. The longer the tour, the more difficult it becomes to unwind – even on a day when there's no concert. Movies allow total mental escape.

However, over dinner in the Samurai Japanese restaurant in our hotel, the Delta Bessborough, there's been a bit of low-level fall-out – no hard feelings, just a bit of banter bordering on bicker. Karl's off the scene altogether. He's presumably doing what he does best after drumming, having imported a date from Edmonton earlier in the week. Johnny and Beardy want to go drinking. Benny wants, as usual, to go Skyping.

The restaurant – or at least the hotel – has been here since 1935. It's clearly very popular and we don't have a table reservation.

'Shall I go and sort it?' I ask.

'No,' says James, 'let's just get a table like normal people.'

'Sorry, we're full,' says the waiter. 'Can you come back in an hour or so?'

'We're guests in the hotel,' James says politely. 'We're going out later and we need to eat right now. Can you ask someone?'

He shakes his head and goes off to talk to the manageress. She looks across at James, does a double take, and her jaw drops momentarily.

'A table for five? Just step this way, please.' Amazing what having the right face and a name to go with it can achieve. We're ushered into a three-sided booth that opens onto the main floor of the restaurant.

'Hi guys,' says the waitress, handing out menus and filling water glasses, 'what are you all doing in town?'

'We're travelling minstrels and this old guy here is our drummer,' says James. She gives me a strange look and hurries off to get drinks.

When she returns her face is bright pink. 'That's not fair,' she says to James, 'I feel really stupid now. We'd like to offer you a private room.'

'No, we're fine here,' James replies with a winning smile. Four bottles of *sake* later, we're finer.

Back in the movie theatre there's as much going on behind us as on the screen.

'James Bond and James Blunt? I need someone to pinch me,' says one of the group behind us. James looks across at me and grins sheepishly.

In fact it's not a new scenario. If Johnny was here he'd burst out laughing. Several months earlier in Copenhagen, a Danish model called Pernille Andersen allowed herself to be persuaded by a group of girlfriends to go and see what she thought was a James Bond movie.

'I was tired and I really didn't want to go,' she said. 'I don't like James Bond movies that much. When I got to the theatre I discovered it was not a movie at all but a concert given by someone called James Blunt. I'd sort of heard of him but didn't know his music. I wanted to go straight home but we'd got the tickets and my friend persuaded me to at least stay for the beginning. While I was waiting for the show to start this tall English guy came up to me and said something like: "Hi, are you and your friend on your own here tonight . . .?"'

The man was Johnny Garrison. She accepted the Golden Ticket. Neither of them knew it was the start of a lifelong partnership.

'I just couldn't believe it!' she told me many months later: 'I set out to see Daniel Craig and instead I ended up with Johnny Garrison. I got the best deal by a long way.'

When the lights go up at the end of the movie, James turns to the row behind as he puts his coat on and gives a nod of acknowledgement to the whisperers. They're two boys and two girls aged about 18. One of the girls leans forward, kisses him on the cheek and says, 'Thank you.'

'For what?' he asks.

'For your music,' she replies, heading for the exit, 'for coming to Saskatoon, for being James Blunt, for being beautiful, for lots of things.'

He and I leave and walk the six blocks back to the hotel in warm, companionable silence. There are lots of bad things that happen, but it only takes one little good thing to make this ridiculous life on the road worthwhile.

The next day the band's looking pretty pleased with its collective self. Karl turns up at the venue after 24 hours away from the pack and promptly gets a talking-to from Blunty.

'Where've you been? I know where you've been. You imported a girl here because you failed to pull her the first night. That's called dating. I mean, how am I going to explain to other rock bands that I have allowed this to happen? Do it on the first night or not at all. Otherwise you set a bad precedent.' Karl just keeps on grinning.

I'm leaving and I'm sad. James and the band are going on to Toronto, Québec and St John's in Newfoundland after a lightning trip to New York for Blunty and Beardy for a TV show. But I have to go home.

'Stay with us,' pleads James, 'you don't *have* to go home. Without you, who is going to organize our parties? In a funny sort of way you've become a part of the tour. You know something? We actually almost *like* having you around.'

'We need your wisdom, O Wise Owl,' says Beardy. 'Stay!' It's good to feel that I really belong. But I can't. There's a whole world out there beyond the footlights and the after-shows. Tomorrow I need to go back to my life in real time. But that's tomorrow.

As the band leaves the dressing-room for the show, following stage manager Mark by torchlight around the back of the stage, Blunty beckons me over and includes me in the haka. We link arms and hug, heads together. 'We'll miss you tomorrow,' he says. 'Speak some words of wisdom to us.'

No words come.

'What's your name?' asks this guy at the after-show. I've no idea who he is or how he got here.

'Peter,' I reply.

'It's good to have you all in Saskatoon, Peter Blunt,' he says, and slaps me on the back. Oh God, here we go again. If I've succeeded in doing one thing on this trip, it's making James' father into a hardcore rocker worldwide.

Winnipeg

'I told you 9 o'clock,' says Easy, the driver, turning the key and waiting for the giant engine to die. He looks ostentatiously at his giant silver wristwatch and says: 'I have . . . exactly . . . 9 o'clock.' I high five him and head back into the sitting area.

It's dark outside, but only because we're in a cavernous underground car park beneath yet another venue. Easy has driven 500 miles through the night to Winnipeg while I slept a little and he kept his promise to get me here on time to catch my flight to Toronto and on to London.

I don't know much about Winnipeg and I'm not going to have time to find out whether it's as boring as it has been billed to me down the years. Somewhere I read that it sort of lost its appeal as a boomtown bang in the centre of North America after the Panama Canal opened in 1914. This may seem to be a geographical anomaly, but Winnipeg was the all-important staging post on the Canadian Pacific Railway. With the opening of the canal it lost its strategic importance as a trading centre to Vancouver.

Not surprisingly, this is of zero interest to the domestic little group of pop people half-buried under duvets, drinking coffee and vaguely watching a movie on a giant screen in the bus sitting room, which Easy has just stretched at the press of a button.

Everyone looks a bit downcast. Whether this is due to hangover, homesickness (sometimes it strikes unexpectedly), or the prospect of my imminent departure, it's hard to tell. I grab my computer bag and get a bear hug from Beardy, who's climbing out of his bunk.

'See you, guys. Be good,' I say, and head down the steps to open the luggage compartment and retrieve my suitcase. Blunty follows me outside and I turn to look at him.

It would be good not just for his fans but for his hardcore critics to see him at this moment in this underground car park. The star is wearing a faded T-shirt and the kind of worn-out, striped winceyette pyjama bottoms that you expect to see in an Ovaltine advert circa 1959.

Julian and Dick of Enid Blyton's *Famous Five* would have been proud to wear pyjamas such as these. Makes you wonder if there isn't a favourite teddy secretly tucked in his bunk. You look tired, James. You probably don't know it, but in the course of this 15-month tour, this is your 45th country – and you've still got four months to go. The workload is simply staggering.

'If I don't see you before,' he smiles, 'I'll see you in Barbados. But come to Verbier for New Year, if you can. It's been good, hasn't it? Happy Christmas, Peter.'

'Happy Christmas, James.' I feel like a character who's stepped out of the pages of a mid-Canadian version of *A Christmas Carol* as I head across the concrete underground car park and out into the snow, sadly trailing my cases beside me.

From the bus window Johnny records my departure on video and sets it to music – 'She's Leaving Home'. In fact, I manage to ruin the moment of theatre by walking back in again three minutes later to collect my camera, which I've left on the counter.

'The airport, quick as you can,' I tell the cab driver.

'Watcha think of Winnipeg?' he asks. 'Been here long?'

I have to think about this. I guess it depends on what, in the crazy context of James Blunt, you mean by 'long'.

Barbados

Another tour leg, another two legs – and this time they belong to a bikini-clad Tash, whose perfectly toned body is right now reclining horizontally in the arms of James and the band. I'm taking a photo by the pool in the comfort of the Crane Resort on Barbados' less fashionable east coast. How she got here – I mean to Barbados, not into the arms of the band – I don't know. I guess Sabina and Tash are slugging it out for the title of James' official companion and, as I'd expect of James, both are winning . . . and both are losing.

How James can have any serious relationship when he is never in one place for more than 48 hours is beyond me, but then I guess the nomadic life suits him. It seems to me that no girl, however beautiful, however intelligent, however loving, is ever quite good enough. It's as if he's searching, always, for someone who's not there. When we talk about it, he just smiles. It's always his first defence. I get the feeling there's a story untold. Maybe I'm just imagining it. After this length of time on the road it's easy to misinterpret almost everything.

The trouble with James is that I guess he's really not what you'd call the 'official boyfriend' type. Curiously this doesn't have anything to do with shagging the planet which is, of course, nice work if you can get it, and Blunty's put long hours of studious overtime into this.

No, it's about being Blunt, and that means emotional isolation. Only in his self-imposed solitary state of mind can he create the music and the words he needs to beat the demons and express his feelings. Get too close to him, demonstrate your feelings, and he'll back away in full protection mode.

But his mates are getting married. Maybe he'd like to get married, have a family, put down some roots. I'm good at getting married and putting down roots because I've done it three times and this is of considerable interest to Blunty. One night when we're chilling out in yet another presidential suite in yet another hotel he says to me:

'I'd like to share life with a companion, and to have a family, but it's hard. The more we lose our innocence, the harder it is to find what we dream of. Perhaps some of us just aren't suited to marriage? I have a friend who has three children from three different men – she chose each father for his genetic strengths and has three very different, fantastic children. The children are extremely well-balanced and enveloped in love and strong parenting. Different relationships provide different things. Sadly, if you talk openly about that kind of thing, people simply say, "You can't have your cake and eat it." But why on earth would you have a cake and not eat it?

'Perhaps it would work if I had a wife and kids in two or three different countries at the same time? I could just go between them all and maybe everybody would be happy?' I'm not at all sure to which level he is joking.

'Maybe you would be happy,' I tell him, 'but if my life is anything to go by, not everybody would necessarily feel the same about the situation.'

The fact is that James is extraordinarily self-sufficient. Possibly he is the most complete person I've ever met. He's dependent upon nobody. But this makes him an island. Don't get me wrong, it's a very comfortable island with hot and cold running water, and always at least one Woman Friday on tap. He's very happy to spend time in his own pool, at the piano and guitar, and to run for mental miles along the beaches of his musical mind.

And then just occasionally he'll climb above the jungle across the rope bridge up to the look-out point and glance across the sea to the mainland. He's prepared a driftwood beacon up there, but it's never to be lit because he doesn't want rescue. He's absolutely content with himself. However, being Blunty and his father's son he's got a nifty little speedboat tucked away in a natural little cerebral harbour.

From time to time he pulls off the tarpaulin and roars across the straits to boogie outrageously with other people. But always he returns to his island. It is, if you like, his own intellectual Ibiza.

Barbados seems to have little to recommend it beyond beaches. While waiting at immigration in the airport, new arrivals fall into three distinct categories. Firstly, there's the extraordinarily conservative and well-heeled older group led by grey-haired men in Jermyn Street holiday shirts and genuine Panama hats from Ecuador via James Lock & Co., founded 1676. They have five-star Sandy Lane written all over them. They look down with some disdain on the second and larger group of package holidaymakers who've done Disney in Orlando and are now about to check out the Caribbean. The third group is us – and just to remind the band that we're not here on holiday Blunty immediately on arrival at the hotel calls for a two-hour rehearsal.

However, it's hard not to catch the spirit on a holiday island such as this. We take a trip to a harbour for dinner in a delightful but expensive fish restaurant. We all loosen up over a couple of rum punches and Karl takes about ten minutes to pick up two sisters from Chicago who just happen to be staying in our hotel.

The mysteriously titled '1973' – the year before James was born – is the final track of each show and has the audience rocking in the aisles.

And though time goes by, I will always be
In a club with you in 1973
Singing 'here we go again'

That was the year Pacha, Ibiza's iconic nightclub, was founded and some say the song is an ode to the place where James can often be found on hot summer nights.

'1973 rhymes with "I will always be",' he tells me. 'Sometimes the meaning of a song becomes clearer after I've written it.

'It's about hanging out with a friend every week in the same club and how I miss the simple fun and friendship of it. I wrote it in Jimi Hendrix's old Electric Lady Studios, with a guy called Mark Batson who writes for Dr. Dre and Eminem. He smokes a lot of grass, and thought my name was funny because he smoked blunts – a cigar filled with "the A-grade shit". He made me one, and presented it to me saying, "Mr Blunt, here's your first blunt." I smoked it and five minutes later I think Jimi Hendrix walked in, but we never credited him on the song.'

In the final stages of the song and the show, James closes the lid of the upright piano, climbs swiftly on top, and adopts a surfing pose as the crowd goes wild. During the course of the world tour this act has got increasingly daring, with James managing to sway the piano on to two wheels in one direction and then in the other. 'The only question is "when" not "if",' says Hamish, one of the full-time techies whose job includes tuning and polishing the instrument.

That time is now. For this circus trick James chooses a basketball stadium in, of all unlikely settings, a suburb of Bridgetown, Barbados. The Caribbean island is better known for native reggae than its appreciation of a white balladeer Brit like Blunty. But for another mysterious piece of reasoning on behalf of global booking agents, here we are in the former British colony off the coast of South America in full tropical humidity.

One reason for our presence here is that we are on our way to Brazil and Argentina where James is to be the support act for Elton John at a series of mega-concerts. But what the army of tour planners failed to work out when James was invited to sing at the Barbados Jazz Festival is that, while the island is indeed off the coast of South America and São Paulo is only 2,700 miles away, there's no link by air. Instead, we're going to have to fly 1,600 miles northwards all the way to Miami and then 4,200 miles back down south again to São Paulo.

The second reason is that the island's prime minister, along with most of his cabinet, are said to be huge fans of James. The PM has asked for a private audience at the venue before the show and we arrive in tons of time for the meeting.

'You can't keep a PM waiting,' says Blunty to complaints from those who would rather have had an extra hour of R&R on the beach. In fact, that would have been a painful mistake. We've spent much of the day jumping the Atlantic rollers pounding the shore. Blunty, Tash and I have liberally slapped on sunscreen, but others have not. As a result, Beardy, Johnny and Karl look like freshly boiled Maine lobsters.

If you are a prime minister, you can, it seems, keep Blunty waiting. Or you can go further, as happens here, and fail to show up at all. This is kind of a pity because the preparations for the presence of the PM are intense. A whole team of government minders has blocked off the front row of seats and fuelled their own giant VIP suite with copious quantities of Mount Gay Rum, which is the island's natural lubricant.

In fact the government seems to have taken over virtually the whole of the backstage area, leaving Team Blunty with a couple of small dressing-rooms to stage left. Oh well, relax. This is Barbados, mon, where Saturday night is every night and time goes by at its own pace.

If the permanent guys in the crew have ever for a moment thought that the going got difficult in Eastern Europe, the Caribbean is chaos. James, Johnny and Benny have got their own guitars, but otherwise the band is relying on locally rented equipment for the gig – the logistics of rigging the full stage here and then shipping it all on to Brazil within 48 hours were just too complex even for a stage manager with Mark's skills.

Mike The Sound shakes his head in amazement at the gear from which he must create a successful acoustic platform for James.

The local riggers include a full-back and a winger from the Barbados national football team, along with a cool Rasta who slips into a climbing harness and shins up a 40-foot pole to the lighting canopy as if it were a coconut palm.

On stage, pride of place goes to the silver Korg Triton keyboard that replaces the normal piano. It looks like Blunty has no choice but to keep his feet firmly on the ground tonight for *1973*. At the sound check I saw him circling it and prodding it with distaste.

'I hate this thing,' he tells Mark. 'Why can't I have a proper piano?'

''Cause there isn't one,' Mark replies.

With an hour to go to the concert, the government's before-, during- and after-show has reached fever pitch. The invited guests – and there are at least 75 of them – are not letting a little thing like the absence of the PM or any of his cabinet dampen their fun. Tash and I carry out a commando raid and come away with armfuls of white wine to even up the alcohol distribution between the rival parties.

The show gets slowly under way with the front row still blocked off for the cabinet. Tash and I borrow two of the seats and are promptly accosted by a furious minder. 'You can't sit there,' she says, 'these seats are reserved for the prime minister's party.'

'But he's not here and the show's half over,' I protest. 'Can't we just park ourselves here and promise to move if he shows?'

'No way,' she says, summoning over a couple of security guards. 'That's not the way we do things around here.' Unless we want to explore the cells of an island police station it's time to make a move.

Back in the cramped dressing-rooms, someone else is making a move. In the middle of the show Mark wanders in to use the loo and comes across a guy with his hand inside Beardy's luggage.

'What the fuck are you doing?' he says to the thief, who has been caught red-handed. To each venue James and the band must inevitably bring a number of personal possessions, including valuable items such as laptops, phones, wallets, iPods and cameras, which need to be carefully minded while they are on stage. The normal way to ensure these don't get nicked is to post a security guard on the chair outside the dressing-room door or to actually take them on to the stage. But today we've got a uniformed guard.

'I'm calling security,' says a furious Mark. He then slowly realizes that that the thief *is* security. He's the guy who's been assigned to guard the door. The usual casualties are iPods at after-shows. Ungrateful guests who've been invited backstage have a curious way of expressing their gratitude for all that free booze and chats with Blunty by seeing any music player left around as fair game.

Back in the arena, Tash decides to liven up the proceedings. She responds to the jobsworth government minder by leading an assault on the stage. For most of the show the audience has been sitting politely in their seats. She breaks ranks and starts dancing right up to the edge of the stage – there's no crush barrier in the pit.

That's all it takes. The audience leaps over the empty reserved seats to join her. The security guards are overwhelmed. Hundreds of girls stretch out their arms across the stage, trying to touch James' legs just a few feet away. Come any closer from the guitar mike and he's in danger of being dragged down into the crowd. I give Miss Jobsworth a big smile. She responds with a growl of anguish. 'Do you think the PM will be here in a minute?' I ask. For a moment I think she's going to hit me.

Up on the stage James is at the keyboard, pounding out '1973'. Suddenly, with a wicked look at the band he jumps up on to the fragile keyboard and starts to surf. It's all too much for the Korg. The keyboard legs buckle and collapse – amazingly they do so, to start with, in slow motion.

Here's how a boardie called Pookey described the scene on James' website:

The highlight of the show, for me, came at the end of '1973' when James pushed his microphone back as he does when he's about to stand on his piano . . . he looked at Beardy and Beardy pointed to James' bench with his chin, James looks down at the bench and then you see he's made up his mind . . . he puts one foot on the bench, then the other on the keyboard, puts the other foot, gets his balance and then, in what seemed like super-slow-motion, the piano slowly goes down under James (in my mind it was like a slow-leaking balloon going pppsshhhhhhh). Oh but the looks on the boys' faces were absolutely priceless (I'm surprised they could continue playing they were laughing so hard!!!). James stood still on the collapsing piano, with arms extended out, not daring to move . . . when the piano reached the ground, he went towards a laughing Beardy, gave him a high-five (but missed as they were laughing too hard), went back to the keyboard, grabs his microphone back and ends the song. OMG it was just brilliant!!!

The crowd thinks it's all part of the act and roars with delight. As Hamish said afterwards: 'It should have gone down in one, like an ironing board. There's no explanation for why it didn't, but then James always has luck on his side.' The hired instrument is completely trashed and James is amazed that he managed to stay on his feet, but there's a big bill to pay for the damage and the usually cool locals seem unusually uncool about it.

Much later we head back to our hotel for a late-night party in James' huge suite, which has a roof-top barbecue. The sisters from Chicago are here and I talk on the sofa to one of them while a smiling Karl disappears hand in hand with the other out on to the balcony.

Surprisingly, my one doesn't seem much interested in me. She keeps looking across at James who is talking quietly to Tash and then across to the balcony doors behind which her sister is presumably not talking to Karl.

Barbados

When the rumpled outsiders return Karl looks a little unhappy.

'She bit my shoulder and it hurts,' he later tells me. 'Peter, do all American women bite?' Only when they're really, really hungry, Karl.

Miami

It's like being in a dream where you're running in mud. You try and you try, but the mud holds you back and you're going nowhere. Except this is not a dream. The bus is leaving for the airport in two minutes from now and I'm not on it.

It all seemed so sensibly simple. All I did was walk the 300 metres across the resort to the reception area and check out of my room. But when I got back to my room to pick up my bags the electronic key had already been cancelled and there's not a member of staff to be seen in the whole isolated unit. If there's one cardinal rule on Tour Blunty it's 'always be on time'. Planes don't wait. When you run what amounts to a military operation, tardiness is not exactly a capital offence for a non-essential member of the crew – they just leave you behind. You catch up at your own expense, or you don't catch up at all. The next destination is 5,800 miles away.

Finally I track down a porter who tracks down a supervisor who has a passkey. It doesn't work. Finally, a new electronic key is cut at reception and a bellboy wanders over with it in his own time, admiring the view and stopping for a chat with a friend along the way. A whole half-hour has slipped by since the scheduled departure time and the band will be at the airport by now. I grab my bags and race, in hope more than expectation, the 200 metres to the bus rendezvous point.

James and everybody are all still standing there. This is Barbados, mon, where all time is relative. At that moment the coach arrives.

'What's wrong, Peter?' says Blunty, as I collapse into a seat beside him and Tash. 'You look like you're about to have a heart attack . . . or are you actually having one?' Nothing's wrong, James, except my life right now. I feel a bit like, and I am just as red-faced as, Michael Winner. Calm down, dear.

It makes absolutely no sense to fly five hours north to Miami in order to fly eight hours south again to São Paulo. But this we do. It is easier and much more pleasant to enter any Third World country than it is to beg your way into the United States.

Since the days of transatlantic seaplanes and leather flying helmets, it's always been a sensible and internationally accepted IATA rule of travel that if a passenger is in transit from A to C via B and stopping over for under 24 hours, he doesn't have to actually go through the immigration process of entering country B. You remain airside and technically outside of the country in which you're changing planes.

I once used this to my advantage at the height of the Cold War when my newspaper got news that a British spy was being released from years of imprisonment in the USSR. We knew the time and number of the flight on which he was being deported, but I had no visa for Russia. I flew from London to Paris and then booked a flight back to London . . . via Moscow. After 16 hours airside at

Moscow airport (and a two-hour interview with a curious but finally amused KGB officer), I boarded the plane to London, sat beside the spy, and got his exclusive story.

However, in his infinite wisdom, in the waves of security hysteria that followed 9/11, George W. Bush arrogantly changed the rules. If country B above is the US of A, you're buggered. Uncle Sam – after all, he's the guy who invented Extraordinary Rendition – insists you go through the full immigration process, even if, like us, you're only going to be Stateside for 45 minutes. Uncle Sam demands to know every detail of who is passing through his airports so that he can, if he doesn't like what he sees, cuff you and send you straight to Jail without passing Go.

So here we are in a two-hour immigration queue at Miami airport with the clock ticking for our onward flight to Brazil. You know, you just know, that the ex-marine immigration officer sitting in his glass booth is going to have real fun with such a shaggy bunch of guys.

'If they don't let us in,' says Glen The Lights, 'they'll hopefully deport us on the next flight . . . which is the one on which we're booked.'

James is up first. The immigration guy is not a music fan. The name means nothing to him. 'White is the wrong form,' he says. 'Go away and fill in the green one.'

'No,' says James, 'white is the right one. I come here every other week.'

'You tryin' to tell me how I do my job?' he asks threateningly. This could take a long time. Most of us wouldn't dare to question a guy like this. But Blunty's got a top artist's visa and that carries weight.

'Absolutely not,' says James, 'but there's a whole bunch of people behind me with the same form . . . so could you just double-check with your supervisor?'

White is right. The guy doesn't apologize. He just stamps the form with an extra bang and waves him through. Welcome, briefly, to the American Dream. I like being here, but Jesus I hate coming here. Around the luggage carousel the dogs are circling and sniffing. I've got nothing to hide, none of us has. Uniforms make me nervous and, looking around me, I'm not alone. My absolute belief in the honesty of every American policeman ended 40 years ago on the streets of San Francisco. Plants are not necessarily things that grow in Golden Gate Park. Still, the dogs are nice.

On this leg of the tour everyone is responsible for carrying an extra item of baggage when they check in. The guitars are lightest and go first. I'm left with the final round bag that contains the cymbals. *Now* I know that the sucker *always* gets the cymbals. They're impossibly awkward to carry and they're really heavy. Somehow we retrieve the bags and recheck them across the terminal, and make it to the gate with minutes to spare. Farewell America, we've been here a couple of hours – and this time it was a couple of hours too long.

São Paulo

It's 42 years since I've been here and the city is now four times the size it was – 20 million people live in the metropolitan area. Every day 1,000 new cars hit the streets and it has what are rightly considered to be the worst traffic jams in the world. It explains why this vista of gleaming skyscrapers and contrasting abject poverty has more private helicopters than anywhere else on earth – they make 70,000 flights each year just across the city. If you want to get to a meeting on time, you have to go by air. We go by road – slowly – from the airport.

Gazing out through the darkened windows of our people carrier I don't expect to recognize anything at all from the 1960s. Even then, I'm not sure that my visit to this bustling city had any lasting visual impact. I have just a blurred recollection of buildings and people, a brief backpacking staging post between the wonders of Rio and the powerful majesty of the waterfalls of Iguazu, which I reached in a 1957 Oldsmobile. The smell of the leather seats and the pungent scent of coffee hog the surface cells of my memory. My hitch-hiking host stopped every 20 minutes at a roadside stall for his next intake, drunk black and sweet from tiny, cracked, once-white cups. There's an awful lot of coffee in Brazil.

'Always hold it left-handed,' he ominously advised. I am left-handed.

'Why?' I asked.

'Because syphilis hides in the cracks to the left of the handle, but not on the right. Nobody in Brazil is left-handed.' Rubbish, but I've never drunk right-handed since.

It was all so long ago. But suddenly, sandwiched between blocks of urban concrete, there it is: the unmistakable shape of a white colonial building dating from the 1900s. It's the secondary school where for a week or two, back in 1966 a few months before Bobby Moore lifted the World Cup in London, I taught English in exchange for board and lodging. Well, to be more exact, I chatted authoritatively while knowing next to nothing about Liverpool, Carnaby Street and the King's Road to teenage Brazilian boys not much younger than myself. They couldn't work out whether they worshipped most a god called Edison Arantes do Nascimento or John Lennon or Mick Jagger. Edison, better known as Pelé, only won on points because he came from the city of Três Corações, which is only 185 miles away as opposed to 6,000 miles.

So here I am nearly half a century later with James and Elton John. Did I mention him? This is billed as a double-headline tour, but in reality James is going to be the support act for The Master at a series of giant concerts across Latin America. The first is tomorrow here in São Paulo and the whole city is buzzing with excitement at the prospect.

The Elton connection is a close one. Elton spotted Blunty at the very beginning of his career – or, rather, Todd did. Todd is James' manager who works for 21st

Artists, which also happens to manage Elton and to be owned by Elton. 'Todd's dynamic and has a quality that's rare in the music business,' says James. 'He has integrity.

'In the early days he heard a demo and then I did a gig for him and some other managers at a place called the 12 Bar in Soho.'

Todd takes up the story: 'For me, hearing James live that first time was a life-changing moment. When I heard his voice live it was what I had been waiting to hear for all my professional career. I just knew that this guy had the potential to be truly world class. It was a quite extraordinary experience.'

'I owe Elton and Todd a lot,' says James. 'The senior manager at 21st was Derek McKillop and I think he and Todd ran just about everything past Elton. Todd said to him: "We like this."

'Elton completely got behind it. I was given the chance to support him at two shows, one in Ipswich and one in Aberdeen in the football stadium there. It was an amazing opportunity, and then I did some other shows for him around the UK and now we're here in South America. After the first album came out, whenever Elton did interviews he would say really positive things and that of course helped me enormously.'

But where is The Master? I thought it was going to be pretty cool, this leg of the world tour, me reminiscing away with Elton and all, him being my age. 'Hey, Peter, you remember when "Rocket Man" was first released?' Sure, I do.

Our paths have crossed on only one previous occasion.

It was March 1976 and we both by chance had rooms on the same floor of the old Hilton Hotel in Sydney. Elton was there, I guess, to give a concert. I was there with Lord Snowdon who, when he wasn't playing royalty, was a down-to-earth, friendly photographer on the *Sunday Times*. His marriage to Princess Margaret had just ended.

Anyway, Elton and I briefly shared the same hotel corridor, which seemed strangely populated at all hours of the day and night by most of the young male population of what is now Sydney's Oxford Street neighbourhood. One evening as I was going into my room, one of his minders asked me and my photographer to a party.

'We can't come,' I told him, 'we've got Lord Snowdon with us.'

'Tony? Great! Bring him along as well.' We didn't, for which the Kensington Palace PR machine should probably thank me in retrospect. Publicity over Tony and the royal split was already at its scandalous peak – without bringing young Elton into the picture.

It's been a normal sort of journey to South America – two of the guitars and the suitcase belonging to Jonny, one of the key technicians, are missing and, like the corpse at an Irish wake, we're still carrying around the shattered keyboard from Barbados.

'Tonight,' says Blunty to the band and me when finally we reach our glass and steel hotel in the heart of grid-locked downtown, 'we're invited to a *very* smart private party. It's going to be deeply flashy and therefore possibly about as shallow as you can get. So dress up in your finest gear.'

Dress up? Examining the poor selection of crumpled

clothing spewing out of my suitcase and onto the bed, I do my best. While travelling around the world on a daily basis, the mundane business of laundry is a never-ending problem. The stickier the climate, the less chance there is of shirts, boxers and socks drying overnight in hotel bathrooms or on balconies. You end up carrying around bin bags of damp clothing. Bobble weaves washer-woman magic for James and the band. I imagine that a condition of him paying the enormous corporate hotel bill in each port of call is that a small army of local laundresses slave throughout the night. But that's only for the band. The rest of us must cater for ourselves as best we can. The secret is to carry as few raw materials as possible. That way, there's less to get dirty.

When we assemble in the bar before dinner, the band and I have all managed to turn out in black rather than blue jeans and shirts, which I guess is the first rung on the ladder to 'smart'. I've even succeeded in ironing my shirt, while the same cannot be said for Benny who has clearly opted out of the last executive laundry run. We order drinks and then Tash arrives looking a billion *reales* – that's the currency here – in a sleek, body-hugging designer dress and killer heels.

Finally the boss puts in a late appearance. Blunty? Blunty's wearing his oldest, most faded jeans and an equally tired T-shirt. His cowboy boots are so hopelessly scuffed you would think he'd just broken in a wild mustang in them. I guess he can afford to make statements like that. I guess when you get to be a high 'n' mighty world-class star with platinum celebrity status, you can wear what you like and say what you like about anyone, even your mates. Everyone expects it of you. Well, that's what you might think. But the fact is that Blunty simply doesn't care about clothes and has total disdain for dress convention. He wore jeans to have tea with the Queen.

I guess it must be difficult living up to other people's expectations. It's hard enough living up to your own. But you have all those people out there hunched in front of their laptops in a feeding frenzy off the World Wide Web noting what you are wearing and hanging on every word you say as gospel. Relative truth is just a bit scary. I remember once in a radio interview in Florida he was asked: 'James, what's the most romantic thing you've ever done?' Without hesitation, he replied: 'I hired a helicopter and dropped 100,000 red roses on my girlfriend's house, picked her up and took her to Paris for the evening.'

Headlines zoomed around the world: 'Roses are Red – and "You're Beautiful", says Blunt'. Complete and utter bullshit, of course. Can you imagine what it would have cost? And, anyway, the weight of them would probably smash the roof.

'James!' gushes our glamorous thirtysomething hostess, putting a proprietorial arm around him after we make our way at midnight through a barrage of photographers to the front door of a magnificent house in the smartest residential quarter of the city. 'So wonderful that you could make it!'

The rest of us are not, obviously, included in the greeting. Tash looks tigerishly uncomfortable at the way in which her role as official companion is being instantly and openly usurped. She wants to leave immediately.

The room into which we are shown is quite

extraordinarily large. It's made up of two giant sitting rooms with enormous white armchairs and sofas. In the middle, between them, there's a full-length pool which is open to the sky. Both halves are packed with sleekly groomed players of the calibre you find in Monaco or at an international polo match.

São Paulo is the largest financial centre in Latin America and these are the people who live and work in it. Now they are at play. It's been said that if São Paulo were a country it would rank among the richest in the world, ahead of both Abu Dhabi and Hong Kong. The harsh poverty that tugs from its suburban shanty towns is not invited tonight. An army of liveried waiters dispense champagne and vodka.

'We'll just stay a short while,' says Blunty, back with a mollified Tash. But actually, now that we've settled in, we stay for much of the night. None of the locals seems interested in talking to us, not even to Blunty. But, as always, we're really quite content with our own company. Karl jousts with a few pretty girls, but doesn't seem to be able to give his full attention to the usual bed quest, probably because it all gets a bit blurry. At one stage a group of 30 diminutive miners in silver overalls and wearing head-torches dance and sing what I suppose are Inca-esque folk songs on the far side of the pool from where we were standing. Tash is looking at Blunty as if she's prepared to be eaten any time now as part of a human sacrifice to appease the gods of touring.

Miners? How do I know they are miners? They could easily be Oompa Loompas straight from the pages of

Roald Dahl's *Charlie and the Chocolate Factory* shuffling symbolically away on the far side of the chocolate river.

'It seems somehow entirely wrong,' says Johnny, picking up another vodka in a cut crystal glass off a silver tray, 'to leave all these fine people to drink all this free booze on their own.' So we don't.

It's 3am, but outside the palatial front door the photographers are still gathered in force, awaiting James' departure. He's used to this and has various ploys for making a clean getaway. Once in LA the getaway was not so clean. He was driving and a paparazzo falsely accused him of running over his foot.

'You go out first, Peter,' he says, 'and start taking pictures of the paps while we follow and make a dash for the car.'

The cunning ruse works well. I open the front door, half close it behind me, and start firing off my flashgun at the assembled crowd. Momentarily they are bemused at having the tables turned on them in such a way and are stunned by the sudden burst of light. Before they can recover, Blunty and band are in the people carrier and speeding off down the street. But what about me? Am I left to be torn limb from limb by frustrated wolves who've just had the financial kill of the night ripped from their jaws?

'For God's sake, Peter, come on!' shouts Blunty from the moving car while holding open the door. I need no further encouragement and scamper aboard with the pack hot on my heels. There's a squeal of rubber as the driver makes good the getaway. He's seen all the movies.

'Nicely done,' says Blunty, 'but next time try running a bit faster, Peter.'

'The golden rule of touring in South America,' says Bobble at the sound check the following day, 'is that as soon as you've got the stage fully rigged and the sound equipment sorted, the heavens open and it pisses down.' Angry clouds are gathering overhead and he's bobble-wrapped in anticipation in a see-through plastic mac that makes him look like the wolf in *Little Red Riding Hood* in sort of airport X-ray grandma mode.

On cue, a brilliant fork of lightning stabs the sky directly overhead and raindrops the size and weight of snooker balls drop from it with rapidly increasing intensity. The two rigging crews – James' and Elton's – make a grab for sheets of black plastic tarpaulin and try to cover the mikes, amps and James' upright piano at the exposed front of the stage. For our crew, that's the disadvantage of being the first act on stage.

Further back, Elton's mighty grand Yamaha is already under the covers. The giant stadium is awash. Water streams off the long cordon of security guards lining the pit. However, quite what they are doing here already is frankly a bit of a mystery. There are still a couple of hours to go to the concert and the stands and seats are entirely empty except for a fleet of workmen who are now virtually swimming for cover.

But in this tropical land where rhythm rules, rain – for at least part of each day for some of the year – is a normal event. You don't let it get in the way. The sound check goes ahead before a soaked but fascinated audience of workmen, caterers and security. I watch two police-women dancing languorously to *Give Me Some Love*, while a guy in a white hard hat takes two hammers from the tool-kit belt strapped around his waist and bangs out the beat on the crush barrier he is supposed to be assembling.

Later, when James is hanging out as usual at this time of day in his dressing-room with its sumptuously tented walls, I sneak a peek around Elton's door. His room is even more magnificent, but that's nothing compared to the entire separate room that houses his flamboyant stage wardrobe. Row upon row of outfits hang on rails and tables are piled high with sunglasses, earrings, and all the other outrageous accessories we've come to expect of Elton down the decades. The whole mobile department store is managed by two personal dressers.

But where's Elton?

He's nowhere to be seen. In my naivety I thought he'd be the central figure of the tour, another person who we would laugh and joke away with during the long hours between performances. Instead, we share our backstage area with four of the great musicians of my lifetime. Elton has brought along members of his original tour band from the 1970s and I find this makes my life much easier. For the first time in a year on the road, no one dreams of asking me who I am. If he's that old, he must be an authentic, wrinkly part of Elton's entourage.

The eternally youthful figure of lead guitarist Davey Johnstone, still with his trademark chest-length 'blond' hair, is 58. Nigel Olsson, one of the legendary drummers of all time, is just coming up to the 60 mark. At 53, Guy Babylon, keyboard, and Bob Birch, bass guitar, are mere youngsters. Tragically, and none of us of course know it at the time, this is to be Guy's final tour with Elton. He died suddenly six months later from a heart attack while swimming in his pool in California.

The rain has stopped and 45,000 hugely excited people have now crowded into the Arena Skol Anhembi stadium to see James and Elton perform. The buzz of anticipation is as big behind the scenes as it is in the audience. No one knows quite what to expect. An army of security men and blue-suited emergency teams take up strategic positions along the pit and in the crowd jammed up against the crush barriers beneath the giant stage.

I knew James had a passionate following throughout Latin America, but just how big he is in Brazil becomes apparent the moment he steps on stage. The crowd goes wild and surges against the barriers. I'm standing in the pit and the grim-faced guy in charge of the mean-looking line of muscle staring out at the crowd nods to me with respect. I nod back.

'We don't do trouble,' he says into my ear. 'If anyone tries to get on the stage we deal with him immediately and in our way.' I believe him. I worry a bit about the 'immediately' and more about the 'our way'. He prowls around his men with the menace and grace of a jaguar in the Amazon jungle. He looks as if his former career before civilian crowd control was in special forces. I ask him. It was.

The reason why I'm in his territory and he hasn't already eaten me for supper is that just before the show begins I'm talking to Blunty when Mark, his show manager, brings the guy over.

'I thought it wise to introduce you, just to avoid any mis-understandings in the heat of the moment,' Mark tells me. Mark always thinks of my safety as I move about taking pictures during the show. In other countries I've occasionally been pushed, manhandled, and even briefly ejected when overzealous security have failed to heed my 'all areas' pass.

'This is Peter,' he explains to the security chief, 'he's to go anywhere any time he wants. When you move the local photographers out of the pit at the end of the second number, Peter stays. Please explain this to all your men.'

The guy slowly nods – he's got the nod down to an art form. This time it says: 'So, Mr Peter is special, but I don't know why. Who is he really? He's too old to be a pop photographer. The camera he's carrying is obviously a prop.'

Blunty promptly provides the answer for this unspoken question. 'Peter's in charge of my personal security,' he says, with a straight face. The man looks me up and down appraisingly and nods again. Clearly he finds me wanting.

Bruno, our own very charming and athletic-looking real head of security, the man who is quietly responsible for the safety of James and the rest of us during our stay in Brazil, looks tremendously put out by this. When we're on our own, I explain James' sense of humour.

'That's great,' he roars with laughter and slaps me on the back, 'I get it. You're too old and clearly far too unfit to guard anybody! You're the man most unlikely to really have my job, right?'

Well, I suppose, yes, sort of right – you can see, Bruno, that I find this unflattering description of me to be an absolute giggle, right? Annoyingly he can't stop chuckling. Blunty, sometime, you wait, I'll get my own back.

I'm crouching with Tash in the pit looking up at the

stage with James in full spate being worshipped by a crowd that wants to consume him.

'James Blunt: I cured my cancer by listening to your songs,' says the poster held by a man and a woman in the front row. Which one? The woman, I guess. Well, that's a new one. I'll suggest that, when we get to Copacabana, Blunty takes a fresh approach to the band's now favourite sport of wave-jumping and tries his hand at walking on water.

But where is Elton? James' set is almost over and there's no sign of The Master. I make my way backstage. There he is, standing in the wings talking to his veteran, blustery, but likeable stage manager Dennis McManus – likeable to me not least because he's my contemporary. Each evening, just before Elton's performance, he 'sweeps' the wings and backstage of unauthorized venue staff and assorted friends of promoters who've managed to acquire backstage passes but have no working reason to clutter up the space needed by the sound and lighting technicians.

'Off you go, you don't belong here,' he says gruffly, giving a helping hand to anyone who doesn't immediately respond – you need a knowledge of American English to understand him.

'And you, and you.' Then to me, 'I know you, you're OK, just stay out of the way.'

His advancing age and authoritative manner, honed over 25 years of running Elton's stage, makes him the butt of some light-hearted ribbing from a few of the musicians and crew.

'Hey Elvis!' I hear one technician call to him one day in Chile. 'What do you want me to do about . . .'

'MR Elvis, to you, c**t!' comes his razor-sharp response.

His job, as he says, is to make sure the equipment is set up right for the start of the show, making sure that Elton's happy when he's on stage – and, when he comes off stage, making sure that he still feels happy about how everything worked.

I've only ever seen Elton perform once previously. He was giving an outdoor solo recital at Highclere Castle in Hampshire, home of the Earl of Carnarvon. It was a damp and chilly evening in the windswept castle grounds. For us listeners it was a rare privilege to hear a legend at play, but for Elton I imagine it was a routine performance that barely made an impression on the carpet of his long career.

But tonight in Brazil, before an audience of nearly 45,000, The Master clearly feels some of the old rush that has driven him along the yellow brick road for 40 years. Although, I understand, he is deeply affected by the poverty he sees in South America and keeps to himself throughout much of the tour.

He's much smaller than I remember him and of considerably greater girth. In fact, walking up the amp ramp to the stage in his voluminous frock coat he looks like the popular image of Henry VIII in his later years – a portly king, but one with dangly diamond earrings.

While James' set lasts 75 minutes – 15 short of the length of his normal concerts – Elton's is to last an extraordinary two and a half hours, which is phenomenally hard work for his voice. In the heat, the crush at the front of the crowd is frightening. Once you're in position there's no way out until the end of the show. I pity the cancer victim and others packed behind the crush barrier.

Rio de Janeiro

The brooding rain clouds have disappeared and Rio is looking just as magnificent as I remember it. I was last here in the 1980s and, at first glance, not a lot has changed. The seafront is still dominated by low-rise 1960s buildings, but glass and steel blocks have added substance to the skyline. A smattering of old colonial homes and offices cling on to the changing fabric of the city in the streets leading back up towards the *favelas* at the top of the hills. These shanty towns, with an apparently ever-cheerful population living in what amount to little more than human dog kennels, made at best from raw concrete and at worst from packing cases and sheets of corrugated iron, look just as fascinating and forbidding as ever. In Brazil the cost of living is rising, but the hotel-lined beaches (well, most of them) are still free.

It's Sunday and the people in their thousands are at play on the sands that border the bay. Beach football, soon to be outlawed, is everywhere. A thousand barefoot baby Ronaldos and Ronaldhinos bend it barefoot, their brown bodies glistening in the midday tropical heat. On Copacabana and Ipanema the girls glisten, too, naked except for thongs and thimbles of fabric. To be a Brazilienne you can see why you need a Brazilian.

Sugarloaf Mountain and El Cristo, the 40-metre statue of Christ the Redeemer, looks benevolently down on this essentially erotic city from the summit of Corcovado. Blunty, Tash and her friend Naughty Nicola – who's just joined us and is coming along for the Brazilian ride – look utterly enchanted by it. At the traffic lights we come across a mono-cyclist who is managing to juggle and skip at the same time. I guess if you're not a visiting rock star you've got to earn a living somehow around here – or maybe he's already in training for a new exhibition sport at the 2016 Summer Olympics.

Our hotel's on the beach and some 45 of Elton's people have already checked in. Elton's booked the presidential suite, but as usual The Master himself is nowhere to be seen. The booking's just a back-up in case he needs a rest.

The two crews are already hard at work preparing for the big concert at Praça da Apoteosa, the quite enormous stadium used for Rio's annual carnival. Tiers of seats on either side stretch back 500 metres from the stage. The sound system is so amped that you must be able to hear the performance all over the city.

Some 40,000 people fill the front half and never have you seen a bigger contrast between rich and poor. Those with money and power don't pay anything at all as they sip cocktails in the Bank of Brazil's air-conditioned, covered hospitality area. Just occasionally they take a peek at the performance. The rest pay just a dollar or two – or manage to sneak in for free – and then jostle for a postage stamp glimpse of the stage from the top tiers of the stadium. The atmosphere is quite extraordinary. Here, once again, James gets a huge welcome and 'Carry You Home' has the whole packed stadium in its thrall.

'James Blunt is one of the most powerful performers

we've ever seen,' says Davey, Elton's guitarist. 'The crowd love him and it's a hard act for us to follow.'

The story behind 'Carry You Home' gives some considerable insight into how Blunty goes about composing.

'It all came out of a funny writing session in Stockholm with Max Martin, who is very famous. He wrote "Baby One More Time" for Britney Spears and songs for Pink and Avril Lavigne. He called me up and said, "I have an idea for you." I flew over to Sweden for a three-day writing session and he sang it to me.

'It went like this:

Tell me I'm wrong, tell me I'm right,
Baby I'll love you into the night.

'That was kind of it. I was thinking to myself: "Wow, shit me! Whatever we write, the label will put it on the album, no matter how bad, because it's Max Martin."

'We were reduced to just staring at each other in silence. After two and a half hours of almost complete silence, I felt like I was dying. Eventually it just felt like, oh – *I'm watching you breathing, for the last time.* And that was enough to trigger the song.'

An hour before his entrance, Elton arrives in a giant motorcade from the airport. It turns out that he's staying on a private estate somewhere miles away near Porto Alegre and flies into each gig – no matter in which country or the huge distances involved – and then immediately back again. He's got the top suite booked in each hotel that we stay in but he rarely uses it. In South America he's got a bigger status than any president and a police escort for his motorcade before and after each concert.

Tonight I stand in the wings less than five feet from Elton and his gold-wheeled Yahama grand as he plays 'Candle In The Wind'. I feel the need to pinch myself that this is really happening. The atmosphere created by the enormous crowd that has already been psyched to the point of hysteria by Blunty is overwhelming. The music – all two and a half hours of it – is clearly ingrained on his psyche, but not all the words – guess it's a lot to remember. I'm surprised to discover that, discreetly hidden out of sight from the audience, the lyrics are all written down on a rolling teleprompt of the kind used by TV news presenters. I'm gently but firmly dissuaded from the idea of reprogramming it for him.

'Do you think James and everybody would like to take a trip out to my house in the rainforest tomorrow?' says a young Brazilian guy who I get talking to at the after-show.

'I don't know,' I say with measured discretion as I hand him a beer, 'but it's a day off and everyone's pretty tired so I imagine they'll want to sleep late.'

'Oh, I meant in the afternoon. I could send some helicopters for you. Nothing formal, just a barbecue around the pool with a few friends.'

Did he say 'some helicopters'? He did. Who *is* this guy?

'He's the richest man in the region. The house is very famous for its tropical gardens . . . the most famous gardens in the country.' Bruno, our bodyguard, fills me in.

'Yes,' says James without a moment's hesitation, when I tell him. I like a man who is decisive.

Naughty Nicola apart, we've now got other camp followers. Firstly, there's Roman, a Blunty Tour regular who is actually from Argentina but lives in Ibiza. He does the PR for Pacha, and has become a valuable friend. Before Roman, Blunty was just another visiting star to the island. Now the club owners understand what a huge business asset he is and give him top celebrity status.

Tonight Roman is organizing the after-show party in a five-star hotel along the beach. He's managed to get lots of beautiful people – we've absolutely no idea who they are – into this really smart bar and the booze seems to flow endlessly, along with the fun.

'Who's paying for all this?' I ask Beardy, accepting another vodka and cranberry from a passing waitress.

'Don't ask,' he replies, 'Roman is a complete mystery.'

Johnny is chatting to two beautiful Scandinavian girls who Roman picked up in the hotel and invited. Clearly Johnny likes chatting to Scandinavian girls because when he's off stage he's rarely off Skype, talking to his permanent and lovely Danish girlfriend.

But even Johnny can't resist the visual delights of Rio. I guess you can look in the cake-shop window, but you don't have to eat the cakes.

'I'm from Sweden, but now I live in Copenhagen,' says the prettier of the two, smiling eyes at Johnny.

'Oh, my girlfriend is from Copenhagen,' says Johnny.

'Really? Where does she live?'

'If you walk up B***** Street and take the second on the left,' says Johnny.

'Not Pernille?' she says, disbelievingly.

'You know Pernille?' he says, also disbelievingly.

290

At the moment when, 4,650 miles away in Washington, Barack Obama is being sworn in as the 44th president of the United States, James and I are swimming in a natural pool in a pleasantly cool stream in the Brazilian rainforest just ten miles outside Rio.

'It doesn't actually get much cooler than this,' he says, glancing around at the sumptuous but low-key villa behind us. The acres of surrounding gardens have been sculpted out of raw rainforest by Robert Burle Marx, the twentieth-century Capability Brown of the Brazilian tropics. The profusion of orchids and other rare plants, trees, lawns and walkways fill an oasis of light cut into the jungle that is fed by the stream in which we bathe. You get the feeling that if the team of gardeners who tend the grounds left for only a few weeks this whole perfumed foothold on nature would simply disappear as the canopy of the rainforest closed overhead once again.

On the terrace, uniformed chefs prepare a barbecue while a helicopter makes a calculated landing on a lawn within a couple of metres of a stand of palm trees. James and some of the band and crew get an airborne tour of Sugarloaf, El Cristo and the whole dramatic skyline of Rio.

The scenery closer to home around the pool is equally magnificent – tanned, wave-toned skin and micro-bikinis contrast startlingly with the white bulbous flesh of Bobble, the band and, of course, me. Only James, Tash and Naughty Nicola blend seamlessly into these glorious corporeal surroundings. The starting-to-slim Bobble still looks, for all the world, like some albino hippo basking in a water hole . . . except I'm pretty sure they don't have hippos in Brazil. But everyone's glad, for once, to get away from the endless rhythm of hotel room and dressing-room and tune into the heartbeat of real Brazilians. Karl is, of course, taking this quite literally and getting to know the prettiest.

One of the party-goers invites Nicola to take a tour of the one-storey villa that is carved in sustainable local hardwoods and covered in rich fabrics all cut from the pages of the glossiest lifestyle magazine. The tour ends in the jungle of the master bedroom where the guy drops his Speedos and pounces on Naughty Nicola, demure but, as always, knickerless beneath her cotton summer dress.

'Oh, no, I don't think so,' she says, casually fending him off and dancing free. 'Not the time, not the place.' Nicola's so multi-faceted she could get a job in any circus – big cat tamer, bare-back rider and clown all rolled into one.

Back in town the beat gets better. We're sitting inside a bar by an open window with a group of new friends, at least one of whom is a survivor from the party in the rainforest.

When we arrive at 10pm the pub, far from the tourist areas, is completely deserted.

'Let's go somewhere else and find some action,' says Benny.

'Let's have a drink here first,' says the girl who brought us here. 'People will come, you'll see.'

Very soon, we can hardly see at all. The trouble with caipirinha, Brazil's signature cocktail, is that it's innocuously smooth and has a kick like Ronaldo. Cachaça, its main ingredient, is an alcohol distilled from sugar cane juice and traditionally the drink of the poor. If you've ever had the misfortune to try your hand at harvesting a sugar-cane plantation with a machete – I did once for about 15 minutes – you need a strong drink just to quell your fear of the snakes that writhe away from the line of flashing blades. Teetotal farmhands should head for Mauritius where they have similar sugar cane, but no snakes.

Caipirinha means 'little hillbilly' and after the first half dozen Beardy and Johnny look set to play the banjo duel in *Deliverance*. I try to decide which one is the redneck and which is the inbred savant. But, like I said, I can't see straight myself.

The bar's now bursting with young Brazilians and the wild beat of samba fills the dance floor.

Karl, who has already pulled our interpreter, now performs the balcony scene from *Romeo and Juliet* – in reverse. He's sitting by the open window of the pub looking out on to the street.

The brunette joins us at the table just as seconds are out for the next round of the how-many-can-you-drink caipirinha contest.

'Hi, I'm Francesca,' she introduces herself, squeezing with difficulty into a chair beside him. Karl gives her a helping hand by putting his arm around her.

'Hi, Francesca, my name's Karl. Karl Brazil,' he replies.

'You're kidding, right?' she looks incredulous. The interpreter looks furious.

'Karl Brazil? What a tosser!' she thinks. 'Still, he does look quite fit, he's got a nice smile, and unlike his friends he's not completely rat-arsed. Anyway, *What's in a name? That which we call a rose, by any other name would smell as sweet.*'

'No, really,' he says, digging into his pocket and producing his Barclaycard as proof. 'Let's have a dance, love.' It's a crying shame that Shakespeare never came up with lines like Karl's.

Being called Brazil while travelling in South America can cause confusion. Later, when we are staying in Buenos Aires, Beardy rings down to reception from his room and says: 'Can you put me through to Karl Brazil, please?'

There's a pause from the receptionist and then she replies: 'You want me to *call* Brazil for you?'

But by Round Eight of the caipirinhas the girl interpreter has rallied and is fighting her corner against the brunette with a series of sharp verbal jabs that are slap on target. Karl looks a bit confused.

'Which one, Uncle Peter?' he whispers.

'Both?' I mumble incoherently. If I'm in a state, Johnny is much worse. Benny's disappeared and Beardy is just warming up on the dance floor with new-found friends-for-life.

I stick my head out of the window.

Night's candles are burnt out, and jocund day
Stands tiptoe on the misty mountain tops.
I must be gone and live, or stay and die.

Time to get the hell out of here and stop quoting Shakespeare. Johnny and I roll into a taxi and somehow manage to remember the name of our hotel.

Buenos Aires

'Don't look around you now, James. But I think we're in a brothel. Well, actually, I know we're in a brothel,' I tell him. Karl and the rest of the band look up from their beers and glance around them. It's 6pm on a sunny weekday afternoon slap in the centre of Buenos Aires. The bar was virtually empty when we arrived. But now every table is taken with girls – and judging by the make-up and the clothes, they're not office workers on their way home. The atmosphere's pretty relaxed. The girls are passing time doing their nails and talking to each other in low voices. I suspect it's the sort of place where middle-aged businessmen drop in on their way home for a bit of *cinco a siete* nooky before settling down to a giant T-bone steak and chips with the wife.

James and the band, not necessarily myself, attract a few admiring glances, but otherwise the girls keep pleasantly to themselves. No hard sales technique here. It's more *Belle de Jour* than the railway arches at King's Cross.

'How,' says James, putting his elbows on the table and looking across at me, 'do you know we're in a brothel, Peter?'

'Well, for a couple of reasons, James. Firstly, it may be perfectly normal for you to be in a room jammed with admiring girls and no men at all because they've come to see you sing. It's fairly safe to assume that this is not the case here.

'Therefore I'm working on the idea that they think you've – we've – come to see them. Karl, judging by that boy-in-the-sweetie-shop look on your face, you like what you're seeing.'

'And the second reason?' asks James.

'Oh, I had a job in a brothel once,' I say, chucking a brick in the pond. The guffaws of laughter turn all eyes in the room towards us.

'Bet you didn't get many takers,' says Benny amid more hoots.

'It wasn't that kind of a job,' I explain. When I was 18 and bumming around the world I worked for a week or two as a doorman at a dirty little joint in Panama City. Prostitution is sort of legal in Panama, but this brothel was unlicensed. My job, in exchange for free board, was to keep an eye out for the cops. If they raided, I was to lock the heavy iron grill that serves as a front door and do a runner out the back along with the girls and customers. Fortunately, that never happened.

'And did you get freebies?' asks Johnny, cutting straight to the point.

'No, but I got free laundry.' One night, I got up to pee at about 4am and the corridor outside my room was as crowded as Oxford Street on the last Saturday before Christmas. Girls and their clients were coming and going at a rate of knots. The best ones could turn a trick in less than five minutes – and hook twice in 15 minutes on a busy night when lots of ships were in port.

As I headed sleepily for the loo I met the girl who lived and worked in the next-door room to me coming the other way. Maria was from Costa Rica and couldn't have been more than 20, but back home in San Juan she had a six-year-old daughter and her parents to support. Her body, she said, was the only way open to her.

'Peter, I forgot to tell you earlier,' she said to me in Spanish. 'I've washed your jeans and shirts – *and* I've ironed them.'

'You didn't have to iron them. But thanks anyway,' I replied. At that moment a hand that weighed about the same as the anchor of a Royal Navy Type 42 destroyer landed on my shoulder and I found myself staring into the bloodshot eyes of a sailor. How did I know he was a sailor? He was wearing a sailor's cap that said HMS *Fornication*, or somesuch.

''ere!' he said, in a strong Liverpool accent. 'What d'you think you're doing chattin' up me girl?' Fights, sometimes vicious ones, were commonplace in the brothel and I was suddenly fully awake.

'Sorry, mate,' I said, trying to calm him down. 'I wasn't trying to chat her up. I live here, see.'

'Blimey,' he said, trying to focus through drunken eyes on the sweating, paint-flaking walls and dirty bare boards of the floor. 'You live here? Fuckin' paradise!'

The anchor was removed and then swung with full strength across my back in a gesture of comradeship. Maria tugged him by the arm and he wandered off down the corridor, shaking his head at how the dice of life had rolled in my favour rather than in his.

As a penance for bringing us here, I pick up the beer tab. Judging by the telephone number prices, it most certainly is a brothel. We make our excuses and leave.

Yes, I suppose like other cities on this leg of the tour,

four decades have eased by since I was last in Argentina. Madonna has since become Eva Peron. Together we've sunk the *Sheffield* and the *Belgrano*, and Maradona's made us all as sick as a parrot with his Hand of God. As I walk the streets of BA I keep getting flashbacks – a building, a bar, a girl. It's all so weird. Of course, the reality is that the building's been torn down, the bar's closed, and the girl's now a toothless granny.

Las Nazarenas, one of the most famous restaurants in a city famous for its beef, seems the sensible choice. The head waiter is thrilled – he's a big fan along with his staff and asks for a photo for the restaurant wall, which is happily given. He's at least as old as I am, so I ask him how long the restaurant's been here. '28 years,' he tells me proudly. Only 28! Shit, I thought I recognized it.

The restaurant has the most amazing steaks, so tender that you can cut the meat with a fork. In the knowledge that it will be enormous, I order the smallest option. Beardy, who can never really resist this sort of thing, goes for the full cow. Unlike Desperate Dan, he can't even begin to eat it all.

I've rarely seen James so relaxed. Clearly he and Tash are having fun. After dinner they go off together and the rest of us head for Kilkenny's, an 'Irish' bar that is a long way from south-east Ireland. It's late, but there's a live band with two girl singers. Karl and Johnny seem mesmerized. I can't make out if it's the alcohol consumed, the girls, the music – or a combination of all three.

'We want to play,' says Johnny. 'Go sort it, Peter,' says Karl. Oh well, makes a change from handing out Golden Tickets, I guess. Normally in Buenos Aires, I learn later, it's seriously uncool for visiting musicians – even famous ones – to ask to do this. But at the Kilkenny, apparently, anything goes.

'Sure,' says the band leader. 'We've got 15 minutes left before 2am when our music licence runs out. Go for it.'

Go, they do. The two girls seem utterly unfazed by finding themselves singing with two world-class musicians and launch into an entirely novel version of 'Long Tall Sally'. Karl and Johnny, not to mention everyone else in the crowded bar, love every moment of it.

'Would James have done that if he'd been here?' I ask Johnny.

'He'd have been the first guy to ask. There's nothing he likes more than the impromptu gig.' By now the entire resident band – and in particular the girl singers – are our lifelong friends. We hand them all tickets for the gig tomorrow night and somehow find our way home.

Maradona poses happily with Johnny for a picture. This comes as no surprise as the owner of the infamous Mano de Dios is a silent dummy statue in one of the horde of supporters' shops that surround the giant stadium that is home to Boca Juniors, one of BA's most famous football teams. Forget Chelsea, Liverpool and Manchester United – this is the home of impassioned football fanaticism.

Elton has just arrived and makes a surprise appearance by putting his head around our dressing-room door when James is absent. There's just me there, along with Tash and Naughty Nicola.

'Hi,' says The Master, casually. 'James about?'

'Hi,' says Nicola, jumping up and flashing freshly exposed flesh at him. Save your energy, Nicola.

'Hi, Elton,' I say. 'I think he's just gone to Catering.' Did I just speak to Elton John? Yeah, I did – but the door had already closed behind him by the time I replied. It's frustrating, but he's not becoming the close pal of my dreams.

Nigel Olsson is much more forthcoming. For a guy who has spent around three years of his life over four decades on stage with Elton he looks incredibly nervous in the two hours before he goes on, massaging and re-massaging fingers that clearly are beginning to feel wear and tear. With Elton, says his band, you've got to get it right – always – on the night. He doesn't do error. If you err you get a mouthful. Err twice and you're out.

Nigel looks just as nervous as if it was his first gig. 'How many gigs have you played?' I ask him. He looks at me in a puzzled sort of way, as if it was a question he had never before even considered.

'I've no idea, Peter, the first was back in 1969.'

1969? No one in our dressing-room – apart from me, of course – was even born then. That was the year I saw Janis for the last time in London. Heroin had taken hold and I hardly recognized her. I guess I, too, must have looked very different to her. We met on the corner of Waterloo Bridge just down the Strand from the Savoy.

'You got yourself a real job, a haircut and a suit,' she said, fingering my tie and touching my cheek with her hand.

'For me? For me, it's just the same old fuckin' day, man.' I never saw her again. She died from a drug overdose the following year.

Nigel and I have fared an awful lot better down the years. But imagine being that nervous before you go on stage – almost every night for 40 years! Sir Laurence Olivier suffered so badly from stage fright that at times during the final years of his performing life he had to be pushed on stage. James doesn't have that problem. Being a celeb is never a buffer from these afflictions of the workplace. Lord Nelson was arguably Britain's first pop star. He pulled capacity crowds and beautiful women wherever he went – and our greatest sailor suffered from chronic seasickness all his life. Supposedly, he chundered on the morning of the Battle of Trafalgar. Mind you, can't say I blame him. I'd have done the same, especially if I'd known how the day would end.

Tonight Nigel's wearing a bright yellow silk stage shirt that clashes vividly with his orange suntan, which looks like it just might owe more to a bottle than to the California sunshine of home. And later, when he's settled at his drum kit and Elton has taken his seat at his piano, The Master leans across and says: 'Christ, Nigel, what are you wearing? You look like a bleedin' M&M.'

Santiago

She's *very* pretty, with long legs, a short skirt, and the kind of face you might find on the cover of *Vogue*. In fact, she has top fashion model written all over her . . . along with stalker.

'Hi,' she says, with the kind of warmth that could easily melt a heart as hard as mine has become. 'I'm a friend of James. He said to come on up, but I've forgotten the room number.'

We were standing at the time by the lifts in the lobby of our hotel in São Paulo. I'm just about to answer her when Karl speaks first:

'Didn't he tell you that there's been a change of plan? Too many groupies. James isn't staying here – you'll find him over at the Intercontinental in suite 901.' She clacks off on her heels, giving us a little wave as she heads for the revolving door.

'Put the water on for the bunny, please,' says Karl, as the elevator door closes and we head on up to James' room.

I'd never have known, but I'm learning. No one who'd really been invited would ever forget James' suite number. Since then I've seen her hanging around the stage door in Buenos Aires, and now here she is again in Chile. As James' new-found head of security the least I can do is not invite potential murderesses into his dressing-room or bedroom. Trouble is, they're not always easy to spot.

Just because they're pretty doesn't mean they're safe or sane. As I've discovered, get talking to this one and she makes no sense at all.

The gig's in the giant and modern Movistar Arena. I thought we'd be at the National Stadium of Chile, which was used as a notorious concentration camp during the 1973 coup d'état when the infamous General Pinochet deposed Allende. Maggie's pal Pinochet had some particularly nasty torture techniques for the mass intimidation of his political opponents. These included rape with animals, welding torches, boiling oil, and pulling out fingernails with pliers. Chile's had a roller-coaster history in recent decades.

Just then James' friendly Chilean promoter comes up to me.

'See that girl over there, Peter,' he says, indicating Ms Stalker. 'She very nice, isn't she? Good-looking girl, and she's James' No. 1 fan in all of South America. We should give her a Golden Ticket to the after-show tonight, no?'

'I'll tell you what, Alfonso,' I say. 'You go over and talk to her for 30 seconds and then come back and tell me she's as nice as you think, and then I'll give her a ticket.'

He comes back to me, shaking his head: 'OK, so maybe we don't take her backstage.'

Chile's fun, but James is in a dark mood and there's little to distract him. We've left Tash, Naughty Nicola and other friends of his back in Brazil. Life's one great goodbye and sometimes it can get even him down. There's a plus side to these moods – when he gets these particular blues he's at his most creative, spending hours at his piano or his laptop with headphones on.

It's as if he's restlessly searching for something or someone who isn't here . . . When I ask him about it he doesn't give a straight answer.

'I was just thinking,' he says, taking off his headphones and looking startlingly young, a little-boy-lost look.

'What were you thinking about?' I dare ask.

'Someone,' comes the non-committal reply. Then he firmly puts on his headphones again as if to shut the whole world out of his very private thoughts about some 'someone', whoever that person may be.

I'm not sure he knows who or what he wants. I know what I want – a month at home with my wife. I'm not sure James has a home. He has a lovely house in Ibiza, but home is much more than bricks and mortar. Sometimes I think there is no relief for him from the words and the music going around and around in his mind and the women circling his body. The more I know of his life, the less I envy it. Mind you, I wouldn't mind a bit of the dosh.

Santiago lacks the raw energy of Rio and BA, but the mild Mediterranean climate gives the city a holiday atmosphere. When James and the band arrive at the stadium they're given the most enormous and sumptuous dressing-room, but quickly realize that this is for Elton, not for them. Instead, we're relegated to two small rooms that have a latrine-like smell to them. Magically, Bobble manages to conjure up a couple of scented candles and Catering is a real restaurant with tablecloths, place settings and excellent food.

The show is a riot, much the wildest and most enthusiastic audience so far, making James a very hard act indeed for Elton to follow.

Guy Babylon tells me: 'James is probably one of the best and definitely the most professional act we've ever worked with in all the years. I can see why Elton is such a big fan.'

The Master himself, too, congratulates James as he comes off stage and I summon up the courage to ask Elton for a picture of him and Blunty together.

'Don't, it's not cool,' whispers James. But I guess if I'm his head of security, I can sometimes overrule his wishes.

'Sure, go ahead,' Elton says. Give me an inch. I push the whole band into a second picture with Benny pulled fresh from the shower and wearing only a towel.

In all the excitement, I've accidentally asked two hardened Australian groupies backstage along with two good-looking Chilean girls. The good ones leave after one drink and the other two abusively demand pictures and autographs. They have to be virtually ejected.

'What kind of a head of security are you?' asks James, as we watch the first half of Elton's gig together. 'When you give out passes, you should use your other eye.' Not again! Sticks and stones, Blunty, but I get the picture, don't I?

We head back to the hotel for a drink, first in the bar and later in James' suite, the inevitable late-night venue. It seems a shame that just as we are getting slowly to know Elton's lot we are leaving them to go back to Brazil. But we'll see them again later in Mexico.

It's late afternoon when James rings my room. 'You're alive? We thought you'd died in the night.' The plan is to go out to dinner somewhere where James won't be hassled. Bobble, the previous evening, has found an outstanding non-tourist restaurant in a park, a 20-minute walk away from where we are staying. Bobble has the curious ability of a truffle hound to sniff out offbeat restaurants with really good food – and this proves to be no exception.

James seems more relaxed but very tired. However, as always, the concept of an early night doesn't come into his thinking. He's left in peace here with barely an inter-ested glance from families on other tables who either don't recognize him or are too polite to ask for autographs.

Later on, it's not the same in Bellavista, the hottest part of town with its fashionable restaurants and bars. Three Mexican boys ask for pictures with him and once the flashes fire, it's an end to anonymity. As the crowd gathers, security guards intervene, but Blunty waves them away. The guards have no idea who he is. But if he's being mobbed by strangers, he must be Someone and therefore they feel they should protect him.

'Who are you?' one of them asks, as we climb into taxis for the ritual race through the streets back to the hotel.

'I am nobody, nobody at all,' says James.

Porto Alegre

James is down! One moment he's on stage singing the Slade cover 'Coz I Luv You'. The next he's ploughing his way through the audience to the back stage, when he stumbles and appears to fall. As a set piece of his act he's carved his way through the audience before at least a hundred times. Security guys are meant to run with him, not behind him, but they're heavyweight forwards who can't duck and weave with Blunty's fly-half dexterity. Usually he's in control while urging the crowd to help rather than impede his passage to the safety of the sealed-off enclosure at the back of the arena with the sound desk. His destination is the hoist that will raise him and his piano above the heads of the crowd for the second part of the song.

But this time it all goes wrong. He's seriously under-estimated the Latin passion of this capacity crowd in a stinkingly hot former aircraft hangar, alarmingly close to the edge of the main runway at Porto Alegre airport. I'm standing, helpless, five metres away in a sea of writhing bodies as a richly sun-tanned Amazonian at least six inches taller than Blunty grabs him in a head-lock and pulls him down, raking her long fingernails across his lip and gripping him in a deadly anaconda embrace.

But, come to think about it, how many books are

there that tell you how to defend yourself from a rabid pack of sexually hyped girls who want to devour you?

He grabs the top of the Amazon's front-buttoned white blouse and at the same time forcibly shoves her away. The blouse rips open. Instinctively she releases her grip to cover herself . . . and Blunty's off through the crowd again.

Blood's trickling from the cut on his lip, but even while he's still moving he's thinking. He's got no tissue, so he uses the back – not the front – of his tie as a handkerchief to staunch the flow. Once up on the stage he wipes his lip on the microphone. He's soaked in sweat and one of his leather shoes is torn, but he resumes the song without missing a note. Amazingly his white shirt escapes unstained and the majority of the audience remains unaware of the drama.

This is real, raw Brazil, man. Forget the contrived razzmatazz of the giant football stadiums he's played with Elton. We're back in more modest arenas with a smaller, younger, but more passionate audience. At least 70 per cent of them are girls and by early evening the galleried hangar is packed to capacity and you can scent the sexual tension in the air.

'We need a massive after-show tonight,' says James. Karl, Beardy and I quarter the audience in search of suitable guests. There's a whole group of uniformed girls promoting cigarettes or beer or something. It's someone's idea, I'm not taking all the blame here, to invite the lot.

At the end of the show, when the majority of the audience has filed out into the night, the floor of each arena looks sad and soulless as the cleaners sweep up mountains of discarded plastic bottles and glasses and the roadies furiously dismantle the set and load the trucks. But tonight at least a couple of hundred fans throng the entrance to the canteen where the party is taking place. My presence at the front of the stage during each concert so far has been noted by the caucus of hardcore fans. They've long since worked out that I'm a catalyst for getting backstage.

The difficulty is in sorting the grain from the chaff – there are so many different categories and sub-categories of fan. Obviously I've failed tonight because as boardie MissJoy reports on James' website: 'And in the after-show party, not one fan! That makes me really upset, coz only slappers were invited.' Well, I've guessed, as I later discover, that you've got a point there. Although, in a small way, maybe she's missing the point. Fans are about the music, and this is after the show, and it's certainly not about the music.

Tonight I'm approached during the show by a tough-looking guy who says he used to be in the Brazilian army. He falls clearly into the bracket of 'local fan', or more likely boyfriend of local fan.

'I've followed a remarkably similar career to James and we have a lot in common,' he tells me. 'I really want him to meet my fiancée. It would mean so much to her.' The international bond of military brotherhood is a card that falls regularly.

Personally, I think it would mean more to him than to her. His motive is solely to impress her. The girlfriend looks nervous. No, she looks frightened. She really doesn't care if she meets James or not. When, later, I tell him, gently, that it's not possible, he scowls with anger and stomps off. I hope he's not waiting outside for me.

Inside, the party – slappers or not – is going a bomb. In one corner in what is normally the venue canteen we have a group of professional lap dancers whose boss has invited us back to his club. Brazen and sexy, let's just say they aren't the sort of girls that I'd take home to my old mum.

In another corner we have two girls who are both called Anna. I have to say that an extraordinarily dispropor-tionate number of Annas fill the world of James Blunt and I have absolutely no explanation for this. Yes, it's one of the ten most popular girl's names in a host of countries from Argentina to Belarus. But then where are all the Gracielas, Constanzas, Agnieszkas and Guorúns. Guorúns? (Iceland, silly.)

The fact is that every time I meet an Anna, including my own daughter, I ask her: 'Do you like James Blunt?' Eight out of ten say yes.

These two Annas, one blonde and one dark, say they've been inseparable friends since they were five years old. One of them is celebrating her 26th birthday today and, in the best spirit of Annadom, the other had bought her a ticket to the concert as a present. They're having a grand evening and they politely thank me for inviting them to the after-show. At this stage of the evening it looks as if I *could* take these two home to Mother.

The party moves from venue to hotel bar. Blunty goes off to show his suite to the most inviting of the strippers, but is back down again after only ten minutes. Karl on the other hand is in a panic. Two girls, who obviously get on with each other, want to give him a show, and are trying to convince him to take them upstairs. 'I can't watch my laptop, and the lap dancers,' he explains in a broad Brummy accent. 'They'll nick it in a flash!'

'You should all come back to our club,' says a dancer. 'We have parties . . . and then we have private parties.' The boys look tempted but it turns out that the 'club' is a 40-minute drive away. In Brazil-speak that's at least an hour away and more probably 90 minutes.

Meanwhile Blonde Anna is making a rival pitch. 'Why don't you all come back to my place? It's my birthday. I'm having a barbecue party with my boyfriend and a group of friends, and you're all welcome – I live only 15 minutes away.' And if you believe any of that, you'll believe anything.

It's 2am and all reason has disappeared in copious amounts of champagne, vodka and beer. Not one of us stops to reason that if Blonde Anna was really throwing a birthday party she would, at this time of night, have been at it – not having a night out with us.

I'm in Dark Anna's car with Johnny and Beardy when, as honorary head of security, the first warning bells slowly start to ring. Actually, they've been there all along, but there seems to be a loose connection tonight between my befuddled brain and the danger signal. I mean, if I was a real head of security I should at this point reach into my shoulder holster, remove my Heckler & Koch 9mm sub-automatic pistol and fire all ten rounds into my own head, just to avoid the inquest.

'So, let's get this straight. Your client is a wealthy inter-national rock star? He's touring the Kidnap Continent of the World. It's 2am in a strange country that's in the world top 20 for violent crime. You allow him to be driven off by a strange and apparently crazy woman to a "party" at an unknown address somewhere in the suburbs? You don't even travel in the same car? Oh, and he's also brought along a girl who describes herself as "nightclub hostess".'

Another bell's just sounded. As we leave the bright lights of the city centre, Dark Anna is driving faster and faster. We run a red light at 60mph and then another and another, narrowly missing one car.

'Shouldn't you slow down a bit, or maybe stop at the lights?' questions Johnny tentatively from the front seat.

'What – are you crazy? If I stop, we'll get car-jacked in seconds. It's pretty dangerous around here.' You're not kidding. She's got her foot flat on the accelerator, one hand on the wheel, and is talking rapidly into a mobile phone with the other, asking for directions.

'But what about the police?' says Johnny.

'The police? They are the worst criminals. They're the biggest danger of all,' she replies ominously.

Ding dong. Here's another bell. If Dark Anna's been best friends with Blonde Anna for 20 years . . . how come she doesn't know where she lives?

Finally we arrive at what . . . phew . . . is a perfectly acceptable suburban apartment. There is no party, just Blonde Anna's boyfriend and a girl of about 20 who she introduces as her 'daughter'. Hang on, if she's really 26 this doesn't exactly add up.

The boyfriend sees nothing unusual in seven strangers, one of them an international celebrity of superstar status and another a bloke in his sixties, turning up in the early hours with his girlfriend who's missed her birthday party.

'Hi, Honey, what kept you? The barbecue's over.'

'Oh, Fernando, I forgot to say I had these tickets for James Blunt. We went to the show and then one thing led to another, so I sort of thought I'd bring him home with me. The band, that old geezer over there and the stripper just tagged along. My, just look at the time! How it flies when you're having a good time!'

'No worries, Annie, I'll get us all a beer.' Why look! Here's Dark Anna's boyfriend. He's just got out of bed, dressed, and driven across town to join us.

I mean, like, what is going on? We've no idea where in the hell we are and we just don't know what *is* going on. James?

'All seems pretty cool to me,' he replies, 'let's just not worry too much. Peter, find us a way of getting back to the hotel before 9 o'clock when we leave for the airport. We don't want Bobble to have a heart attack.'

Up on the roof-top terrace my gaze pans the endless vista of darkened suburban housing where, behind double-bolted doors, the less eccentric inhabitants of Porto Alegre are sensibly deep in slumber at this witching hour.

But there, slap in the middle of my vision, is a Tardis. Or to be more exact, a whole line of Tardises, drawn up one behind the other and all with green lights on their roofs. Yes, it's a taxi rank. Why the drivers are sitting there at a time when there's zero chance of finding a fare is a mystery. Maybe they're awaiting the first commuters. Maybe they've got nowhere else to sleep.

I go downstairs and break the news to James. If he's

even slightly surprised, he fails to show it. I've simply done what he asked me to do – to find a solution to the current, pressing problem. In his eyes, there is always a solution. Failure is simply not an option.

'Don't leave, Johnny!' says Blonde Anna, her arm around her boyfriend and her daughter as we say our goodbyes. 'Stay with us and have some fun.' Johnny looks a bit startled. So far on this tour, foursomes have usually been limited to tennis.

São Paulo (Again)

I've been here three times in 42 years – twice in the past week – and it's all too much. I want to go home. How can anyone keep up this pace?

'Football,' says Karl. So instead of catching up on the sleep that I missed out on entirely last night in Porto Alegre, I find myself in the dug-out of a São Paulo sports ground pretending to be a football photographer. Karl's team, which includes Beardy, Johnny, Ben and Mike The Sound, hold their own with credit against a local club in a match that had been arranged during our previous visit.

Blunty's back at the hotel catching up on his zeds with Tash, while Naughty Nicola is nursing a hugely swollen foot that's fallen foul of an infected mosquito bite. This is strange. Normally, Nicola does the biting.

Too much – that's what Mike The Sound and Glen The Lights think the following night. Here we are in another arena crowded to capacity. James is due on stage in exactly three minutes' time and stage manager Mark has just gone back to the dressing-room to collect him. The level of excitement in the audience has reached fever pitch. And then . . . bang . . . the entire lighting and sound desk blows up with puff of blue smoke.

There's a half-hour delay while six people manhandle another desk into place and Glen quietly earns his keep, rewiring with no assistance forthcoming from the locals.

I remember once in Mexico he spotted a guy walking down the corridor carrying a screwdriver in one hand and a pair of pliers in the other.

'Are you an electrician?' he asks him.

'Sí, señor,' replies the man, happily.

'Well, all the power's failed in the dressing-rooms. I need to find the fuse box.'

'No, me not electrician,' says the man, and walks on.

Much later, after the show, we go to a private party in a club. We're shown to a roped-off corner by the stage and I can't help but feel that rather than being guests, we are the entertainment. Everyone dances up to have a close look at us. Naughty Nicola makes faces back at them and waves her bandaged foot like a club. She and Tash are off back to England in a few hours' time, when we leave Brazil for Mexico, and I can't but help feel a little sad.

'You have to look forward in life, not back to what was or what might have been,' says James during a reflective moment, 'something that I don't always allow myself to do.' I'm not sure what he means by this. When I ask him, he just shakes his head and changes the subject.

Mexico with Elton promises to be fun but, nevertheless, I'll miss Tash and Naughty Nicola. But I'm looking forward to seeing Sabina again in Peru. These people have become my friends, but of course they're not my girl-friends. The more I see, the less I understand how Blunty works the emotional switchboard. Peace through pain? Satisfaction through stress? Sometimes I think unhappiness is a deliberate choice for him. Only then do the words and music flow for him.

Once, not long before he died, I interviewed Peter

Sellers at his flat in Mayfair. He greeted me at the door in the persona of the Indian doctor in *The Millionairess*. By the time we reached the sitting room he'd switched to Dr Strangelove and on to Inspector Clouseau. For 45 minutes I sat writing barely a word as he raved on.

'Who is the real Peter Sellers? Does he exist at all?' I kept asking myself. The pointless interview was then interrupted by a mighty bang at the door. Sellers opened it to reveal the figure of Spike Milligan dressed in the full uniform of a German *Wehrmacht* corporal, complete with steel helmet.

'*Kommen Sie mit mir, schnell!*' he roared, grabbing us both and manhandling us to the door and down the stairs to the street. '*Mein* tank awaits!' The tank proved to be a convertible Morris Minor with the roof down. Sellers drove with me in the passenger seat and Spike standing behind him, giving the Nazi salute at traffic lights and shouting staged German insults to bemused passersby.

'I hope you know a bit more about me now than you did before we met,' said Sellers in a Ve-hav-vays-of-making-you-talk Gestapo accent when he finally dropped me off outside my office.

No, much less actually. I couldn't help but feel that Sellers lacked an essential sense of happiness. I feel the same way about you, Blunty. Before you make anyone else happy, you're going to have to make yourself happy. Lay to rest whatever it is in your past that's troubling you. But if you're happy, I'm not sure you'll be as great an artist.

Mexico City

'Just look at that bunch of convicts over there!' says one of a BA cabin crew just arriving from London as they join the agonizingly lengthy queue for immigration at Mexico City airport. In Mexico, everyone queues. Clearly they learnt their immigration art from Big Brother America up north. OK, so we've just flown ten hours north after one hell of a farewell party for Tash and Naughty Nicola. We don't look good, but we don't look *that* bad.

'Hang about, guys,' says Debs, the purser of the 16-person crew, taking a closer look at these bedraggled Brits, 'they're not convicts, they're my mates.'

I guess it's inevitable that if you travel as much as James and the band – and more by BA than any other airline – you'll run into the same cabin crews who tend to over-night in the same city centre hotels and have the urge to party just as hard. This is a meeting of old friends. Beardy and Debs are pals from way back.

When God first left Mexico City in 1521 the Spanish *conquistadors* raised it to the ground after the Aztecs rose against them. When He left for the second time, around the start of the twenty-first century, He took all law and order with him.

When I last set foot in Mexico City as an 18-year-old, I hitchhiked in a cattle truck that had carried me all the way from the ancient city of Oaxaca. It wasn't a journey of which the RSPCA would have approved. In exchange for the ride I hung on the side of the truck with two other boys, squirting bottles of water at the tightly packed heifers whenever one fell to its knees from heat exhaustion and kicking it back up on to its feet.

In the waistband of my jeans, I carried a .32 revolver. That may sound pretty strange by today's standards, but without a gun I'd have been the exception. Latin America hadn't moved much since the days of Butch Cassidy, but there seemed to be some kind of delicately balanced peace and decency in a land that's always had a bit of the *bandido* about it throughout its long and often bloody history.

Since then Mexico has descended into a pit of drug-war violence, becoming one of the most dangerous places in the world – and that's without swine flu.

Only a couple of days before we arrive, a French businessman is murdered for his wallet, a mile from the airport. There's since been a spate of such attacks. Lookouts are posted at the airport currency exchange windows to tip off armed gangs as to likely victims. The gangs, high on crack cocaine, then follow the target, box in his car, rob him – and then sometimes kill him just for the hell of it.

A middle-aged Mexican friend of mine was sitting in a midday traffic jam on Paseo de la Reforma, the long and wide avenue that cuts across the heart of the city. He was in the middle of the modern banking quarter and lost in thought when there was a sharp tap on the driver's window. He looked left, into the barrel of a gun. He looked right, at a second gunman on the passenger side.

Both guns were pointed unwaveringly at his head. Without hesitation he opened the driver's window and – with exaggerated slowness – handed over his wallet. He was lucky. The gang moved on to the next car in front of him. When that driver refused, they shot him.

All of this in a capital famed for its kidnaps is a complete nightmare for Elton's team and for Bobble. We leave the airport in a cavalcade. Paramilitary police armed with an arsenal of automatic weapons guard key crossroads, and flashing blue lights are everywhere. No, it's not just for us. It's just the dramatic daily show of force on the streets. But if by this the authorities hope to curtail the activities of the drug-fuelled gangs, they are not succeeding. Some 5,300 people died in 2008 in what in some areas of the country amounts to open civil war. Astonishingly, 1,600 of these killings took place in just one city – Ciudad Juarez, near the US border.

Right now I've got other problems on my mind – money. We check into the Four Seasons Resort and order drinks and food at the bar. When I see the figures on the tab, it makes my blood run cold. I thought this was meant to be a poor country? On tour James pays for all the basic expenses of the band and the rest of the travelling group. Flights, accommodation and meals at the venue on working days are all taken care of, but each person is responsible for other food, drinks and hotel extras such as phone bills, movies, internet, laundry and room service. The smarter the hotel, the bigger these extras can be.

At that moment, as I am looking at the tab, Bobble comes into the room, puts his hand on my shoulder and whispers: 'Just sign it. Elton said he will comp the lot – all hotel expenses.'

'The lot?' I say in amazement. Picking up the bill for 60-plus hotel rooms is remarkable, but paying for everyone's booze and food is a quite extraordinary act of generosity! I mean, we haven't even been formally – or otherwise – introduced.

'The lot,' says Bobble. 'You don't have a hotel bill. None of us do.'

Phew. Then I learn even more about big money. We're here to play at a private party the following evening. James will be on stage for just 45 minutes and Elton for 75. The fee? A cool $3 million. Not bad work if you can get it. But if you're going to be as generous as Elton you probably need that much. Then I learn that James and Elton are giving the whole lot to charity.

It seems remarkable that the city where I lived for the longest all those years ago is the one I remember the least. But then a series of earthquakes, including the catastrophe of September 1985 that killed 10,000, has changed the city almost beyond recognition.

The gig for which we have travelled all this way is a private corporate party for 1,000 guests of Buchanan's whisky. This is not a big drink brand in Britain, but it's the drug of choice among the wealthy in Mexico, Venezuela and Columbia. Judging by the scale of preparations for the party, Buchanan's must have sold rather more than a wee dram or two. All the money raised by the event – along with the performers' fees – is to go to help the poor through local charities.

At first glance, it doesn't look to me as though too

many of the poor are involved in the actual proceedings – unless you count the steeplejacks far above my head who are putting the finishing touches to a giant $1-million temporary dome covering the magnificent eighteenth-century quadrangle of Colegio de San Ignacio de Loyola Vizcainas. This private school is the stunning venue for tonight.

It does seem to me like a lot of cash to keep the cold out for one evening. The ancient cobbles have been richly carpeted and golden carp now swim among flowering water lilies in the central fountains. Guests will watch from the 'floor' and from sofas and armchairs on each level of the surrounding mellow, stone cloisters. The lighting rig is revolutionary and bathes the whole building in surreal shades of colour.

In a world where albums make little money because of piracy, touring for any artist is the financial name of the game. The occasional private party is the icing on the cake. The price seems to be the equation of what the client is prepared to pay against what the artist is prepared to accept. One party wants to tell wife, husband or the world how rich he or she is, the other has to weigh up the convenience and the cost of flying musicians, technicians and often a whole stage-set halfway around the world for a 90-minute concert and a tête-à-tête with the hosts.

I was with James once in the sitting room of his house in Ibiza when the telephone rang.

'No, sorry, I'm afraid as I've already told your agent, I can't do that right now,' he says politely. 'No – it's not about the money . . . it's just that I'm on holiday.' After an exchange of pleasantries and the promise of a future visit, he cuts the connection and returns to his piano and the song he is writing.

'What was that?' I ask.

'One million dollars for a private party next week,' he replies, casually.

'You turned it down?' His friend, Nin, and I look at each other in blank astonishment. Maybe I could quickly grow a beard, lose 30 years, and have a go as his double?

'Yup,' he replies.

'Why?' I ask incredulously.

'Because it's in Macau . . . *and* I'm on holiday,' he smiles. I wish I could afford to smile like that. In fact, although the sum is huge, half would go in expenses. Probably it's also unrealistic to think he could assemble band, technicians and set at such short notice. But I guess it must feel good not having to try.

The Buchanan's party tonight is in stark and dull contrast to the capacity-filled stadiums of South America. Karl has only an acoustic set of drums to play with but drama strikes at the sound check.

'Where are my drumsticks?' he asks. Brazil's drumsticks are still in Brazil and shortly to move on to Peru. A furious row ensues with Karl blaming a technician and vice versa.

This is the kind of man management that Blunty, thanks to his army training, handles with considerable skill. Time and again he will calmly take the heat out of a potentially dangerous flare-up between members of the touring squad. When a group of individual artists and professionals are thrown together in such a highly stressful, fluid environment over many months, such fracas are inevitable.

Blunty is the commanding officer even though he doesn't wear a uniform. The two other ranks concerned, one drummer, one senior crew member, are called into the CO's dressing-room which doubles as his office. Both sides get to state their case and he adjudicates. In this case both of them should have shared responsibility for remembering the sticks. Both get a strip torn off them and they walk out, gradually resuming their friendship. 'Keep Calm and Carry On', as Blunty stickers on some of the packing cases backstage proclaim. Lingering sulks are not permitted on tour.

Elton, James, 60 other people and a Yamaha grand piano have flown ten hours for the night. Elton goes leisurely on from here to Las Vegas. But, unbelievably, before dawn we're flying all the way back down to Peru.

What's more, now the concert has started, I see that nobody really wants to listen. Decked out in their finery, they want to drink and talk with a little music in the background. Only about a hundred people, those standing up close to the stage, are quietly enthusiastic.

Give me some love, sings James. But the crowd are not showing any sign of it. This song's very tongue-in-cheek. 'It's me laughing at them laughing at me trying to be cool. Sort of,' James explains to me.

'I'm saying, "Why don't you give me some love?" I've taken shitloads of drugs – as if that would convince them to like me!'

But all these subtle nuances may be lost tonight on the Mexican audience, which seems for the most part interested more in what they have got in their glass than in their ears. It's the same later for Elton, but no one minds at all.

'It's always like this at private parties,' says James. 'Normally you just have to see it as a pay cheque. Tonight we have the privilege of sharing a stage with Elton.'

After the show we have a few drinks and then all go back to the combined after-show party, which is at the hotel and hosted by Buchanan's. This is when it all gets a bit hazy. The combination of jet lag, lack of sleep and alcohol takes its toll. The next day Johnny says it was the whisky. I don't remember any whisky.

What I do remember is Bobble pounding on my bedroom door. 'Peter, we're going to Peru NOW!' Before that, all I recall is going up to my room at 3.15am to bring my bags down. I sat on the bed to change my shirt and then nothing.

I come to with a start. It's 3.45am and James and the band are waiting downstairs in the bus. 'And where the fuck is Peter?'

James texts me: 'Peter, we're off to Peru NOW. See you around sometime,' and tells the driver to head for the airport. But Bobble, good old Bobble, intervenes. Ringing my room has no effect, so he comes up and kicks the door.

Finally I make it to the bus to raucous shouts of derision. They're all as tired and as drunk as me, but they just didn't fall asleep at the critical moment.

Forget armed bandits on the streets around the airport. If we are attacked we will only have to breathe on them to knock them out. It takes every ounce of my concentration to handle ticket, passport and immigration papers at the check-in desk.

'Sober up, everyone,' warns Bobble, 'or they're not

going to let us on the plane.' Somehow we flop into the business-class section of the aircraft, bound firstly for San Salvador, and order more drinks. It's the first time in my life that I've been on a plane that runs out of its full supply of tonic water before it even leaves the stand.

If the going was tough before, it's just got a lot tougher. We've flown 4,612 miles from São Paulo to Mexico City, spent 34 hours on the ground there, and now we're on our way to Lima in Peru, which is 2,636 miles away – oh, and there're 10,000 people gathering there to hear James in concert *tonight*.

'I wanted to leave you back there,' Blunty tells me, over the final vodka and tonic. 'We were already late and Bobble going in search of you made us even later.' Being late, keeping them waiting, is an unforgivable sin.

'I'm really sorry, James,' I say, feeling like a boy apologizing to his headmaster – except pupil and teacher are both pissed, 'it won't happen again.'

'Still, I'm glad you made it, mate,' says Blunty, finishing his drink and settling back in his seat with his hoody over his face. 'You wouldn't want to miss Peru . . .' And he falls dreamlessly asleep to order.

Wouldn't I? Little did I know it, but a day that started badly is about to get much, much worse.

Lima

I awake as we're coming in to land. My mouth tastes like the proverbial vulture's crutch and, looking around me, we are all in a similar state. It's fiercely hot on the tarmac, and my clothes stick to me. All I want are cool sheets and 12 hours of air-conditioned slumber. If I can't have that, I'll settle for a shower and a swim in the sea or my hotel pool before another long night out.

But neither option is open to me. In the baggage hall, one by one the band and the crew collect instruments and suitcases as they appear on the belt. I get that deep sinking feeling in the pit of my stomach. Somehow, long before the belt stops, you always intuitively know when it's your case that is the one that missed the flight. Did I even check it in? In the rat-assed state that was me at Mexico City airport, anything is possible.

Oh well, you gotta roll with it I guess. What's in a suitcase? My whole world right now. Miriam from the local promoter's office is extremely helpful. We move from desk to desk filling in countless forms. If the suitcase didn't, for whatever reason, make the plane, the last thing I want is for it to be sent on to me here because – absolutely unbelievably – we are flying back to Mexico City tomorrow morning. I give them the address of our next hotel there.

'No problem, señor,' says the airline person. 'We've already found your case in Mexico and we'll deliver it today to this address.' I'm pretty sceptical, but there's nothing more I can do. Already I've kept the band waiting in a minibus for half an hour on two occasions today – in two different countries.

Miriam and I walk through customs, with me wheeling my carry-on bag. In Latin American customs halls they play a kind of Russian roulette. I'm not sure it does much in the War Against Terror or the War Against Drugs for that matter, but it does make travel a game of chance. Each passenger is invited to press a button as they put their luggage through the scanner. If this turns on a green light, you're free to leave the hall. If it randomly turns on a red one, you're searched.

Yes, the lamp lights red. It's just not my day. But luckily or unluckily, I don't have a suitcase to search. My wheelie bag contains only my cameras, my two laptops, and assorted cables and chargers. Wearily I hand over my passport, along with the customs declaration form that I completed on the plane.

I mean, how much of the small print on customs declaration forms do you actually read?

Are you carrying firearms? NO
Are you in possession of illegal drugs? NO
Have you visited a farm within the past 14 days? NO
Are you carrying more than one personal computer? NO.
If the answer to Question 4 is 'Yes', please note that importing more than one personal computer into Peru is punishable by life imprisonment and/or death by firing squad.

Shit, I didn't read that bit.

'You've got two computers!' says the outraged woman officer, pressing an alarm bell so that I am immediately hemmed in by two grim-faced uniformed men. As I'm holding both my laptop and my lightweight electronic notebook in my hand, I guess it's pretty obvious that I have.

'You've signed here,' she says, indicating my signature on the form, 'swearing that all the statements above are correct.

'In short,' she smiles triumphantly, 'you lied, señor. In Peru, that is a very serious offence indeed.'

This, I decide, is probably not the moment to point out that my BlackBerry is a computer, my watch is a computer, and I've also got a couple of hard drives tucked away in one of the side pockets.

Once inside the security office, belligerent bureaucracy gives way to a heated exchange between my interpreter and a new weasel-like official.

If I'm correctly getting the gist of this pistol-shot *castellano*, we've reached the backhander stage of negotiations. In exchange for an enormous amount of US dollars, my inadvertent law-breaking can perhaps be overlooked.

But just then another officer – judging by the amount of scrambled egg on his shoulder, a senior one at that – puts in an appearance. My interrogator looks uncomfortable. But he's not as uncomfortable as I am. I'm hot, tired and fed up.

'I'll tell you what,' I interrupt. 'Why don't I just give you one of these fucking computers as a present, and then we can all be happy and I can go to my hotel.'

I'm quite serious; one laptop is half-dead anyway and

nearly all the material from it that I need is already on the other one.

'No, that's not possible,' says Weasel Face with a look of pure indignation tinged with bitter disappointment. Certainly it would have been possible in exchange for a few greenbacks a couple of minutes ago, before the arrival of Sr Scrambled Egg.

In the end, it's agreed that the offending laptop is to be sealed, painstakingly slowly, in bubble-wrap. I may retrieve it in time for my flight to Mexico in the morning – and then I will be formally deported from the country for importing contraband. Good, I can hardly wait.

By the time I join the rest of the band at the hotel, more than an hour has slipped by. Sensibly, they'd given up waiting for me.

At the hotel I've got just half an hour in which to check in, shower and change before going to the gig with the rest of them. Change? Into what? I find a T-shirt, underwear and toiletries in the hotel shop. I dash up to my room and strip off for a shower when there's a knock at the door.

'Your suitcase, sir, the airline has just delivered it,' says the bellboy.

My luggage had been on the flight all along.

Exhausted, I meet up with Bobble and Blunty in the lobby. 'Maybe, after all, you should have stayed in Mexico,' Blunty says, his face deadpan. Definitely, you're right.

But the long night is only just beginning. We head out to the Jockey Club where the gig is taking place. I'm so tired I don't know what to do with myself and everyone else looks in a fairly similar state. After the sound check

Blunty crashes out on the sofa. I put four upright chairs together in the unused dining area of what is a pretty swanky dressing-room and fall into a troubled sleep.

It's just amazing the effect that three suntanned, long-legged and fresh-faced girls can have on collective exhaustion. Sabina and a friend from Ibiza, along with a pretty dark-haired Peruvian girl, come bursting into the dressing-room. Like Alka-Seltzer dropped into a glass of water, James and the band start to fizz. Sabina, a pack of the inevitable Marlboro's nestling in the top of each of her thigh-length boots, gives me a big hug and then lies down on the sofa next to Blunty. He looks pretty happy about this. Actually he looks just about thrilled. She is one cool lady. The three girls have been on holiday together in Peru for three weeks. They've done Cusco, Machu Picchu and the Inca Trail, and now they're going to do the Blunt concert. It's the climax of their stay, and they're determined to enjoy every precious minute. Precious? We've got about ten hours before we fly all the way back to Mexico.

At times, I ask myself agonizingly what I've got out of this prolonged romp around the world with Blunty and Co. Material for a book? I've been talking about this for so long that no one on the tour takes it seriously.

'Peter, we have absolutely no idea at all why you are here. Why are you here?' says Beardy tonight, pouring himself a glass of red wine, before going on stage. He often says this and then he thinks he might have offended me, so he adds: 'Don't get me wrong, we like having you around. Things happen when you're around. But shouldn't you be somewhere else, like at home with your wife?'

I feel like I'm at the Mad Hatter's Tea Party. I think I'll have a drink, too.

'Have some wine,' the March Hare said in an encouraging tone.

Alice looked all round the table, but there was nothing on it but tea. 'I don't see any wine,' she remarked.

'There isn't any,' said the March Hare.

'Then it wasn't very civil of you to offer it,' said Alice angrily.

Did Lewis Carroll ever go to Peru? On the one hand I'm daily offered the richness of revisiting the hazy, crazy world of my youth in a way that no old geezer of my age can hope for in his wildest dreams.

I mean, like last night, there I was with Elton chatting to a couple of supermodels at a sumptuous private party in Mexico City. Tonight, here I am watching the show in the VIP area in Lima and flirting with three beautiful women half my age before this giant audience. Meanwhile, James struts his stuff on stage in a manner that is quite incredible – given the fact that he has had virtually no sleep for 48 hours.

I can imagine the conversation behind me. 'I tell you, *compadre*, whoever that wrinkled senior *señor* out there is, he must be pretty damned important to have three cheeky *chicas* like that. See how they laugh with him and put their arms around him for the pictures. Who is he? Is he James Blunt's father? Is he a billionaire sponsor? The owner of a record label, perhaps? Is he a *famoso* fashion designer like Roberto Cavalli from Milano? *Hombre*, he's old enough! *Pero*, what would I give to laugh and dance like that with three hot, hot half-naked *muchachas*. Eh?' That's about all the Spanish I can manage.

On the other hand – and it's a big other hand – I'm reminded of the downward, desiccating passage of years. Be honest, even if you wanted to, Pedro, the only thing you're going to pull tonight is a toilet handle. I don't know if Ol' Roberto ever gets the blues like that. Maybe he does, and maybe he doesn't. Cheers Roberto! There's nothing like a pisco sour for lifting your spirits before and during a show. Pisco's the local liquor, made from distilled grape juice, and I can tell you I've had a few . . . and boy what a catwalk we've got tonight with these three beauties. Roberto, I'm really sorry you're not here because you are the only person I've met on five continents on this tour who is actually older than me.

On stage, James starts to sing the next number: *Goodbye my lover, goodbye my friend* . . .

When we finally leave the show our car is mobbed by a hundred fans banging on the sides. Now I can imagine, a bit, what it felt like to be a Beatle.

'You are to be deported from Peru,' says yet another over-serious official at the airport the following morning. Can't wait.

'OK, but can I have my laptop back first?' I feel like a small boy who has kicked his ball into the neighbour's garden and must now endure a familiar lecture before it is handed over. Miriam and I walk the length of the terminal three times after being redirected to different offices for different stamps. Then, to my astonishment, the bubble-wrapped laptop is produced.

But now we are in another catch-22 situation. My armed guards – they sort of materialized in quite a friendly way at around stamp two – want me on my way airside right now. But I am responsible for carrying one of the guitars and I can't check my bags in until all the instruments have cleared customs. This brings us back to office one where the whole laptop episode began and where Mark is now quietly fuming over the pile of boxed instruments.

Finally the desire to see the backside of the convicted *contrabandista* outweighs the desire for a further backhander from Mark. Across the airport I go with my guards once again. At the check-in a quietly amused Blunty is waiting and watching.

'We should have left you in Mexico,' he says.

'Well, this lot also seem to think the same,' I reply, indicating my escort. I am taken to immigration, where another stern official looks at me as if I have committed treason. He stamps my passport.

'Can I come back again another time?' I ask him. 'Or is this goodbye forever to Peru?' He shrugs. I'm not sure if that's a 'yes' or a 'no'. Then my guards release me. Like a carrier pigeon I wing it out of the wicker basket and on to the gate before anyone changes their mind.

Mexico City (Again)

If you want to strike it rich in Mexico, all you've got to do is set up a factory making flashing blue bulbs. Once again there are police cars parked on every road junction from the airport. Now that we are on our own without Elton, we head for a rather more discreet hotel than the Four Seasons.

The security problem is close to everyone's heart. James, with his cheap plastic watch, can always tell the time. ('This pink watch is really so stylish . . . maybe someday it will be possible to buy such a watch in his merchandise shop,' posts a Chilean boardie.) The rest of us take local advice and don't wear any jewellery at all or carry more than a few small banknotes on the streets. But the big question, as always, is what do you do with your valuables? However respectable the hotel appears to be, locking them in a room safe poses a chain of problems.

Firstly you've got to be able to reopen the safe, which isn't always as simple as it says on the instructions. Secondly, you've got to remember – before you take your bags down to check out in a haze of exhaustion – that you put them in there in the first place. Thirdly, you've got to assume that potential thieves haven't already acquired the master codes.

We've long ago decided that the safest bet is to hide them in obscure corners of your luggage, put the Do Not

Disturb sign firmly on your door, and do without any housekeeping during your short stay. Making your own bed is a small price to pay for hanging on to your wallet and passport.

Teatro Metropolitan is a 1940s movie theatre that's been converted into a rock venue and James has two nights here. One proves quite enough for me – as I learn in the early hours of the following morning.

'Ping' goes my mobile. It's a text from James:

'Please don't invite any more high-profile groupies backstage. Take a look at my website.'

I've committed the cardinal sin – I've allowed security to be breached.

Daniela, half-French and half-Mexican, seemed such a nice girl, too. But never judge a book by its cover. The whole idea behind the after-show is that it's a chance for James to meet people in private. 'No cameras, no autographs', it says on the Golden Tickets. It should also say 'no internet posting'. I only invited her and her 'boyfriend' because I was happy she was a local fan. How was I to know that the 'boyfriend' was a stooge? She's written a graphic account of what happened backstage – and later in a bar – and she's put it, along with a heap of photos, on James' website. I'm in the doghouse.

Nervously, I click on to the message board: 'Hi everyone, I'm new on this board although I've been reading it for a while. I wanted to tell you about the amazing time I had last night.' Oh my God.

The concert was great, of course. James has so much energy. He kept saying that he loves the Mexican audience cause we're so loud. At some point he and the band were wearing Mexican sombreros, so the people went crazy.

But the best part was after the show. I went with a friend and we managed to meet him backstage and, well, spend some time with him . . . until three in the morning!!! It was an incredible night, I still can't believe it!!!

I'll tell you all about it later . . . I have to upload the pictures.

How could I be so naive? I feel sick inside. But Daniela's just warming up:

Before the concert started we were already at our seats and I noticed a guy with a staff badge that was standing near to us (we were in the second row). I didn't pay much attention to him, but then during the concert, as I was really singing at the top of my lungs with so much enthusiasm, that guy kept staring at me.

He was in the front taking pictures of James and the band. Then when the band went off stage, before the encore, he came to me and said, 'You know there are three more songs.' I replied that I knew that and asked him if there was any possibility to meet James after the show. He said, 'No, no, sorry it's not possible.' I knew James wasn't going to come out for autograph signing cause I had already asked one of the security guys. So I was resigned to not meeting him this time.

The concert ended and we were leaving but we noticed that the same guy was still there looking for something or someone. So we stayed there, too, curious about what he was doing. He eventually saw us and came over to talk to us. We chatted for a while, he was asking us where we were from and stuff like that. He turned out to be a really lovely guy.

He said, 'You know what, I'll give you these two passes'!!!! Needless to say that we were in SHOCK! We followed him backstage and he took us to a side room with sofas and a table full of drinks!!!!

Now, for those who are wondering, the guy's name is Peter, he is writing a book about his experiences on tour with James, and he is a really lovely man. I can't thank him enough.

So there we were, waiting for someone to show up. The first to come in was Beardy. He instantly welcomed us and said, 'Hey, help yourselves to drinks!' Then came in Paul and Karl and other guests. AND FINALLY JAMES!! At that point I wasn't nervous at all and I was really very excited to see him. There were like 20 people in the room waiting for him. He eventually made his way over to us and we got introduced by Peter.

Well, what can I say? James was lovely! He is just great! He didn't even ask what we were doing there considering that we were the only people non-friends, non-staff. We stayed there about two hours and chatted with him a lot. He was telling us all kind of funny stories. I even shared a cigarette with him!!!!

I told him that the last time I saw him was in Paris and now that I was back to Mexico he was here too, to what he replied: 'Yeah, I've been stalking you.' My friend told him that I was a little bit jealous because he kissed all the other girls in the room and not me. He looked at me and said, 'Aww, come over here', and kissed me on both cheeks. All the band was really friendly and easy to talk to. I was really impressed. We had a great time! I'll never forget it!

Later, Beardy started mentioning that they might be heading elsewhere. He told us to join them and gave us the address of the bar. We followed them to the exit and since it was forbidden to take pictures backstage (I don't know why) I asked James for one next to the vans. Karl was nice enough to take it for us!

So we got the car and headed to the bar. I think it was too much going there cause there were only like ten people who all seemed to be close friends of the band so we felt a little apart. James was with a tall blonde girl who had all his attention so we didn't get a chance to talk to him again. We had fun though, Peter was there too and Ben is a really funny dancer! So we stayed there until about 3 o'clock.

I still can't believe all this happened. I couldn't sleep when I got back home, I kept picturing all these moments in my head. It was an amazing experience. All I can say is THANK YOU PETER!!!!!!!!! I hope you read this board.

Daniela, I just did – and so did James, which is why he's pissed off with me, and me with you. The barrier between public face and private life has been seriously breached, and it's all my fault.

A couple of days later Blunty has a private chat with me beside the hotel pool in Guadalajara. He's annoyed, but he's more relaxed about it now.

Daniela's post opened up a whole thread around the world on her 'amazing' experience and on how to get backstage. One easy way seems to be to keep an eye out for Peter. The whole topic only draws to a conclusion when someone – probably James himself – switches the subject: 'By the way . . . a stupid question: Is James allergic to peanut butter?' Not, so far as I know – nor jelly, either. Just now I don't much care.

'Why did you give her a ticket?' Blunty asks me . . . er . . . bluntly. I realize that while I may be clad in swimming gear and dripping wet, I'm in the army on the carpet in the colonel's office.

'Well I *think* I met her before in Paris, although now I'm not quite so sure – and she looked like a genuine local fan and as she seemed to be with her boyfriend I was pretty sure she wasn't a stalker.'

'I know it's difficult sometimes to tell,' says James, 'but the fact that you thought you'd seen her before should have rung a warning bell. You've got to take more care when handing out the passes. Pick ones that we – not you – would like to meet.'

Then he smiles. I've had a sleepless night, I've apologized. Knuckles have been suitably rapped and the incident is clearly now to be forgotten and forgiven. I feel good about that. Blunty's man management skills are out-of-sight.

But hang on, wait a minute – what damage did Daniela actually do? I mean, she got backstage and got a kiss on the cheek from Blunty. It still seems to be that she's a dedicated fan, not a loony. She followed us to a bar where she saw that Benny was a funny dancer, and no one can deny that's true. At the end of the day she wrote – on James' *official* website – about what a ball she'd had and chatted to other boardies about her night out with Blunty. It doesn't seem to matter much, does it? This is a fan who is sharing her adoration of you with other fans. Aren't you overreacting, James?

On the other hand, now that I've spent several months myself living in the paranoid atmosphere of the goldfish bowl I can see how this breach of privacy gets to him. No one cares a fig about me, and anyway I've been getting to leave the bowl for weeks on end and live my own private life in another world where no one is watching my every move.

Each time when I return to mundane reality, I'm sad to go but secretly just a little relieved to be out of the bowl.

But on tour, James never escapes the bowl – and only rarely does he when he's off it. A line in the sand between his public and private lives is essential, but it will always be vulnerable. Paying the price of fame doesn't always come easy.

A month later, 17 concerts in 14 countries down the line, another boardie hands me a letter in Athens during the final gig of the tour. It had been sent from Mexico and it's from Daniela.

Hi Peter, my intention was actually to send a gift as a thank you for giving us backstage passes, but I had no way to contact you. I can't thank you enough for getting us there and introducing us to everyone. I was resigned to not meeting them that night. I can't believe how lucky we were that you were there right next to us during the concert. I'm guessing that I was singing too loud and that's why you noticed me. I was thrilled to see how everybody among James' crew is so nice. Take care, Daniela.

Not a stalker, a nice girl – but, yes, I'm on my guard now.

'Oh my God, I was sure for a while back there that I was being kidnapped,' says Karl, his normal smile missing for once. He looks genuinely shocked and takes a giant gulp from the drink that I hand him. It's 2am back at the hotel and Karl has been missing for nearly two hours in one of the most dangerous cities in the world.

'She kept driving with one hand on the wheel and talking rapidly in Spanish on her mobile to a man who was issuing instructions,' he says. 'We were way off the centre and I didn't recognize any of the streets. I thought of throwing myself out of the car.'

'Just as well you didn't,' says Johnny. 'Otherwise someone might have found you and properly kidnapped you.'

It's after the second concert in Mexico City, where I've been reluctant to offer any Golden Tickets at all. Why do I bother anyway? The whole party scene is a bit depressing.

'Come on,' says Karl. 'You made a mistake. We all make mistakes. We'll invite all those promotion girls.' Sol Cerveza appears to be a sponsor of the show and they've fielded half a dozen girls in slinky yellow outfits to hand out pens and baseball caps. And he does.

When the rest of us all leave to go back to the hotel by limo, Karl is willingly whisked away in the car of one of them.

I'm oblivious to all this because just as the show is getting under way I see this guy walk into the foyer of the theatre. He looks like Rick Wakeman. It is Rick Wakeman. Rick is playing the venue the following evening and he's come to see the show and check it out.

'That,' he tells Blunty after the show, 'was an amazing performance. You had the whole theatre on fire. I'm a big fan.'

When Blunty and everyone finally say goodnight to Rick and head for home, Karl is nowhere to be seen. That's because he's heading across the city with this wild blonde at the wheel. No, as it turns out, she's not kidnapping him – she's asking her boyfriend for directions to our hotel. Paranoia now rules. Still, you can't be too careful.

Our hotel, the Condesa, is a fine old colonial mansion, which has been turned into a boutique hideaway for visitors to Mexico who want a change from the usual swanky American-plan four- and-five stars.

It's also a pretty cool place to stay in more ways than one – especially if you visit between November and February when the temperature at night in the city drops to single figures Celsius. Trouble is that the central atrium which houses the restaurant is open to the sky. Well, that's what James says. As we sat down to a chilly dinner I looked up to the moonlit funnel of sky above the building and I could have sworn there was a glass roof. 'Look,' I said, 'I can see specks of dirt on the clouds. There must be a roof.'

'Whatever you're on, can we have some of that?' says Benny.

'Peter's finally lost it,' says James. Perhaps he's right. It's definitely time for me to go home. Either way, it's bloody cold. Much later that night we sit drinking in the roof garden of Blunty's penthouse suite. It's freezing. Perhaps staying here is a deliberate ploy by Bobble to acclimatize them all for Russia and Finland next week, where there'll be snow and sub-zero temperatures?

In the early hours James sends everyone in the band a round-robin text about a story he's just read on the BBC website. Doesn't he ever sleep? Ron is a 73-year-old grandfather who has been blind for 30 years. Doctors have fitted him with a bionic eye and he is starting to see again. Blunty's text includes a quote from him:

'"My one ambition at the moment is to be able to go out on a nice clear evening and be able to pick up the moon" – one man's admission that he has been smoking the same stuff as Peter.' OK, so maybe I have lost it.

But otherwise the hotel is a great, if eccentric, place to stay. On my floor that night, a couple of workmen repaint the white walls of the corridor . . . by torchlight. I've picked up my laundry from the laundrette down the street, I'm trying to squash everything once again into my scuffed suitcase, and annoyingly I've mislaid a shoe in Peru or somewhere.

Room service, too, is unusual but impeccable. We're gathered by the front door of the hotel the following morning and are just about to board the transfer limo to the airport when Blunty suddenly turns to me and says: 'Peter, do you think you left something behind in your room?'

All eyes turn to the lobby. Coming down the stairs and then heading for the reception desk is the hotel's resident brown Labrador. Proudly carried in its mouth, like a freshly retrieved cock pheasant, is one of my green Converse shoes.

Beirut

For a guy who says he doesn't need special security and doesn't like having guards with him, it does seem a bit ridiculous. Blunty turns up for the sound check in the Lebanese capital surrounded by no fewer than 20 heavies who marshal him on to the stage. The band and the crew can't stop laughing. This is the celebrity who is famous for saying that he doesn't like having any security people around because it only draws attention to him. But, hey, this is Beirut, once the hostage capital of the world. Even his harshest critics wouldn't wish him chained to a radiator like John McCarthy and Brian Keenan for the next four years.

But in the event that evening, 20 guards weren't nearly enough to keep control of the crowd.

'We saved the best for nearly last,' gasps James afterwards as he and the band collapse in the dressing-room. 'That has to have been the best fun and the best audience of the whole tour.' The band all agree.

Since I left them in the sunshine of Guadalajara less than three weeks ago, they've played Moscow, Helsinki, Tallinn, Riga, Vilnius, Warsaw, Bucharest, Sofia, Belgrade, Muscat, Dubai, and now we are in Lebanon. But when I make my usual unannounced appearance in the lobby of their hotel as they gather for the ride to the venue, they seem hardly to have noticed my absence.

Unlike Sarajevo it seems incredible that a city, ravaged so badly by 15 years of a bitter civil war that ended in 1990, has managed to reincarnate itself as an even livelier and more fascinating Mediterranean tourist centre than it was before. The redesigned historic centre is hardly recognizable without the barbed wire, barricades and bombed-out buildings that littered the dangerous streets during my last visit in the 1980s.

It's a tribute to the culture and the resilience of these extraordinary people, and tonight they're turning up in their thousands to queue for entry to the 6,000-seat Forum de Beyrouth.

'Seeing James' guitar leaning against a speaker on stage feels strangely reassuring, as well as seeing the guys' gear,' posts boardie Pacha on James' website. Hang on, there's a hat-trick coming up.

'Isn't that a fez he's wearing on his head?' posts TrixieF.

Yes. Mark the stage manager has magicked it Tommy Cooper-style out of nowhere just before the show. Just like that. From sombreros in Mexico to fur hats in Moscow, a bit of local colour always goes down well.

From the moment the 6,000-strong capacity crowd starts to stream into the hall, you can tell by the incredible warmth of the atmosphere – even before the lights go down and the wall of sound both on and off stage rises – that it is going to be a big one.

Moments before each performance Blunty goes through his Marmite ritual: he eats a whole spoonful of the spread, which he believes helps him hit the notes. Tonight, in the last stages of the tour, his voice is in serious need of R&R and he's brought the familiar yellow-topped jar on stage with him, placing it on the floor beside his water bottle.

When the spotlight picks him out and he starts into 'Breathe', the whole hall simply explodes in excitement.

Faced with such a fury of screaming Lebanese girls, the 20 security guards lined along the edge of the stage simply give up and retreat to the safety of the sides. They know that they are outnumbered and overpowered. The girls surge forward on to the edge of the stage and for a few moments chaos reigns.

James tells the story from his perspective by the guitar mike:

'They start to grab bits of the stage; the wires; my bottle of water. I've got one girl holding on to my leg and another one hanging on to the microphone and I'm still playing my guitar. I turn to Brian who looks after the guitars and is standing in the wings and yell, "Save the Marmite!"

'Brian comes storming over and the crowd expect him to pull these screaming girls off me. But, no, he grabs the Marmite and runs off.'

Almaty

Where? Kazakhstan, of course, the formerly obscure Central Asian republic that was thrust ridiculously on to the world stage by Sacha Baron Cohen's *Borat*.

Almaty's not even the capital (although it's the largest city) and the big mystery is: Why is James going there at all? It's a helluva long way to go for a single gig, isn't it? It's 2,500 miles east of Istanbul and it's even got a border with China. I mean, has anyone really thought this through? But James believes passionately that he has a kind of duty as a musician to go to as many of the obscure corners of the world as possible.

Almaty is a modern city that, until the recession, was expanding at high speed. Now it is dominated by silent cranes and half-built office blocks along with a legacy of some brutalistic Stalin-esque architecture from the heyday of the USSR. The wine, which I sample over lunch, is most definitely not made with urine as Borat says – it just tastes like it.

Borat may be outrageous fiction but when we arrive at the airport, the spirit of farce seems alive and well. The male border guards wear giant outsized military hats in a kind of caricature of their Russian counterparts. Elton would love to have one. The strikingly pretty girl guards wear a khaki uniform . . . with razor-sharp, Jimmy Choo-style stilettos. Our visas have all been organized and paid for in advance, but there is, it seems, 'a problem'. An hour later we appear to be no nearer to solving it.

Finally, an infuriated Bobble digs into the voluminous pockets of his shoulder bag and bangs down a wad of notes on the counter. 'I don't mind paying a bribe once,' he tells me, 'that's normal. But paying the same bribe twice is quite unacceptable. Greedy bastards.'

Blunty, as always, has asked for discreet transport. If you want to live any form of a normal life it makes sense to travel as anonymously as possible. When we finally get out of the terminal and into the cold we find we're to travel in true Borat style . . . in two of the biggest stretched white Hummers I've ever seen. Ours is so long that the driver is almost out of earshot.

Only 1,700 people turn up for the concert. 'James is huge in Kazakhstan,' says a fan I get chatting to, 'but hardly anyone knows this is happening tonight. I only found out because of a friend who works at the Holiday Inn where you are staying.'

Audience size really doesn't bother James. If the arena is half-empty, like tonight, he tries to draw them all down to the stage and seems to make an even bigger effort than usual to involve them. To the fury of the local security guys, who tried to insist everyone stay in their seats, he has them dancing almost on the stage.

The following morning at first light, and with a hard rain falling, our ridiculous stretched Hummers make it through the traffic to the airport . . . but not to the plane. We have to claw our way through a barrage of bureaucracy that engulfs the export of recently imported music instruments, not to mention musicians.

'That's why other artists don't go to Almaty,' says James. 'Nice people, but it's difficult to get into and even more difficult to get out of.'

Kiev

'Where,' says Blunty, 'is the chicken? We've been here for 24 hours and we haven't seen a single one.' We're sitting in Catering once again with just a couple of hours to go to show time.

I know what he's thinking. Chicken, hot wings of, are rarely far from Blunty's thoughts. You don't find wings often in Eastern Europe. But if someone's cooking up a Kiev, which just involves the body of the bird along with breadcrumbs and garlic, there must be some wings going begging. It's true that chicken Kiev is notable by its absence from the menus I've seen so far since I arrived in the Ukrainian capital. Of course, that could be because the dish comes from Russia and not from here at all.

'Food historian William Pokhlebkin claims it was first cooked up in Edwardian times in the Moscow Merchants' Club,' I tell James and the others at the table. 'I just thought you'd like to know that.'

'The wheel – no, the wheels – are coming off the chariot now,' observes Johnny, absorbing the conversation with a weary shake of his head and settling for some suspicious-looking meatballs.

He's right. After 14-and-a-half months on the road and just three gigs to go, the whole tour has taken on a manic, surreal quality. Like a spacecraft that's just re-entered the earth's atmosphere, touchdown is now inevitable and the landing and its aftermath are uppermost in everyone's thoughts. The exterior of the Bubble is white hot and the crew (not to mention the band) are hanging on to their controls by their fingertips.

There's now an almost hysterical note to the proceedings. *All The Lost Souls* seem suddenly to be in danger of being just that. Only Blunty remains firmly on the bridge with his hand on the tiller, steering the craft onwards towards the final concert in Athens . . . and for him a long summer relaxing by the pool in Ibiza before getting seriously into writing the new album.

But for the band and all the technicians, there's the uncertainty of release from something that's curiously like a long stay in prison or in hospital or in both – Bedlam springs to mind again. For 15 months none of them, with the obvious exceptions of tour and stage managers Bobble and Mark, have had to think beyond the glass walls of the Bubble. Indeed, it's become increasingly difficult for any of them to do so.

All routine daily cares have been airbrushed from their lives. Visas, flights, transfers, meals, beds and even laundry have been arranged and paid for by James. All they have been required to do is keep pace with the tour and perform each night to the highest standard.

Now, as the craft plummets towards touchdown, each finds himself racked with thoughts of what the future may hold, back in the real world.

Ben's booked his flight to Perth in Western Australia and is counting down the hours to his reunion with Sam, who is scheduled to give birth to their son, Ollie, in just a few weeks' time.

'My biggest worry,' he tells me, 'is what the hell happens if she goes into labour early? I can't get there in time . . . and I can't leave the band until the final gig is over. "Hang on, Sam," I tell her every day. Just a few days now and I'll be on my way to our new life together. We're getting married in November.'

My worry is how big-hearted, wild-man Benny will adapt to that serene new life on the other side of the world. During the whirlwind course of the tour he's fallen in love with Sam, whom he met in a bar during a stopover in Perth. Remarkably, they've managed to carry on this courtship via Skype and the odd snatched days in hotels and on tour buses. Blunty's worried, too. Will this be the start of the break-up of the band?

Once, before he met Sam, Benny joked as we chatted in Sacramento in California, surrounded by beautiful women at yet another after-show: 'It comes with the job, Peter. It's my duty to shag as many as I can. If I don't, I'll be letting down my fellow rock musicians.' Now for the moment he's forsaking the music and the rock lifestyle for a quiet family life in Oz.

Johnny, too, has fallen head over heels during the course of the tour. Pernille is a model from Copenhagen and, judging by the time they spend on Skype together, the relationship is about as serious as it gets.

Pernille's coming to Athens for the finale. Then they, too, will go off to make their lives together, dividing their time between Copenhagen, London and New York. Unlike Benny and Sam, they'll remain in the centre of the music universe, allowing Johnny to work as a session and tour musician for the likes of Natalie Imbruglia and Leona

Lewis, as well as producing and promoting his own solo album. What he can, at this stage, have no way of knowing is that life for him is also irrevocably changing. By this time next year they will have a son, Viktor.

Beardy is also nervous about the future. 'We've done this for so long, I can't really remember any other life. I guess there'll be a long holiday. Then James will write the third album, we'll record it, and the tour will start up all over again. But right now that's a long way away and I'm looking forward to spending some time at home with Nat.' Again, what he doesn't know is that he will be spending much more time with Robbie Williams, becoming the MD of his touring band and playing keyboard for him at gigs including the *X Factor* final.

Karl, ever smiling Karl, is apprehensive. 'Touring is a drug, and when you go on a tour of this length and importance, you become totally addicted. You go home, you wake up in the morning – and you just don't know what to do with yourself. Your family has been taken away from you and at the back of your mind is the thought that you may never get them back.

'It's the same for the crew, who all have new jobs to go to. It's an anti-climax, so I'm trying to line up lots of sessions and stuff. I've had a lot of fun, met a lot of wonderful women, but you know something? I envy these guys with their long-term relationships. Maybe it's time to settle down a bit. But I guess I just haven't met the right person yet, the girl I want to spend my life with.'

What he doesn't know is that within weeks he will meet Esther. She's a schoolteacher from his beloved Brum. She, too, by the end of the year will be expecting their first child.

That leaves James. 'What about you? What happens to you now when the tour is over?' I ask him. We're sitting alone in his dressing-room in Kiev's Palace of Sports, the venue, if you must know, for the final of the 2005 Eurovision Song Contest.

'In a few days' time the Bubble's going to crack open and you're all going to come tumbling out . . . Benny goes to Australia and a baby and then a wife. Johnny goes to Copenhagen, Karl goes to Birmingham and Beardy to London. Will you all ever work together again?'

'Definitely, I'd like to think so,' he replies. 'We've been to a lot of places and we work well together. If you can take the pressures we've all had to take and are still talking to each other, then we're friends for life. I'd like to think that now we'll all take some time out and then get back again for the next album and the next tour. It's been a load of fun, hasn't it?'

Yes, but it's taken its toll. James looks exhausted and painfully thin. Recently he's become more introspective than usual and I sense his thoughts are already turning towards the next album.

If he wants to keep on touring he needs a new successful album. The endless travel and the nightly performances help to keep this unspoken personal demon at bay, whatever it is.

'Lots of good has come out of the past 15 months,' he continues, 'there have been benefits that we could never have imagined. Look at my band, Ben and Johnny have both fallen in love and now Ben's having a baby.

'We've basically said to people all around the world: "Look, we're having fun, do you want to come and join in?" That was the deal. And they did. All these people have been hanging out with me and the band just because they got the music, not because I'm good-looking or funny. The people we've met are enjoying life for today.'

I'll take everything in this life.
I'll join everyone. When I die.

'We've said to them, "Seize the moment – live for today!" And lots of people have joined us in seizing the moment. We've all had fun and, thank God, we've managed to hang on to an appreciation of just what amazing fun it's been.'

'But what are you going to do now? Are you going to miss working almost every night?'

'No,' he smiles. 'Firstly, I'm going to take a break in Verbier and then I'm going to spend a long time at home in Ibiza and I guess I'll be composing – I've already got a few songs.

'My manager and my label say, "Take your time, take a year off, then write the third album. There's no hurry." But, as you know, that's not me.'

'Will you do another world tour as challenging as this one?'

'Sure, but even bigger and better. There's a hell of a lot more places we have to visit as well as returning to see old friends.'

That's James sorted then, but I guess there's also me.

Halfway through the concert, I'm standing beside Gerry on the lighting stage listening to James singing 'High'.

Beautiful dawn – melt with the stars again
Do you remember the day when my journey began?

Yes, I do. I remember sitting in your mum's car in her driveway listening to 'High' for the first time on your first demo disc. Why were we sitting in the car? Because there wasn't a CD player in the house. That's the musical background you came from.

My own strange journey through this tour has taken a pretty circuitous route. It began over four decades ago in San Francisco with Janis Joplin. When she was my friend and lover she was almost entirely unknown outside Northern California. Yet her voice and her music to me were hauntingly different from anything I'd ever heard before. But if you'd told me she'd become a superstar, I'd have laughed.

Back on that driveway in Hampshire, no one, least of all me, could have imagined then that 'High' would become part of the Bestselling Album of the Decade. But when I listened to the music I didn't laugh. This time, much later and maybe a little wiser, I decided to follow my instincts and to see where they led. So that's why I've been here with you. In a short time now, I'm going back to my own life.

But this tour's not over yet. Kiev is a beautiful city, full of golden domes, minarets and stunning women.

'Make it 16 max,' says Blunty as the band and I head off to hand out Golden Tickets for one of the last times. 'Any more and you'll scare off the good ones.'

In fact it is almost impossible to find any. I ask a couple, but they shake their heads in confusion and turn quickly away. Maybe this is a cultural thing? Maybe they just don't appreciate being propositioned by this bloke old enough to be their father? Maybe they think that this is the first rung on the ladder to being spirited away into the white slave trade? Who knows? Maybe they don't speak English? In the end we make do with a lively bunch of Norwegian medical students on an exchange visit to Kiev University.

'How did we get home from that second club last night?' Johnny asks me the next morning.

'How did we get *to* that second club,' I reply. Blunty had been determined to explore Kiev by night to the full. Somehow we end up in what appears to be a professional karaoke club with a live band. It seems that anyone can get up and sing – and either the standard is fantastically high, or the vodka is telling me that it is.

We have a private room upstairs overlooking the action, but the band are in a fevered state. Blunty seems a bit lost. Karl's sitting there drumming his fingers on the table. Suddenly he looks up at Blunty and raises his eyebrows in silent question. Blunty nods 'yes'.

'Fix it, Peter,' says Karl. Without the vodka it might have been embarrassing. I wander downstairs and, between songs, talk to the band leader.

'Excuse me, do you speak English?'

'Of course.'

'Do you know James Blunt?'

'Of course. Do you want to sing one of his songs?' Now there's a thought. I could empty this place in three minutes and we could all go home to bed.

'No, he's in the room upstairs and he wants to sing two of his songs. His band want to know if you would very kindly lend them your instruments.' He looks me up and down as if I am completely mad or very drunk. Possibly, I am both.

'James Blunt is here, in my club? You're making a joke, right?'

'No, I'm serious.' A slow smile of delight blooms across his features. He rubs his chin thoughtfully.

'"You're Beautiful" and "Goodbye My Lover"?'

'"Same Mistake" and "1973",' I say. He pumps my hand.

I signal the gallery and then watch as James and the band begin to set up drums, keyboard and guitars. It must be way after 2am and the vodka-fuelled audience, which appears to be made up mainly of musicians, look stunned as recognition slowly beings to dawn.

I'm standing on the edge of the central stage beside a tall girl with long pre-Raphaelite hair and her boyfriend who's got matching tresses. They turn to me. 'Omigod, is this really happening? You're with them, right?' I nod.

'We tried and tried to get tickets to the show tonight – but it was impossible. We were very disappointed because we love his music so much and he has made the effort to come here to Kiev where he has so many fans.

'We thought we'd come here instead and maybe someone would sing one of James' songs. Now he's standing here beside us, and he's going to sing.' I nod.

I'm getting good at that. I could give masterclasses in nodding.

As the first chords of 'Same Mistake' echo across the room, she reaches over and kisses me lingeringly on the cheek. At least, I think it was her.

Athens (Again), March 2009

'Last week, I'd never been to Turkey in my life,' says Benny. 'Now I come here every other day.' It's true. James and the band have spent so long in Istanbul airport they're on first-name terms with the girls in the airline lounges. They spent half a day here on their way to Muscat, Dubai and Lebanon – and the same on the way back. We stopped over for ages after Kiev, and now here they are again for their fourth five-hour stay in a week.

'I just want to get to Australia and Sam,' he goes on. 'What if the baby comes today?'

'If she's hung on until now – she'll hang on for another 48 hours and then you'll be on your way,' I tell him.

It's nine months since the Blunty show was last in Athens, when local politics forced the cancellation of both his concerts and James swore he'd never set foot in the country again.

'What happened wasn't the fault of the fans,' he says as the plane begins its descent. 'They paid good money to see us play and we weren't allowed to. So that's why we're here. It seems a good note on which to end.'

Later at the hotel James issues some final orders. 'We stay in the hotel tonight. No clubbing,' says Blunty. He rarely issues orders of this sort, but when he does, he means it. I guess we're almost there, it would be foolish to slip at the last.

Karl looks quietly put out by this. 'Just because you've imported yours, I'm meant to go without. Is that right, James?'

'That's right,' Blunty replies. It looks like the CO might have a last-minute mutiny on his hands. But at that moment a whole bunch of friends that the band made on their last visit turn up and a party in the hotel quickly gets under way. Much later we ask the waitress for the enormous bar bill so that we can divide it up.

'Oh, don't worry,' she says, 'I've put it all on his room,' indicating me.

'Why my room?' I protest.

'Because you're James' father,' she replies.

Much, much later, just before dawn, I'm chilling out with James in his roof-top suite and gazing across the city to the floodlit magnificence of the Acropolis, still bearing witness to 26 centuries of Greek history.

Blunty's sprawled across the sofa, half-listening to a strange haunting folk song that I don't recognize. He's in a mellow, reflective mood. In a few hours' time he'll run out on to the stage of Athens Faliro Pavillion and launch into 'Breathe' for the last hurrah. In 2004 the hall was the Olympic venue for taekwondo which, believe it or not, is the most popular martial art in the world.

For me, too, after all these months the show is over. Tomorrow, I'll leave James and fly back to my own life. I've learned a lot about him along the way, but I feel that I will take with me on the plane to Heathrow more questions than answers. It seems strange and not a little sad that someone who does, as I have witnessed, bring happiness to millions all around the world should not be permitted his own fair share. I guess someone has to lie on the barbed wire while others climb over the top. Deep down, I think he's alone and lonely. The music is the only partner to whom he can fully give himself.

Early in the day at a press conference, a local TV reporter had asked him: 'James, do you have a girlfriend, or people that you especially love in life?'

'Yes,' came the instant reply, 'my mother and my father, who have done – and continue to do – so much for me.' The Blounts are an incredibly close-knit and supportive family.

'Who else do you love, James?' I ask him now. 'Who do you really love? There must be someone?'

Blunty goes silent for a full couple of minutes and I feel that finally I've overstepped the bounds of our friendship, I've knocked uninvited on the door of his privacy. At first I don't think he's going to reply at all. He seems a long way away, lost in thought. But then he does.

'I say a person's name every single day,' he replies. 'She is my last thought when I go to bed at night and the first when I wake up in the morning.

'She was my first love, and she's who I was supposed to be with through life.'

Outside the window, at the start of another day, the city built in tribute to a goddess who never took a lover is slowly springing to life.

'So where is she? Why aren't you with her?' I ask gently.

'We went out with each other for three years at university,' he says. 'But she's married now with two children.'

'The *real* girl on the subway in "You're Beautiful" and "Goodbye My Lover"?' I venture. 'But I've met people, girlfriends of yours, who clearly believe that those songs are about them.'

'Yes, some other people think that "You're Beautiful" and "Goodbye My Lover" might be about them, and of course everyone close to me has huge influence on the songs. But they don't need those songs to tell them that I care about them.

'But she's in all the songs. That's the irony. We met when we were young, when my ambitions were too naive. As a boy, no one goes to school or university saying to anyone or even to themselves, "My ambition is to fall in love and have a family." I wanted to join the army, become a musician and taste everything that life has to offer. So I've done all that, and I've tasted a fair bit of life, and after all that, I've realized that what I failed to see was that the sweetest thing that life had to offer was right in front of me.

'But it's too late. Life has moved on too far to reach back and grab at what we once had. She's carved her own path now, and it's not for me to interrupt that. It's just not how you expect life to end up. The true love of my life exists but she is not with me. No one ever writes their own book like that, do they?

'So I get to achieve my ambition, and the price is to sing songs about her.'

I leave him, standing alone by the giant plate-glass window of his suite, looking out on his troubled world. As I close the door and wearily head for my room, I can't help but feel that James will always stand alone, cushioning the void with his music and his lyrics. Being alone is what makes him what he is.

The lyrics of the new song he's been composing echo in my head:

When you marry and you look around
I'll be somewhere in that crowd
Torn up that it isn't me.

When you're older and the memories fade,
I know I'll still feel the same,
For as long as I live.

If time is all I had,
I'd waste it all on you.
Each day I'll turn it back.
It's what the broken-hearted do.
I'm tired of talking to an empty space.
Of silences keeping me awake.
Won't you say my name one time
When the song is over?

Much later that same day, the three-song encore of the final concert of the 58-country *All The Lost Souls* World Tour 2008–2009 is about to begin.

Tash, who has flown in specially, comes bursting into the dressing-room and asks me:

'Do you think James would mind if I paint "The End" on my bare bum and moon in the finale?'

'Why not?' I reply. 'That's the most sensible thing I've heard anyone say around here in the past 15 months.'

Acknowledgements

I'd like to thank everyone who worked on the *All The Lost Souls* and *Back To Bedlam* world tours for tolerating my frequent and unannounced intrusions into their working lives with kindness, humour and friendship. In particular my thanks go to tour manager Robert 'Bobble' Hayden who took me under his then ample wing to ensure I got to the next venue on time and didn't get left behind, and to show manager Mark Reuben who gave me unlimited access to his stage and regularly saved me from over-enthusiastic security guards; and also to Mike Hornby, Hamish Laishley, Brian Murray, Gerry Wilkes, Glen Johnson, Scott Essen, Jonny Gallagher and all the other technicians and crew. My thanks also go to James' managers Todd Interland and Stuart Camp.

My special thanks go to my agent Gordon Wise at Curtis Brown who continued to believe in the project during the long months when others did not; to Jane and Charlie Blount for their support and faith from the outset; my long-suffering editor Carly Cook, who expertly weaved the manuscript and photographs into shape, along with Jo Whitford and everyone else at Headline; Val Hudson who originally commissioned the book; my family for putting up with my frequent absences; to Paul, Karl, Benny, Johnny, Malcolm, and above all to James.

Music Credits

I would like to offer my thanks to EMI Music Publishing Ltd for allowing me to reproduce lyrics from some of James' songs. My thanks also go to his co-writers and their publishers for granting music licences.

'1973'
Words & Music by James Blunt & Mark Batson © 2006 EMI Music Publishing Ltd (50%)/Universal/MCA Music Ltd (50%). All rights reserved. International Copyright secured. Used by permission of EMI and Music Sales Ltd.

'So Long, Jimmy'
Words & Music by James Blunt & Jimmy Hogarth © 2003 EMI Music Publishing Ltd (50%)/Dalmatian Songs Ltd/Universal Music Publishing MGB Limited (50%). All rights reserved. International Copyright secured.

'Annie'
Words & Music by James Blunt & Jimmy Hogarth. Published by EMI Music Publishing Ltd (50%). © Universal Music Publishing MGB Limited (50%). All Rights Reserved. International Copyright Secured. Used by permission of EMI and Music Sales Ltd.

'I'll Take Everything'
Words & Music by James Blunt & Francis White. Published by EMI Music Publishing Ltd (50%). © Universal Music Publishing Ltd (50%). All Rights Reserved. International Copyright Secured. Used by permission of EMI and Music Sales Ltd.

'Wisemen'
Words & Music by James Blunt, Jimmy Hogarth & Sacha Skarbek. © 2004 EMI Music Publishing Ltd (50%)/Bucks Music Group Ltd (25%)/Universal Music Publishing MGB Ltd (25%). All Rights in Germany Administered by Musik Edition Discoton GmbH (a division of Universal Music Publishing Group). All Rights Reserved. International Copyright Secured. Used by permission of EMI, Bucks Music Group and Music Sales Ltd.

'Carry You Home'
Words & Music by James Blunt & Max Martin. © Published by EMI Music Publishing Ltd and Maratone AB, administered by Kobalt Music Publishing Ltd. Used with permission.

'You're Beautiful'
Words & Music by James Blunt, Sacha Skarbek & Amanda Ghost.
© Published by EMI Music Publishing Ltd and Bucks Music Group Ltd. Used with permission.

'Cry'
Words & Music by James Blunt & Sacha Skarbek. ©

'Goodbye My Lover'

'No Bravery'

'Tears And Rain'

'One Of The Brightest Stars'

'Same Mistake'

'Out Of My Mind'

'I Can't Hear The Music'
Words & Music by James Blunt. © Published by EMI Music Publishing Ltd. Used with permission.

'Love, Love, Love'
Words & Music by James Blunt & Francis White. © Published by EMI Music Publishing Ltd and Sony/ATV Music Publishing (UK) Ltd. Used with permission.

'High'
Words & Music by James Blunt & Ricky Ross. © Published by EMI Music Publishing Ltd and Warner/Chapell Music Ltd. Used with permission.

Untitled lyrics (p.366) © James Blunt. Used with permission.

Picture Credits

All images © Peter Hardy, James Blunt, John Garrison, Felice Hardy, Charles Blount, Anna Georghallides.